THE DEAD SEA SCROLLS READER

THE DEAD SEA SCROLLS READER

PART 6

ADDITIONAL GENRES AND UNCLASSIFIED TEXTS

Edited by Donald W. Parry & Emanuel Tov
With the assistance of Nehemia Gordon

BRILL
LEIDEN • BOSTON
2005

Printed on acid-free paper

Cover Art: Lika Tov, Jerusalem ('The Men behind the Scrolls')
Cover Design: Coördesign, Leiden

Transcriptions and translations published in the series *Discoveries in the Judaean Desert* and in J.T. Milik, *The Books of Enoch* (Oxford: Clarendon Press, 1976) are reproduced by permission of Oxford University Press and/or the individual editors.

New transcriptions and translations prepared by M.G. Abegg, Jr., J. Bowley, E. Cook, and M. Wise are reproduced by permission of the authors.

Translations published in M. Wise, M.G. Abegg, Jr., E. Cook, *The Dead Sea Scrolls: A New Translation* (San Francisco: HarperSanFrancisco, 1996) are reproduced by permission of the authors.

Transcriptions and translations from Y. Yadin, *The Temple Scroll* (Jerusalem 1983) are reproduced by permission of the Israel Exploration Society.

Translations and transcriptions published in F. García Martínez and E.J.C. Tigchelaar, *The Dead Sea Scrolls Study Edition*, vols. one–two (Leiden/Boston/Cologne: Brill, 1997–1998) are published with permision from the authors.

The Hebrew text of 1QM (J. Duhaime) published in J.H. Charlesworth (ed.), *The Dead Sea Scrolls: Hebrew, Aramaic, and Greek Texts with English Translations:* vol. 2, *Damascus Document, War Scroll, and Related Documents* (Tübingen/Louisville: J.C.B. Mohr (Paul Siebeck)/Westminster John Knox, 1995) is reproduced with the permission of J.C.B. Mohr (Paul Siebeck).

Library of Congress Cataloging-in-Publication Data
LC Control number 2003062757

ISBN Part 6: 90 04 12646 5
ISBN Set: 90 04 13578 2

Printed in The Netherlands

CONTENTS

(For the contents of the complete edition see the back of this part.)

General Introduction*

The Dead Sea Scrolls Reader (*DSSR*) presents for the first time all the non-biblical Qumran texts classified according to their genres, together with translations, in six separate parts.[1] Some twenty-five previously unpublished texts are included in this edition (see notes 6, 8). The purpose of *DSSR* is to enhance the research facilities of the individual texts within their respective genres.

The nature of the Dead Sea Scrolls publication project was such that texts belonging to the same literary genre were published in different volumes in the *Discoveries in the Judaean Desert* (*DJD*) series, although those from cave 4 were often published by subject. The dispersion of these texts in several different volumes complicated their analysis, a problem that is now overcome in *DSSR*.

The great majority of the Hebrew and Aramaic texts included in this edition represent the content of the FARMS database of the Institute for the Study and Preservation of Ancient Religious Texts, Brigham Young University. This database is based on the totality of the non-biblical texts included in *DJD*, supple-

*This is an updated and corrected version of the Introduction published in parts 1, 2, and 4. Following the classification of Lange-Mittmann (*DJD* XXXIX, 115–64), some texts in parts 1, 2, and 4 are segmented in the presentation as belonging to different literary genres, as in 1QS I 1–III 12 in part 1A. In this case, the other segments of 1QS are presented elsewhere. In *DSSR* parts 3, 5, and 6, the segmentation pertains only to the listing in the Table of Contents, since the complete text editions are always presented in a single place, accompanied by a note like "Complete text of 4Q**205** provided."

[1] Several persons helped us in this cooperative effort. Irena Abramian, principally, incorporated the bulk of the material into the FARMS database (see below) over the course of many years, aided by programming provided by J. Doug Bayless. Irena's insights and careful treatment of the texts provided the basis of the present edition. FARMS and Brigham Young University are to be thanked for their part in the preparation of the Hebrew transcriptions, which were originally prepared for the electronic publication: E. Tov, ed., *The Dead Sea Scrolls Database (Non-Biblical Texts)* (The Dead Sea Scrolls Electronic Reference Library, vol. 2; Prepared by the Foundation for Ancient Research and Mormon Studies [FARMS]) (Leiden: E. J. Brill, 1999). M. G. Abegg and E. Cook kindly provided us with electronic copies of a sizeable number of additional texts (originals and English translations) which had not been included in the original FARMS database. A few texts in *DSSR* present completely new text editions prepared by Abegg, Cook, and Wise (see n. 8). These texts were originally prepared by these two scholars for Abegg's database, which forms the basis for the Qumran module in the Accordance computer programme (Oaktree Software, see http://www.oaksoft.com/) and his preparations for the printed concordance: M. G. Abegg, Jr. with J. E. Bowley and E. M. Cook, *The Dead Sea Scrolls Concordance I. The Non-biblical Texts from Qumran* (Leiden: E. J. Brill, 2003). E. Cook and M. Wise kindly agreed to review our corrections of their earlier translations of Aramaic texts, and to finely tune these translations. Several sections and lines were missing in the translations by Wise, Abegg, and Cook as well as those in *DJD* I–VII. These have now been skillfully added by N. Gordon of Jerusalem, who incorporated his new translations together with corrections to the original translations into those of Wise–Abegg–Cook. In such cases, the name of N. Gordon has been added to the acknowledgements. Ayelet Tov-Sagi proofread all the *DJD* texts against the printed volumes. It is our impression that no detail escaped her trained eye, but we take blame for all oversights. In the Provo office, D. Fry, Carli Anderson, and Mindy Anderson copy-edited and formatted the transcriptions and translations skillfully and professionally. In the Jerusalem office, Janice Karnis copy-edited large parts of the edition applying to them her good sense of style. Shelly Eshkoly proofread large segments of the editions, and she also improved the notation of the parallels.

mented by a sizeable number of previously published and unpublished texts in new editions by M. G. Abegg, E. Cook, and M. Wise (see note 8 below).

Classification. The classification in this edition closely follows the list published by A. Lange with U. Mittmann-Richert in the introductory volume to the *DJD* series.[2] Recognizing the subjective nature of any classification, we accept this one with a limited number of changes,[3] since the inner logic of a classification should be adopted in its entirety.

The subjective nature of each classification proves to be problematic. Scholars conceive of several compositions in different ways, often resulting in their classification under different headings. Some of these compositions admittedly belong to more than one literary genre, so that they may be classified rightly in different places, or often in two places at the same time. As much as possible, a classification needs to be based on insights into the content, at the same time leaving the door open for different views visible through double classifications and/or a series of notes. A classified list differs from a text edition in that the former can allow itself to present texts in different places, while the latter obviously will present a text only once. A text edition based on a classification therefore needs to provide appropriate cross-references (see the introductions to the individual parts) recording alternative and additional options of classification. The main purpose of this publication is to present a convenient edition of all the Dead Sea Scrolls, and their classification is only a secondary goal. The problematic aspects of this method of organization are recognized, but its advantages outweigh its disadvantages.

Following the classification by Lange–Mittman-Richert, some Qumran texts representing more than one literary genre have been segmented into different elements and presented in different parts of *DSSR* parts 1, 2, and 4. For example, sections of 1QapGen are presented in three segments in part 1, while parts of 1QS are contained in parts 1 and 4. In these cases, cross-references are provided in *DSSR* to enable the unbiased study of these compositions. This procedure has been discontinued in parts 3, 5, and 6, as well as in the combined edition (see n. 1 in the Table of Contents).

Coverage. DSSR covers all the non-biblical texts from Qumran, that is three-quarters of the Hebrew and Aramaic texts found there,[4] excluding the biblical texts from that site.[5] A few Greek texts are included as well. The pre-

[2] "Annotated List of the Texts from the Judaean Desert Classified by Content and Genre," in *The Texts from the Judaean Desert—Indices and an Introduction to the Discoveries in the Judaean Desert Series* (ed. E. Tov; DJD XXXIX; Oxford: Clarendon, 2002) 115–64.

[3] Note the addition of 4Q**168** to part 2, the addition of 4QReworked Pentateuch (4Q**158**, 4Q**364–367**) and 4Q**365a** to part 3, the removal of 4QPsalms[e] (4Q**87**) from the genre covered by part 5, and the addition to *DSSR* of all the texts listed in category 15.2 of Lange ('Texts Not Included'). In addition, the internal sequence of some sections of parts 4, 5, and 6 has been changed. The segmentation of texts has been discontinued in parts 3, 5, and 6 (see n. 1 in the Table of Contents), involving, among other things, the combination of all the Enoch texts in part 3.

[4] A sequential list of the Qumran texts covered by the various parts in *DSSR* (a 'reverse list' of the contents of the parts) is published in part 6. The parts themselves cover all the non-biblical texts listed in *DJD* XXXIX, 27–114.

[5] The biblical texts are scheduled to be included in *The Qumran Bible* edited by E. Ulrich (forthcoming).

sent edition focuses on Qumran, excluding the finds from other sites in the Judean Desert: Murabba'at (see *DJD* XXXIX, pp. 97–104), Naḥal Ḥever, and Masada (for both, see ibid., 104–14). While not including all the texts found in the Judean Desert (also named the Dead Sea Scrolls), the present edition does contain the great majority of the literary texts from among the Dead Sea Scrolls. The sites other than Qumran preserve almost exclusively documentary papyri, such as contracts, letters, and lists of goods (for the documentary texts from Qumran, see part 6).

The edition includes all fragments published with an identifying title, such as the large group of texts recorded in part 6G ("Unclassified Manuscripts with Specific Names") containing, for example, 4QpapFragment Mentioning Festivals (4Q**478**). So-called "unclassified" or "unidentified" fragments (without any identifying title) which have been listed in *DJD* XXXIII have not been included in *DSSR*. In addition, the edition includes texts identified in 2003 and 2004 by E. J. C. Tigchelaar and H. Eshel–E. Eshel.[6]

As in *DJD*, *multiple manuscripts* of the same composition are presented separately without attempting to create a composite edition on the basis of the various fragments. The only composite edition appearing in the *DJD* series is that of the manuscripts of 4QMMT (4Q**394–397**, **399**) in vol. X, reproduced in part 1 of *DSSR*.

Biblical and Non-biblical Texts. DSSR covers only the non-biblical Qumran texts based on a formal understanding of what constitutes a biblical text. The canonical biblical books are excluded from this edition, while Ben Sira (2Q**18**) is included. However, due to the fragmentary character of the Qumran compositions, it is often unclear whether a small fragment contains a biblical or a non-biblical composition,[7] but *DSSR* follows the decisions on the nature of the texts made by those who edited them. Furthermore, the distinction between what is considered Scripture and non-Scripture in the wide sense of the word is often difficult, especially in 4QReworked Pentateuch (4Q**158**, 4Q**364–367**) included in part 3. Since this text was published in *DJD* XIII as a non-biblical text, it is presented as such also in *DSSR* 3.

Editio minor. DSSR serves as an *editio minor* of the Qumran fragments, while the full apparatus relating to these editions is not repeated from the official editions: introduction, information on the photograph numbers, apparatuses of notes on readings and content remarks, photographic plates. Since the con-

---

[6] E. J. C. Tigchelaar, "Unidentified and Identifiable Fragments on PAM 43.680: A New Manuscript of *4QNarrative and Poetic Composition*, and Fragments of *4Q413, 4Q269, 4Q525* and *4QSb* (?)," *RevQ* 21 (2004) 477–85; idem, "Minuscula Qumranica," *RevQ* 21 (2004), 643–8; E. Eshel and H. Eshel, "New Fragments from Qumran: 4QGen^{f}, 4QIsa^{b}, 4Q226, 8QGen, and XQEnoch," *DSD* 11 (2004), forthcoming.

[7] Some of the very fragmentary texts which have been named biblical may actually have been parts of compositions which included, among other things, long stretches of Bible texts, such as *pesharim* and other commentaries, or paraphrases such as 4QReworked Pentateuch (4QRP^{a-e}). For example, 4QGen^{k} 5 may actually belong to 4QRP^{a} (4Q**158**). Likewise, the text which has been published as 4QpapIsa^{p} (4Q**69**) contains only a few words, and therefore could have been part of a *pesher* like 4Qpap pIsa^{c} (see J. R. Davila's discussion in *DJD* XII, 75). 4Q**168** is presented in all lists as 4QpMic?, but it could be presented equally well as '4QMic?'.

cordance by M. G. Abegg and others (see note 1) covers more than the individual volumes of the *DJD* series, it may be more accurately considered a concordance to this volume, than to the volumes of *DJD*.

Sources. The table of contents lists the source for the texts and translations included in *DSSR*. Most of these sources have been published, while for a few texts provided by M. G. Abegg or E. Cook[8] this is their first publication. Usually one source is provided in the table of contents, such as "(*DJD* XIX, 1995)," implying that both the transcription and translation are quoted from *DJD* XIX. If two sources are listed, such as "(Abegg; WAC [Wise, Abegg, Cook])", the first entry refers to the source for the transcription, and the second one to the source of the translation.

The *text* of the Hebrew-Aramaic compositions follows exactly that of the *DJD* editions when available (but see below regarding minor corrections). This applies to the great majority of the texts in *DSSR*, with the exception of 11QTemple[a] and the Enoch texts quoted here from their standard editions,[9] and the large texts from cave 1, as well as several additional texts,[10] that are adduced from the transcriptions by M. G. Abegg and E. Cook[11] and those edited by J. H. Charlesworth.[12]

Languages. In all its sections, *DSSR* contains both Hebrew and Aramaic compositions.

The *translations* provided in these parts are those accompanying the *DJD* editions, and in the case of texts not included in *DJD*, we resorted mainly to translations published by Wise–Abegg–Cook,[13] as well as a few unpublished translations by these scholars. Some of the translations have been supplemented and revised by N. Gordon in Jerusalem, as indicated in the acknowledgements for each text. Use of the *DJD* translations was more complicated than had been anticipated since, in the early volumes, many lines or sections of the texts had not been translated at all, necessitating the addition of new translations in the present volume.[14]

---

[8] See the table of contents. This pertains to a few texts in the cryptic A–C scripts and 4Q**551–578**.

[9] Y. Yadin, *The Temple Scroll*, vols. 1–3 (Jerusalem: Israel Exploration Society, 1992); J. T. Milik, *The Books of Enoch* (Oxford: Clarendon, 1976) for 4Q**201–202**, 4Q**204–207**, 4Q**210–212**.

[10] 1QH[a], 1QpHab, 1QS, 1QSa, 1QSb, 1QapGen, 4Q**317**, 4Q**324d–e**, 4Q**551–578**.

[11] These transcriptions were prepared for the Qumran module of the Accordance computer programme as well as for the Qumran Concordance (for both, see note 1 above). In the texts from cave 1, Abegg leaned much on the edition of E. Lohse, *Die Texte aus Qumran Hebräisch und Deutsch*, vols. 1–2 (Darmstadt: Wissenschaftliche Buchgesellschaft, 1964, 1971), supplemented by additional editions, as explained in the 'Readme' file in the Accordance programme (see n. 1). 1QapGen in Abegg's text is based on the following editions: M. Morgenstern, E. Qimron, D. Sivan, "The Hitherto Unpublished Columns of the Genesis Apocryphon," *AbrN* 33 (1995) 30–54; F. García Martínez and E. J. C. Tigchelaar, *The Dead Sea Scrolls Study Edition, Volume One* (Leiden: E. J. Brill, 1997). See further notes in the edition itself.

[12] For 1QM: J. Duhaime in the valuable edition of J. H. Charlesworth (ed.), *The Dead Sea Scrolls: Hebrew, Aramaic, and Greek Texts with English Translations*: vol. 2, *Damascus Document, War Scroll, and Related Documents* (Tübingen/Louisville: J. C. B. Mohr (P. Siebeck)/Westminster John Knox, 1995).

[13] M. Wise, M. G. Abegg, Jr., E. Cook, *The Dead Sea Scrolls: A New Translation* (San Francisco: HarperSanFrancisco, 1996).

[14] All of the translations included in the 'French' *DJD* volumes (III, VII, XXV, XXXI) have been replaced with English translations.

In order to make the presentation of the translations more consistent throughout the text editions, quotations from the biblical text in *pesharim* and commentaries are presented within quotation marks and in italics.[15]

Nomenclature. The names of the Qumran compositions follow the official editions, as summarized in *DJD* XXXIX.[16] In the system of *DJD*, different *copies* of the same composition are indicated by small raised letters (e.g. the various manuscripts of the *pesher* on Isaiah named 4QpIsa[a,b,c]), while manuscripts representing related compositions are indicated with capital letters, such as 4QapocrJer A, B, etc. This distinction, which admittedly is subjective,[17] was not yet fully developed in the first *DJD* volumes.

In the nomenclature of the texts from the Judean Desert, the following system is used:

The name begins with a reference to its find-site, as listed below

Ḥev	Naḥal Ḥever
KhQ	Khirbet Qumran
Mas	Masada
Mur	Murabba'at
Q	Qumran
Ṣe	Naḥal Ṣe'elim

The different caves at each site are denoted with sequential numbers, for example, 1Q, 2Q, etc. (XQ refers to an unknown cave at Qumran). Appearing after the find-site are references to the material on which the text was written (pap = papyrus), followed by the type of composition (apocr = apocryphon; p = pesher; tg = targum) and/or type of script (paleo = paleo-Hebrew; crypt = cryptic [A, B, C]). The assigned name of the text then appears, followed by the language of inscription (ar = Aramaic; gr = Greek; lat = Latin; nab = Nabataean). All documents are written on leather in Hebrew unless otherwise designated.

Common abbreviations for the classification of the scrolls are as follows:

apocr	apocryphon (e.g. 4QapocrLam A [4Q**179**])
ar	Aramaic (e.g. 4QLevi[a] ar [4Q**213a**])
crypt	Cryptic A, B, C (e.g. 4Qpap cryptA Prophecy? [4Q**249q**])
gr	Greek (e.g. 4Qpap paraExod gr [4Q**127**])
heb	Hebrew (e.g. 4QAccount B ar or heb [4Q**354**]; XḤev/Se papDeed of Sale B ar and heb [XḤev/Se **8**]). N.B. 'heb' *only* appears together with another language and denotes that either the language is uncertain or that both appear in the document. When no language abbreviation appears after the text name, Hebrew is assumed.

[15] Some *DJD* authors make use of italic print without quotation marks for questionable translations (e.g. in *DJD* XXXIV).

[16] The reader is referred to a description of the nomenclature of the Qumran scrolls in *DJD* XXXIX, 10–11.

[17] Thus in *DJD* XXXI, the rather similar, yet different, cycles of pseudepigraphical works ascribed to Ezekiel and Jeremiah are conceived of in different ways. The manuscripts of the Apocryphon of Jeremiah are described as a group of related compositions: 4QapocrJer A (4Q**383**), 4Qpap apocrJer B? (4Q**384**), 4QapocrJer C[a–f] (4Q**385a**, **387**, **388a**, **389–390**, **387a**), while 4QpsEzek[a–e] (4Q**385**, **386**, **385b**, **388**, **391**) are presented as different copies of the same composition.

lat	Latin (e.g. Mas papLetter lat [Mas **728**])
nab	Nabataean (e.g. 5/6Ḥev papUnclassified Text nab [5/6Ḥev **38**])
p	*pesher* (e.g. 1QpHab)
paleo	Paleo-Hebrew (e.g. 11QpaleoLev^a [11Q**1**])
pap	papyrus (e.g. 4Qpap paraExod gr [4Q**127**])
tg	Targum (e.g. 11QtgJob [11Q**10**])

Parallels. A visual means for indicating parallel texts was developed fully in the volumes published in the 1990s. This relates to two types of parallels: (1) those between segments in manuscripts of what is supposedly the same composition and (2) those between different compositions. The notion of a 'parallel' is intentionally vague, often rightly so, but in most cases it pertains to texts which actually overlap, although differences in details between the texts are recorded. Such differences are visible upon examination of the exact amount of overlapping as recorded in the *DJD* editions.[18] The recording system used in most volumes indicates very precisely all the letters and spaces which any two texts have in common, so that even the smallest agreements and differences between them are visible when underlined or not. In several cases, three or four different parallels are indicated by three types of underlining as well as overbars, such as in the manuscripts of the *Damascus Document* (part 3 [*DJD* XVIII]).[19]

Quality and Consistency. The main purpose of *DSSR* is to present the texts and translations published in *DJD* and elsewhere over the course of almost half a century. The high standards of these publications have not changed over the years, but here and there a text edition was of a lower quality. Despite these occasional discrepancies, these editions have been reproduced in their original form.[20] Due to the nature of the publication of *DJD* carried out over the course of fifty years on different continents, a certain degree of inconsistency regarding the presentation of the texts proved unavoidable in the original editions. This inconsistency relates to all aspects of the presentation of the texts and their translations: degree of certainty ascribed to partially preserved letters (e.g. what looks like a certain letter to one scholar may be indicated with a diacritical dot by another), amount of reconstruction (some scholars did not reconstruct elements not preserved, while others presented a small number of reconstructions, and yet others reconstructed extensively), translation vocabulary,[21] type of translation, uncertainties expressed in the translations by *italics*, and the presentation of biblical quotations in the translations of the *pesharim* and biblical

[18] The data and difficulties involved are described in detail by E. J. C. Tigchelaar in *DJD* XXXIX, 285–322.

[19] The parallels in 4Q**415–418c**, **423** (part 4B [originally published in *DJD* XXXIV]), indicated by interlinear letters, have not been recorded in *DSSR*, while the references to the parallels have been retained.

[20] It would not be amiss to note that vol. V in the *DJD* series (4Q**158–186**) was published prematurely. In the individual parts of *DSSR*, the texts from that volume are nevertheless reproduced in their original form, but it is envisaged to include the revised editions (from the planned revision of the complete volume, *DJD* Va) in the final volume. The present edition (part 5A) already includes the revised edition of 4Q**179** by M. Bernstein.

[21] For example, the Tetragrammaton is represented in the translation in four different ways: LORD, Lord, YHWH, and Yahweh.

commentaries. The presentation of the texts became more standardized from 1990 onwards.

In the following areas, *DSSR* introduced a greater degree of consistency than *DJD*:

1. Indication of empty lines or segments as *vac(at)*.
2. Indication of partially preserved untranslated words with three spaces in the translation.
3. Indication of the beginnings and ends of lines with right- and left-hand brackets whenever the full column size is reconstructed.
4. In the Hebrew a space usually is used rather than *ellipsis* signs; in translations, *ellipsis* signs are not used in reconstructions, and rarely so in running texts.
5. Indication of top and bottom margins for texts originally published in *DJD* I–V.
6. Indication of scribal corrections and erasures (see below).
7. Biblical quotations, when recognized in the text editions, are represented in italics between quotation marks. Often the references themselves were added in *DSSR*.

Corrections. A text edition in *DJD* is in the nature of an *editio princeps* and it is only logical that such an edition would subsequently be improved upon by its editor as well as by others. New views on the reading of a certain letter, new understandings of the nature of a composition involving new readings and reconstructions, new suggestions regarding physical joins and connections made between two or more different fragments could all improve the nature of the edition. At the same time, as the nature of the art of editing is subjective, that of its correcting procedure is equally subjective. Due to this subjectivity in the correction process, and also to the fact that there is virtually no right or wrong in this area, no corrections can be provided in an edition like the present one, with the exclusion of typographical errors (e.g. 4Q**409** frg. 1 i 7 קדושו [*DJD* XXIX] corrected to קודשו).[22] The only content corrections included in *DSSR* pertain to the few re-editions included in the later volumes of *DJD* correcting earlier *DJD* editions. In these cases, the re-edition has been included in *DSSR*, while the earlier edition has been excluded.[23] A few *DJD* editions such as 4Q**422** (part 3) and several Jubilees manuscripts (part 3) have been included in *DSSR* in a revised version (recorded as: "Corrected, 2004").[24]

A special case is a group of four small fragments that are presented in vol. XXIX as both 4Q**471b** frgs. 1a–d (4QSelf-Glorification Hymn; edited by E.

---

[22] Such typographic errors are corrected in the following way: <DJD: קדושו> קודשו. At the same time, clear typographical mistakes in such matters as numbers and brackets are changed without leaving a trace (there are no more than twenty instances in all the parts). Thanks are due to M. G. Abegg for providing us with a list of typographical errors. Other errors were collected in the Jerusalem office.

[23] The edition of 1Q**23** (1QEnGiants[a] ar) follows the re-edition in vol. XXXVI; that of 1Q**26** (1QWisdom Apocryphon) follows vol. XXXIV, that of 1Q**28a** (1QSa) follows vol. XXXVI, that of 2Q**26** (2QFragment of a Ritual?) follows vol. XXXVI, that of 4Q**269** (4QD[d] frgs. 10, 11) follows vol. XXXVI, and that of 4Q**394** frgs. 1–2 (4QMMT[a], first published in *DJD* X) follows vol. XXI.

[24] These corrections have been kindly provided by J. VanderKam.

Eshel) and 4Q**431** frg. 1 (4QH[e]; edited by E. Schuller). The latter is recorded in part 5.

Acknowledgements. Precise references to the *editio princeps* are provided after the title of each document.

PRESENTATION OF THE TEXT. The system used is that of *DJD*, described in detail by E. Tov in *DJD* XXXIX, 19–22. *DSSR* presents the Hebrew/Aramaic texts on the left page and the English translation on the facing page. In multiple cases, where Hebrew/Aramaic transcriptions consist of only a few letters enabling only infrequent English translations, the texts and their translations appear together on the same left or right page, thus decreasing the amount of white space in the edition.

The structure of individual columns of the text within a given composition, extant or reconstructed, is often based on physically unconnected fragments placed in an extant or reconstructed column sequence. Some scholars were more reliant than others on their own suggestions regarding the reconstruction of the column structure of the scroll made on the basis of the preserved fragments. The columns in a multi-sheet composition, both extant and reconstructed, are numbered with large Roman numerals (I, II, etc.). Different columns found on a *single* fragment are numbered with lower-case Roman numerals (e.g. frg. 1 i 8 = fragment 1, col. i, line 8). Adjacent columns in the scroll or on a fragment are presented sequentially, but when the remains of one of the two columns are very scanty, they are often printed side by side.

Usually the numbering starts with the first preserved column (as opposed to the first column of the composition), while the system used by some scholars takes into consideration putative columns which may have preceded the first preserved column. Thus, 4QOtot (4Q**319**) begins with col. IV, as it is presumed that the three columns of 4QS[e] (4Q**259**) appeared beforehand.[25] The fragments comprising each column are numbered a, b, c, etc.; unconnected fragments are numbered 1, 2, 3, etc. (sometimes subdivided into 1a, 1b, etc.)

The lines of each column are usually numbered 1, 2, 3 etc., starting with the first preserved line. In some cases, when the number of lines preceding the first preserved line or column can be estimated—especially when one or more adjacent columns are preserved—the first line or column may be numbered with a higher number. Some scholars, preferring to retain the number '1' for the first preserved line, number the presumed preceding lines as 01, 02, etc. (thus 4Q**299**; 4Q**423**; 11QT[a]).

Joined presentation. In the case of double presentation in *DJD*, e.g. when fragments a and b are presented separately and also in the joined reconstruction, only the latter is presented.

Top and bottom margins, when extant, are indicated in all the original publications, although inconsistently so in *DJD* I–V. On the other hand, left and right margins are not indicated explicitly, since the absence of square brackets at the right and left indicates the existence of such margins.

Spaces within the text, as well as completely empty lines. Within the text, spaces indicating contextual breaks are indicated by *vac(at)* at the beginning of

[25] See J. Ben-Dov, *DJD* XXI, 195–7.

the line (indentations), in the middle, or towards the end of the lines. As a rule, the exact dimensions of the spaces are not imitated in the printed editions. Areas which are not inscribed due to a rough surface or damage to the leather are indicated in some volumes by *vac(at)* and in others by ///. Completely empty lines are also numbered. This system was not used in the early volumes, where the word *vac(at)* was usually not printed in the spaces.

Writing on two sides. Recto and *verso* are indicated, as well as the 'lower' and 'upper' versions in the documentary texts in vol. XXVII.

The exact position of the inscribed surfaces within the fragments. While an attempt is made to imitate in print the position of the inscribed surface on the fragment, it is often impossible to do so accurately as printed and written letters have different widths.

Supralinear, infralinear, and (less frequently) marginal additions are indicated in the text by raised or lowered characters (often in a smaller font). When longer than a few words, the addition is often indicated by an additional line, which is sometimes indicated with a special number (line 8a [rarely: 9a] would indicate a supralinear addition above line 9). Sometimes, the exact position of the supralinear letter or word cannot be indicated accurately. We follow the *DJD* editions in not distinguishing in the transcriptions between *prima manu* and *secunda manu* additions.

Individual letters or words written in the palaeo-Hebrew script, mainly the Tetragrammaton, are represented in that script. In the translation, these words are represented in **boldface**.

Corrections and erasures are indicated as follows in the more recent volumes in the series:

Superscript letters	שׁזע[ק]תם (4Q**434** 1 i 3)
Erasures on the leather	{כיא הואה} כיא הואה (4Q**417** 2 i 5)
Erasures on the leather (undetermined letters)	/// (4Q**169** 3-4 iii 11)
Crossing out a letter or word with a line	~~אמתו~~ (4Q**405** 3 i 12)
Deletion dots above, below, or around letters	מׄעל (4Q**434** 1 i 1)

Earlier *DJD* volumes did not differentiate the above different types of deletions, representing all of the above by { }. In those earlier editions, this sign is distinct from < > indicating a scribe's omission (see vol. I, 48). *DSSR* has attempted to improve upon these earlier editions, but some inconsistency remains.

Scribal signs, with the exception of *paragraphos* signs, are not indicated in the transcriptions (for a list, see vol. XXXIX, H. SCRIBAL NOTATIONS IN THE TEXTS FROM THE JUDAEAN DESERT). The *paragraphos* is represented as a printed straight line (e.g. 4Q**532** frg. 1 ii, before line 7) and only rarely is the 'fish hook' *paragraphos* presented as such (thus 4Q**428** 10 11; 4Q**477** passim). Other paratextual elements are usually analyzed in the PHYSICAL DESCRIPTION in the introductory material of the various *DJD* volumes: horizontal and vertical ruling, guide dots at the beginnings or ends of sheets, remnants of stitching of sheets.

Letters omitted by a scribe and reconstructed by modern scholars are usually indicated as < > e.g. 1Q**28b** 15 2.

The degrees of certainty regarding the identification of letters are based on each editor's evaluation of the preserved remains of the letters. The following conventions are employed:

א	certain letter
א̇	probable letter
א̊	possible letter
◦ (mid-line circlet)	remnant of an undetermined letter

No consistency is possible in this system, since what one editor considers a certain letter, e.g. א, another editor will denote as א̇. The same fluctuation is possible between א̇ and א̊, and between א̊ and ◦. In a few volumes (especially vols. X and XXXIV), the uncertainty concerning the distinction between *waw* and *yod* and also, rarely, between final and non-final *mem* is indicated by a *macron*: ו̄, י̄, מ̄. Different possible readings of letters are sometimes recorded in *DJD* by stacking the letters above each other, especially in vol. XXVII (documentary texts) or by parenthesis signs (e.g. *DJD* XXV, 95).

Reconstructions are enclosed in square brackets. Brackets at the beginning and end of the lines are often omitted when the length of the line is unclear. Right brackets were not used in the texts originally published in *DJD* XXV.

Summary of the symbols employed

א	certain letter
א̇	probable letter
א̊	possible letter
◦ (mid-line circlet)	remnant of an undetermined letter
ו	either *yod* or *waw*
[א]	reconstructed text
⌈א⌉	reconstructed text (according to a parallel manuscript; see 11Q**19** [part 5])
______	*paragraphos*
< >	a modern correction, sometimes an addition, e.g. 1QS VI 7
{א}, {a}	usually: erased letter(s) or surface; for texts published in *DJD* I-VII rarely: deletion, scribal dots, strike-through
~~אמתו~~, ~~truth~~	crossing out a letter or word with a line, e.g. 4Q**405** 3 i 12, 4Q**266** i e 2
מ̇על	deletion dots above, below, or around letters, e.g. 4Q**434** 1 i 1
(א)	alternative or uncertain reconstruction, e.g. 4Q**524** 6–13 (*DJD* XXV, 95). In the texts of *DJD* VII these parentheses denote reconstructions in parallel texts, e.g. 4Q**509** 8 6
א/ב	different options, e.g. 1Q**25** 2 4 (*DJD* I, 100)
(saying)	in the *translation*: words added for clarity
שׁזע^{ק}תם, ^{six} months	superscript letter or word
///	erasure or damage in the leather (undetermined letters), e.g. 4Q**169** 3–4 iii 11
𐤉𐤄𐤅𐤄	Tetragrammaton (the four-letter name of God represented in paleo-Hebrew letters)
• • • •	Tetrapuncta (the four-letter name of God represented in the text by four [five] dots), e.g. 4Q**176** 1–2 i 6
vac(at)	interval (usually: the writing space was intentionally left blank)
recto/verso	observe/reverse side of a document
top/bottom margin	part of the top/bottom margin has been preserved
italics (in translation)	doubtful translation (usually single words)
italics (in translation)	biblical quotations (usually long stretches within quotation marks)
boldface (in translation)	the Hebrew word for 'God' is either the Tetragrammaton in paleo-Hebrew characters, or is represented by four dots
word 1/word 2 (in translation)	alternative translations (e.g. 4Q**285** 3 4)

ABBREVIATIONS

1. Texts from the Judaean Desert

apGen	Genesis Apocryphon
apocr	apocryphon
Ber	*Berakhot* (Blessings)
Cal. Doc.	Calendrical Document
D	Damascus Document
DibHam	*Dibre Hameʾorot* (Words of the Luminaries)
DM	*Dibre Moshe* (Words of Moses)
En	Enoch
Enastr	Enoch, Astronomical Books
EnGiants	Enoch, Giants
EpJer	Epistle of Jeremiah
Flor	Florilegium
H(od)	*Hodayot* (Thanksgiving Scroll/Hymns)
Hym/Pr	Hymns or Prayers
Hym/Sap	Hymnic or Sapiential fragment(s)
Jub	Jubilees
Kgs	Kings
Lit	Liturgy
M	*Milḥamah* (War Scroll)
Mez	Mezuzah
MidrEschat	Midrash Eschatology
MMT	*Miqṣat Maʿaśe Ha-Torah* (Some of the Torah Observations)
MSM	*Midrash Sefer Moshe*
Myst	Mysteries
NJ	New Jerusalem
Ord	Ordinances
p	*pesher*
par	paraphrase
Pent	Pentateuch
Phyl	Phylactery
ps	pseudo-
Pr	Prayer(s)
PrFêtes	Prières pour les fêtes (Prayers for Festivals)
PrNab	Prayer of Nabonidus
PrQuot	Prières quotidiennes (Daily Prayers)
RitMar	Rituel de mariage (Marriage Ritual)
RitPur	Rituel de purification (Purification Ritual)
RP	Reworked Pentateuch
S	*Serekh ha-Yaḥad* (Community Rule)
Sa	Rule of the Congregation

Sam	Samuel
sap	sapiential
Sb	Rule of the Blessings
ShirShabb	*Shirot ʿOlat ha-Shabbat* (Songs of the Sabbath Sacrifice)
T	Temple Scroll
TNaph, etc.	Testament of Naphtali
Tanḥ	Tanḥumim
Test	Testimonia
tg	targum
TLevi	Testament of Levi
Tob	Tobit
Unid.	unidentified

2. General Abbreviations

ar	Aramaic
col.	column
cr(ypt)A	cryptic script A
DJD	*Discoveries in the Judaean Desert*
FARMS	Foundation for Ancient Research & Mormon Studies
fr(a)g.	fragment
gr	Greek
Ḥev	Naḥal Ḥever
Kh. Q.	Khirbet Qumran
lat	Latin
Mal	Malachi
Mas	Masada
Milik, *BE*	J. T. Milik, *The Books of Enoch* (Oxford: Clarendon, 1976)
ms	manuscript
Mur	Murabbaʿat
nab	Nabataean
ostr	ostracon
paleo	paleo-Hebrew
PAM	Palestine Archaeological Museum
pap	papyrus
Q	Qumran
r	recto
S	Serekh
Se	Seiyal
Study Edition	F. García Martínez and E. J. C. Tigchelaar, *The Dead Sea Scrolls, Study Edition,* vol. 2 (Leiden/Boston/Cologne: E. J. Brill, 1998)

Sir	Sirach
TOC	Table of Contents
v	verso
WAC	M. Wise, M. G. Abegg, & E. Cook, *The Dead Sea Scrolls: A New Translation* (San Francisco: HarperSanFrancisco, 1996)

A. Historical Texts and Tales

1. Historical Texts

4Q**322a** (4QHistorical Text H?) ed. E. J. C. Tigchelaar, *DJD* XXVIII

Frg. 1 (formerly Mishmarot C^{b} 3)

1]◦◦[
2]◦◦[
3]◦[ ]ש[
4]◦[ ]נ֯י֯ת[
5]◦◦ אנש[י
6]◦ ו֯נגד אר[
7]◦מרו בע[
8]שבעים י֯[
9]שהי֯א[

Frg. 2 (formerly Mishmarot C^{b} 5)

1]כ֯בשו֯[ ]ה֯◦[
2]כ ה◦[
3]◦[ ]◦ן֯ וי֯ה◦[
4]ב֯ע֯[ ]◦ אי֯ש֯ ע[
5]י֯ש֯[ ] למ֯[רח]שון [
6]◦שני שמ֯ני֯ם֯[

Frg. 3 (formerly Mishmarot C^{b} 4)

1]◦◦[
2] [
3] [
4]◦◦◦[
5] לע֯[
6] ת֯שע֯[ה

4Q**332** (4QHistorical Text D) ed. J. Fitzmyer, *DJD* XXXVI

Frg. 1

1 [ ]א בעשו֯[ה בחודש הששי]
2]בארבעה עשר בו ביא[ת֯ ידעיה ב֯ש֯שה עש֯[ר בו]

A. Historical Texts and Tales

1. Historical Texts

4Q322a (4QHistorical Text H?) trans. E. J. C. Tigchelaar

Frg. 1

5.] me[n
6.] and opposite [

8.]seventy [
9.]which is[

Frg. 2

1.]subdued[ ] [

3.] [ ] and [
4.] [ ] man [
5.] [ ] of Ma[rḥe]shvan [
6.] eighty[

Frg. 3

6.] nin[e

4Q332 (4QHistorical Text D) trans. J. Fitzmyer*

Frg. 1

1. [ ] on the tenth (day)[in the sixth month]
2. [on the fourteenth in it the entran]ce of (the priestly course of) Jedaiah; on the sixteen[th in it]

* Cf. Part 4 I (Calendrical Texts).

3] בעשרים]ושבעה בחודש[השביעי [
4]] הושיב ג◦[[
5]]אים וגם ◦[[
6] מ]רורי הנפש ◦[[
7]]אסירים[[

Frg. 2

1 ל]תת לו יקר בערב[ים
2 בת]שעה לשבט זה[
3]ה שהוא [ע]שרים בחודש[
4]ביסוד באה שלמציון ◦[ ]
5] להקביל את[
6]ב הרקנוס מרד[בארסטבולוס
7]להקביל[

Frg. 3

1]◦◦ ה◦[
2 ראש הכת]יאים הרג ש[
3 ב]חמישי בידעיה זה[

bottom margin?

4Q**333** (4QHistorical Text E) ed. J. Fitzmyer, *DJD* XXXVI

Frg. 1

1]]◦ עשרים
2]]◦
3] בי]חזקאל שהוא
4]]הרג אמליוס
5] בחוד]ש השביעי
6] ב]י[את] גמול
7] ש]הוא
8]]הרג אמליוס

Frg. 2

1]איש יהודי א[

bottom margin

4Q**468e** (4QHistorical Text F) ed. M. Broshi, *DJD* XXXVI

1 [ס◦◦◦◦]
2 ה]רוג את רוב הגבר]ים
3]פותלאיס והנפש אשר ◦[

bottom margin

3. [on the twenty-]seventh in the[seventh] month [
4. [ ] he settled [ ]
5. [ ] and also [ ]
6. [em]bittered in soul [ ]
7. [ ]prisoners[ ]

Frg. 2

1. to]give him honour among the Arab[s
2. on the n]inth of Shebat, this (is)[
3.] which is the [tw]entieth in the month[of
4.]with secret counsel Salome came [
5.] to confront the[
6.] Hyrcanus rebelled[against Aristobulus
7.]to confront[

Frg. 3

2. the leader of the Kitt]im killed S[
3. on the] fifth in (the course of) Jedaiah, this (is)[

4Q**333** (4QHistorical Text E) trans. J. Fitzmyer

Frg. 1

1. [ ] twenty
2. [ ]
3. [in Je]hezkel, which is
4. [ ]Aemilius killed
5. [in] the seventh [mon]th
6. [the en]tr[ance of] Gamul
7. [which] is
8. [ ]Aemilius killed

Frg. 2

1.]a Jewish man [

4Q**468e** (4QHistorical Text F) trans. M. Broshi

1.] *s* [
2. ki]lling the multitude of me[n
3.]Potlais and the people that [

2. COURT STORIES

4Q**242** (4QPrNab ar) ed. J. Collins, *DJD* XXII

Frgs. 1, 2a, 2b, 3

1 מלי צ[ל]תא די צלי נ֯ב֯ני מלך [בב]ל מלכ֯[א רבא כדי כתיש הוא]
2 בשחנא באישא בפתגם א֯[לה]א בתימן[אנה נבני בשחנא באישא]
3 כתיש הוית שנין שבע ומן [די] שוי א[להא עלי אנפוהי ואסא לי]
4 וחטאי שבק לה גזר והוא֯ יהודי מ֯[ן בני גלותא על לי ואמר]
5 החוי֯ וכתב למעבד יקר ור֯[בו] לשם א[להא עליא וכן כתבת אנה]
6 כתיש הוית בשחנא ב[אישא] בתימן [בפתגם אלהא עליא]
7 שנין שבע מצלא הוי[ת קדם] א֯ל֯ה֯י֯ כספא ודהבא [נחשא פרזלא]
8 אעא אבנא חספא מן די [הוית סבר די אלהין ה[מון]
]ד של֯○]○[/ אן
9 [ ]ת֯ [ ]מיה֯ו֯ן֯[

Frg. 4

1]ל֯ב֯ר המון אחלמת
2]מ֯נה אח֯[ל]ף֯ של֯ם֯ של[ותי יתוב עלי]
3]○ [ ]נו רחמי לא יכלת [
4]כ֯מה דמא אנתה ל○[
5]○ ○○[

4Q**550** (4QPrEsther[a] ar) ed. E. Cook

1 [ומש]ת֯מעין לפתריזא אבוך ○[ ]
2 [ ]א֯ ו֯בעבדי לבוש מלכותא ב[ ]ל[ ]○[ל]מ֯עבד
3 עבידת מלכא ככול די קב[ ]ע֯ין֯ בה בשתא
4 ארכת רוחה די מלכא א○[ס]פ֯ר֯י אב[ו]הי ה֯ת֯קריו קדמוהי ובין
5 ספריא אשתכח מגלה ח[דה חתי]מה חתמי[ן] שבעה בעזקתה די דריוש אבוהי
עניגה
6 [ ]○○[דר]יוש מלכא לעבדי שלטנא די ב֯[א]רעא שלם פ֯תיחת קרית השתכח כתיב
בה דריוש מלכא
7 [למלכין די י]מלכון בתרי ולעבדי שלטנא ש[ל]ם֯ ידיע להוא לכון די כול
אנוס ושקר

2. Court Stories

4Q**242** (4QPrNab ar) trans. J. Collins

Frgs. 1, 2a, 2b, 3

1. The words of the p[ra]yer which Nabonidus, king of [Baby]lon, [the great]king, prayed [when he was smitten]
2. with a bad disease by the decree of G[o]d in Teima. [I, Nabonidus, with a bad disease]
3. was smitten for seven years and sin[ce] G[od] set [his face on me, he healed me]
4. and as for my sin, he remitted it. A diviner (he was a Jew fr[om among the exiles) came to me and said:]
5. 'Pro[cla]im and write to give honour and exal[tatio]n to the name of G[od Most High,' and I wrote as follows:]
6. 'I was smitten by a b[ad] disease in Teima [by the decree of the Most High God.]
7. For seven years [I] was praying [to] the gods of silver and gold, [bronze, iron,]
8. wood, stone, clay, since [I thoug]ht that th[ey were] gods [ ]
9.]their[

Frg. 4

1.]apart from them. I was made strong again
2.]from it he caused to pass. The peace of [my] repo[se returned to me]
3.] my friends. I was not able [
4.]how you are like [

4Q**550** (4QPrEsther[a] ar) trans. E. Cook

1. [ ] would obey Patireza your father [ ]
2. and among those who make the royal garments [to] make/do
3. the business of the king, according to everything that [ ]. At that very time
4. the king was unable to fall asleep, [ ] the records of his father were read before him, and among
5. the books was found a scroll [seal]ed seven times with the signet of Darius his father. On the outside it said
6. [ ] ['Dar]ius the king to those who exercise authority in the earth, greeting.' It was opened and read, and the following was found written in it: 'Darius the king
7. [to the kings who] will reign after me and to those who exercise authority, greeting. Let it be known to you that every oppressor and liar'

4Q**550a** (4QPrEsther[b] ar) ed. E. Cook

1 אנש להן יד[ע] מלכא הׄן איתי [
2 ולא יבד שמ֯ה טבא [ו]הימנו[תה
3 מלכא איתי לפתריזא בר ו◦[
4 נפלת עלוהי אימת בית ספ[
5 אושי מלכ֯א די תמ֯[ר] ותתיהב [
6 ביתי ו֯נ֯כסי לכול מה די ית[
7 התכיל ותקבל עבידת אבוך [

4Q**550b** (4QPrEsther[c] ar) ed. E. Cook

1] א֯[ו]שׄי מלכא די תמר לשר^ה^ת֯א א֯[ ]ת֯ה נד[
2] פׄתׄרׄיזא אב֯[וך]מן יומא די קם ע֯ל עבידת[ה מן]קדם מלכא ◦[
3]ה עמ֯[ה ו]ה֯[ו]הׄ עבד מן קשוט ומ֯ן הי֯[מנו ק]דמוהי [
4]◦אׄ ואמר אושי [
5]נ֯ה ארג[ונא
6]ל[ת]לׄת ש◦[

4Q**550c** (4QPrEsther[d] ar) ed. E. Cook

Col. i

1 ארו ידע אנתהׄ[ ]ת֯ ◦[ ]לי[ ]י ובחובי אבהתי
2 די חטו קדמיך ו[ ]שפא לר[ ] ונגדת ◦[ ]יך גבר
3 יהודי מן רברבני מ֯[לכותא] לה קאם לקבלה ובׄ[ע]א[ ]רא טב[א]
4 גברא טבא עבד [ ]א מה אעבד לכה ואנתה ידעׄ[מה]אפש[ר]
5 לגבר כותי֯ להתבה[לגבר]כׄו֯תך קאם באתר די אנתה קאם [ ]ה א◦[ ]
6 ב֯[ר]ם מה ד֯י אנתה צ[ב]א פקדני וכדי [תמ]ו֯תׄ אׄקׄברנך ◦[ ]
7 עמר בכול אפשר די תע[ל] ית עבידתי ק[דמיך כ]ול די[

Col. ii

1 [ ]◦[ ]שא גזרת ◦[ו]תׄנ֯[יני]א אזלו֯[
2 [ל]מכת[ב ות]ל[י]ת֯י֯א אזל[ו]◦ בלבוש֯[
3 [ ]כליל דה[ב על רי]ש֯ה וחמ[י]שיׄא אזל[ו
4 [ ]ב֯לחודוהי ר[וש]תיתיא אזלו אכׄ[
5 למ◦[כל כ]סף ו^[כ]ל^ ד֯הב[ ]י֯ן די [אי]תי לבגושי בכפ֯ל֯[

4Q550a (4QPrEsther[b] ar) trans. E. Cook

1. a man, therefore the king knows if there is [
2. and his good name and [his] reputation will not perish [
3. the king [asked], 'Does Patireza have a son?' And [
4. the fear of the scri[bal] guild fell on him [
5. the gifts (?) (*or*: pillars [?]) of the king that you shall say and it will be given [
6. my house and my possessions to anything that [
7. are you able to take upon yourself your father's business? [

4Q550b (4QPrEsther[c] ar) trans. E. Cook

1.] the gifts (?) (*or*: pillars [?]) of the king that you should say to Sharhata (?) [
2.] Patireza your father from the day that he stood over [his] business [from] before the king [
3.] with him and he served honestly and relia[bly be]fore him [
4.] and he said, The gifts (?; *or*: pillars) of [the king
5.] him in pur[ple
6.]three [

4Q550c (4QPrEsther[d] ar) trans. E. Cook

Col. i

1. For you know [ ] in the sins of my fathers
2. that they sinned before you and [ ] peaceful and I spent a long time [ ] a man,
3. a Jew, from the nobles of [the kingdom] standing opposite him and asking [ ] a good [ ]
4. the good man has done [ ] what shall I do for you, since you know[what is] possible
5. for a man like me to repay [a man] like you, standing in the place where you stand [ ] [ ]
6. However, whatever you w[an]t, command me, and when [you] die, I will bury you [ ]
7. dwelling in everything, it may be that you would bring my work be[fore you] all that [ ]

Col. ii

1. [ ] I decree [ ] and the se[con]d ones passed[
2. [to] writ[e and] the third ones passed [ ] in the clothing of [
3. [ ] a crown of gol[d on] his he[ad;] and the fifth ones passed [
4. [ ] he alone [ ] and the sixth ones passed [
5. [all] silver and all gold, [ ] that belonged to Bagoshi, in double measure [

6 ושב[יעיא אזלו]◦ על בש[ל]ם בגסׄרו לדרת מלכא ◦[
7 בגושׁׄ[י]ב ל֯[ ]◦בה ר[ ]◦◦[וק]טׄיל אדין עׄל[ב]גסרו לד[ר]ת
מלכא ש◦[
8 ואחדׄה בי[דה] על רישׁׄ[ה]הׄ ונשׁקה ענה ואמר בׄ[גס]רו בגסרו מן [

Col. iii

1]עליא די אנתון דחלין ו[פ]לחין הו שׂליט ב[כול אר]עא כול די יצבא קרוב
ביׄקׄר ל[ ]◦[
2]כׄול אנש די ימר מלהׄ[באי]שא על בׄגסרו נׄ[ית]קטל בדיל די לא אית[י] כׄ[
3]טה אׄנה ל[ע]לם ◦[ ]◦ די ח֯ה כׄ[ ]תרתין ואמר מלכא יכתׄ[ב
4]עׄזׄ[ ]◦[ש]לטׄ[נ]ואנון בדרת בית מלכׄ[א]רׄבתאׄ[
5 י]קׄומ[ו]ן בתר בגסרׄ[ו] קרין בכתׄבא דנ[ה
6 ב]אישׁׄא באישתה תאבה על[ריש]ה כ[
7 זר]עׄה *vacat*

Frg. 2

1]אמריןׄ[
2] לבגוש[י
3 ב]גסרו ער[
4]א בגוש[י

Frg. 3

2]הי ◦[
3]◦יתא ש[
4]ש ושויו◦[

Frg. 4

2]◦◦[
3]דיט◦[
4]שתה די בגו[שי

Frg. 5

4]◦ אקבל

4Q**550d** (4QPrEsther^{e} ar) ed. E. Cook

Frg. 1

1]קדם מלכא אמׄ[ר
2]הלך בקוריאׄ[
3 ע]ל אנפיכׄ[ון
4 ב]גסרו כדׄ[

Frg. 2

1]עבד עׄ[
2] דכרון ◦[
3]ל[

6. and the seve[nth ones passed] Bagasraw came in good health to the court of the king [
7. Bagosh[i] [ ] killed, then [Ba]gasraw entered the court of the king [ ]
8. so he took him by the h[and] on [his] head [ ] and he kissed him. He raised his voice and said, Ba[gas]raw, Bagasraw, who/from [

Col. iii
1.]the Most High that you revere and worship He rules over [all the] earth. All who will, come in honour to [
2.]everyone who says anything [b]ad about Bagasraw [ ] shall be killed, so that there may be no [
3.] I forever [ ] that is proper [ ] twice. And the king said, 'Let it be wr[itten]
4.] ruler [ ] and they are in the court of the great king [
5. those] who arise after Bagasr[aw] will read in this book [
6. who says anything] bad, evil shall come upon his [head
7.] *vacat*

Frg. 3
2.] his (?) [

4.] they placed [

Frg. 2
1.]they say[
2.] to Bagosh[i
3. Ba]gasraw [
4.] Bagosh[i

Frg. 5
4.] I will receive

Frg. 4

4.] of Bago[shi

4Q550d (4QPrEsther^{e} ar) trans. E. Cook

Frg. 1
1.]before the king he sa[id
2.]he went in the city[
3.] on y[our] face [
4. Ba]gasraw when[

Frg. 2
1.] he did (*or*: servant) [
2.] memorandum [

4Q**550e** (4QPrEsther[f] ar) ed. E. Cook

1]א֯ר֯ו מן צפונא אתיה באישתא ◦[ ]

2] ◦בנה ציון ובה יסתתרון כל עניי עמ[ה]

3] *vacat*

4]◦מו עלוהי כריפו בין מדי לפרס ואתור ולימא

5] *vacat*

3. DIDACTIC TALE

Tobit

4Q**196** (4QpapTob[a] ar) ed. J. Fitzmyer, *DJD* XIX

Frg. 1 Tob 1:17

1]]שורא די נ֯ינו֯ה֯[[

Frg. 2 Tob 1:19–2:2

top margin

1 [חד מ]ן֯ ב֯֯ נינוה והחוי למלכ֯[א עלי ד]י֯ אנה קב[ר אנון ו]א֯חוית וכדי ידעת [די] ידע בי

2 [ולי בעה למקט]ל֯ ◦דחלת וערקת֯[[20]כ]ל֯ ד֯[י]הוה לי ולא שביק פ לי כל מנד֯[עם]

3 [ ]ל[הן חנ]ה֯ אנתתי וט֯ו֯ב֯יה ברי [21]ולא הוה יומין א֯[רבעין]

4 [תרי בנו]ה֯י ואנון ערקו לטורי אררט ומלך {ומ[לך} אסרחדו]ן֯

5 [והוא]א֯שלט לאחיקר בר ענאל אחי על כל ש֯[יזפנו]ת֯

6 [מלכותה ולה הוה ש]לט֯ן֯ ע֯ל֯[כ]ל ה֯מ֯רכלות מלכא [22]ובעה אחיקר ע֯ל֯י֯

7 [ארי ואחי]ק֯ר֯ א֯ח֯י֯ הוה ר֯ב֯ שקה ורב עזק֯ן֯ וה֯מ֯ר֯כ֯ל

8 [ו]ש֯יזפן קדם אסרחריב מלך אתו֯ר ואשלטה אסרחדו֯ן תנין לה ארי

9 ב֯ר֯ א֯חי הוה ומן בית אבי ומ֯ן משפחתי [2:1]וביומי אסרחדו֯ן [מל]כא כדי תבת

10 לב֯י֯ת֯י ואתבת לי חנה אנתתי וטוביה ברי ביום חג שבו[עיא הות] ל[י]

11 שרו טבה ורבעת ל[מאכ]ל [2]ו֯א֯קרבו֯ פ֯ת֯[ו]ר֯א לקודמי וחזית נפ֯ת֯ניא די קרבו

12 עלוהי שגיאין ואמר֯[ת לטו]ב֯יה ברי ברי אזל דבר לכל מ֯ן֯ [די ת]השכח באח֯[ינא]

13 [ ]◦◦ ב֯רי אזל דבר ואתהייתה ויכל֯ [כחדא]ע֯מ֯י֯ וה֯א֯ א֯נ֯ה֯

bottom margin

4Q**550e** (4QPrEsther[f] ar) trans. E. Cook

1.] behold, from the north comes evil [
2.] building Zion and in it all the poor of [his] people will take shelter
3.] *vacat*
4.] upon him/it a battle (?) between Media and Persia and Assyria and the sea
5.] *vacat*

3. Didactic Tale

Tobit

4Q**196** (4QpapTob[a] ar) trans. J. Fitzmyer

Frg. 1 Tob 1:17

1. [ ]the wall of Nineveh[ ]

Frg. 2 Tob 1:19–2:2

1. [one o]f the Ninevites, and he made known to [the] king [about me th]at I was bury[ing them, and] I hid. When I knew [that] he knew about me
2. [and was seeking to kil]l [me], I became afraid and I fled. [[20] a]ll th[at] was mine, and noth[ing] was left to me
3. ex[cept Hann]ah, my wife, and Tobiah, my son. [21]And there were not f[orty] days
4. [ ] his [two sons] and they fled to the mountains of Ararat. Then [Esarhaddo]n began to reign
5. [and he] put Aḥiqar, son of ʿAnaʾel, my kinsman, in charge of all the c[redit ac-coun]ts
6. [of his kingdom; and he had c]ontrol over [al]l the treasury accounts of the king. [22]And Aḥiqar interceded on my behalf.
7. [Now Aḥi]qar, my kinsman, had been the chief cup-bearer, the keeper of the signet rings, treasury accountant,
8. [and c]redit accountant under Sennacherib, the king of Assyria. Esarhaddon put him in charge as second to himself. Now
9. he was the son of my brother, of my father's house, and of my family. [2:1]In the days of Esarhaddon, the [ki]ng, when I had returned
10. to my house, and Hannah, my wife, and Tobiah, my son, were restored to me, [there was] for [me] on the day of the festival of Wee[ks]
11. a fine dinner, and I reclined to [ea]t. [2]And they brought in the ta[b]le before me, and I saw (that) the delicacies that they offered
12. upon it were many. [I] said [to To]biah, my son, 'My son, go, get anyone [whom you] will find of [our] kinsfolk
13. [ ] my son, go (and) get (him), and let him be brought in that he may eat [together] with me; and look, I

Frg. 3 Tob 2:3

1] את]חנק [[

Frg. 4 Tob 2:10-11

1] לעי]ל֯ם [11]בעד]נא דן [

Frg. 5 Tob 3:5

1] ל]מ֯עבד ב֯י [[

Frg. 6 Tob 3:9-15

top margin

1] אזלי]בתרהון ו֯ל֯[א] נ֯חזי לכי בר [או ברה לכל עלמין]
2] [10] ובכת וסלק]ת֯ לע֯לית בית֯ [אבוה [
3] [
4] [
5] ולא אשמע ח]ס֯ד עוד בחיי ו[[11] [
6]]לק֯[ב]ל[[
7] ובריך]ש֯מ֯ך֯ קדישא֯[וי]קירא ל֯כל ע֯[למין ו]יברכ֯[ונך כל עובדיך [
8 [[12]וכען פנית ע]ליך אנפי ועינ֯[י נ]טלת [13]אמר לאפטרותני מן ע֯[ל ארעא]
9] [14]אנתה •••• י]דע ד[י]דכיה אנה בגרמי מ֯[ן כ]ל֯ ט֯מ֯א֯ת֯[גבר]
10 [[15]ולא ג]ע֯לת ש[מי ושם אב]֯י בכ֯ל ארעת שבינא֯[יחי]ד֯א אנה[לאבי]
11 [ולא]ב֯ר לה אחרן די י֯ר֯ת֯נ֯[ה] ו֯אח לה ו֯ק֯ר֯י֯ב֯ ל[א איתי] ל[ה די]
12 [אנטר נ]פ֯שי לבר ד[י אהו]ה לה אנתה כבר א֯ב֯[דו]מני שב֯ע֯[ת גברין]
13]]ל֯[[

Frg. 7 Tob 3:17

1] לא]ס֯יא ח[רריא [
2] נהר]ת ש[מיא [
3]]ל[[

Frg. 8 Tob 4:2
Parallel: 4Q**200** 2

1] מו]ת֯ ולמא לא[אקרא לטוביה [
2] ע]ל֯ כס֯פ֯א[דן [

Frg. 3 Tob 2:3

1. [ ]has been strangled [ ]

Frg. 4 Tob 2:10-11

1. [to E]lam. [11]At [that] tim[e]

Frg. 5 Tob 3:5

1. [to] deal with me [ ]

Frg. 6 Tob 3:9-15

1. [Go] after them! May we ne[ver] see a son [or daughter] of yours!
2. [[10] and she wept and wen]t up to an upstairs room of [her father's] house

5. [and may I no] longer [hear such a re]proach in my lifetime, and [[11]]
6. [ ]tow[a]rd[ ]
7. [Blest be] your holy [and ho]nourable name for[ever!] May [all your deeds] bless [you!]
8. [[12]And now I have turned] my face [t]o you and [have lif]ted up [my] eyes. [13]Bid me depart from up[on the earth.]
9. [[14]You, O **Lord**, k]now th[at] I myself am clean fr[om al]l defilement [with a man.]
10. [15]I [have not be]smirched [my] na[me or the name of] my [father] in all the land of our captivity. I am [my father's on]ly child,
11. [and] he has [no] other child who will be an heir to [him]; n[or] does he [have] a kinsman or relative,
12. [for whom I should keep my]self, or a son for who[m I shal]l be a wife. Already seve[n husbands] ha[ve] perished on me.

Frg. 7 Tob 3:17

1. [to cu]re [the] whi[te scales]
2. [the ligh]t of hea[ven]

Frg. 8 Tob 4:2

1. [dea]th, and why [should I] not [call Tobiah]
2. [a]bout [this] money [ ]

Frg. 9 Tob 4:5

1] ו]ביו֯מ֯ך ◦[[
2] הוי דכר ל•••• ואל תצבי ל]מ֯ח֯טא ולמשטה [מאמרה [
3]]ד֯ שק֯ר֯ [[

Frg. 10 Tob 4:7
Parallel: 4Q**200** 2

1] כארך]י֯דך ברי הוי ע֯]בד צדקתא [

Frg. 11 Tob 4:21–5:1

1] •••• א]להך [
2] 5:1 כול די פקד]ת֯ לי אעבד֯] [

Frg. 12 Tob 5:9

1 קרא֯] לי [
2 מהי֯]מן [

bottom margin

Frg. 13 Tob 6:6-8
Parallel: 4Q**197** 4 i 4–19

top margin

1] נונא ואכ]ל ואף לאורחא ש֯וה֯ מ֯ל]יחה שאר]יתיא א]זלו תריהון]
2] 7 באדין ש]א֯ל עולימא למל֯]אכא] *vacat* [עזריה] א֯חי א֯מ֯]ר לי]
3] מה סם ב]לב֯ב֯ נונא וכב֯ד֯ה] [עלוהי ◦]]ן
4] 8]◦]ו]ל]א] יסחרו]
[
5]]ל[[

Frg. 14 Col. i Tob 6:13-18
Parallel: 4Q**197** 4 ii

1] 13 ו]כ֯די נת]וב מן [
2] [
3] [
4] 15 דחל אנה מן שדא דן] די֯ ר֯]ח]ם֯ לה
5]]ש֯ד֯ קטל להן
6] חי]י אבי ואמי
7] לא איתי להון בר אחרן]די יקבר
8 אנון] 16 הלא תדכר לפק]ודי א֯בוך די פקדך
9] וכע]ן שמע֯ לי אחי א֯ל֯
10] בלי]לי֯א֯ דן֯
11] 17 ס]ב מן לבב
12 נונא] 18 וירי]ח֯ שדא ו֯י֯]ערק]
13] וכדי תצבי] ל]מהוה עמה]

Frg. 9 Tob 4:5

1. [and] in your day [ ]
2. [Be mindful of the LORD, and seek not to] sin or to transgress [his command]
3. [ ] wickedness [ ]

Frg. 10 Tob 4:7

1. [according to what is in] your hand, my son, gi[ve alms]

Frg. 11 Tob 4:21–5:1

1. [the LORD, your G]od[ ]
2. [5:1 All that] you [have ordered] me I shall do [ ]

Frg. 12 Tob 5:9

1. Call [for me]
2. trustwor[thy]

Frg. 13 Tob 6:6-8

1. [the fish and at]e (it); moreover he sal[ted] the [re]st for the journey. [The two of them] jo[urneyed along]
2. [7 Then] the youth [a]sked [the] an[gel] *vacat* [Azariah] my brother, tel[l me],
3. [what medicine is in] the heart of the fish and its liver?[ ]about it [ ]
4. [8 and] they will no[t] encounter[ ]

Frg. 14 Col. i Tob 6:13-18

1. [13 and] when we re[turn from]

4. [15 'I am afraid of this demon] which is [in lo]ve with her.
5. [ ]a demon kills them.
6. [the li]fe of my father and mother
7. [They do not have another child] who will bury
8. [them. 16 'Do you not remember the com]mands of your father, who ordered you
9. [No]w listen to me, my brother; do not
10. [on] this (very) [ni]ght
11. [17 t]ake some of the heart of
12. [the fish. 18 and] the demon [will sme]ll (it) and will [flee]
13. [and when you wish] to [be with her]

Frg. 14 Col. ii Tob 6:18–7:6
Parallel: 4Q**197** 4 iii

4 שגיא ר]חמה
[
5 [7:1]עזריה אח]י
[
6 וה]ש[כחו לרעואל יתב ק]דם תרע[דרת]ה ושאלו שלמה לקדמין ואמר[
7 להון לשלם אתיתון ועל]ו ב[שלם] אחי ואעל אנון לביתה [2]ואמר לעדנא
אנתתה]
8 כמה ד]מה עלימא דן לטובי בר דדי] [3]ושאל]ת אנון עדנא
[
9 ואמר]ו לה מן בני נפתלי] די שבי]ן בנינוה [4]
[
10 וא]מרין לה די]ידעין אנח]נא לה
[
11 [5]ואמר טוביה די] אבי הוא [6]וש]ור רעואל
[
12]
[
13]◦
[

Frg. 15 Tob 7:13

1]]וחתם[[

Frg. 16 Tob 12:1

1]די הוה עמ]ך ונתן לה אגרה[[

Frg. 17 Col. i Tob 12:18–13:6
Parallel: 4Q**200** 6 1–3

top margin

1] [18]כדי ה]וית עמכון
2] [19] ל]א אשתית
3] [20] הא אנ]ה סלק
4] [21] למחזה ל]ה [22]והוו
5]מברכין אתחזי להון מל]אך ◦◦◦[◦]
6–12] [
13] [13:3] בה]ון [4]ותמן
14] הוא מראכ]ון והוא
15] [5] על כל חט]איכון
16] [6] ע]לוהי בכל

bottom margin

Frg. 14 Col. ii Tob 6:18–7:6

4. he fell very much [in love with her]
5. 7:1 Azariah, [my] brother[ ]
6. and they fo[u]nd Raguel sitting be[fore the gate of his] dwelling [and they greeted him first. And he said]
7. to them, 'In peace have you come! Now enter [in] peace [my brothers.' And he brought them into his house. 2 He said to Edna, his wife,]
8. 'How [this youth] re[sembles Tobi, the son of my uncle.'] 3 So [Edna] ask[ed them]
9. and [they] said [to her, 'We are of the Naphtalites], who are captive[s in Nineveh.' 4]
10. and [they] sa[id to her], 'W[e] do know [him .]
11. [5 and Tobiah said], 'He is my father!' 6 Then [Raguel] jum[ped up]

Frg. 15 Tob 7:13

1. [ ] and he sealed (it).[ ]

Frg. 16 Tob 12:1

1. [who was with] you, and we shall give him his wages[ ]

Frg. 17 Col. i Tob 12:18–13:6

1. [18 When] I [w]as with you,
2. [19]I did [n]ot drink
3. [20 Look, I] am ascending
4. [21 to see h]im. 22 And they were
5. [blessing there had appeared to them the an]gel of the **LOR[D.]**

6–12. [ ]

13. [13:3 among t]hem. 4 And there
14. [he is y]our [Lord,] and he is
15. [5 because of all] your [si]ns,
16. [6 t]o him with all

Frg. 17 Col. ii Tob 13:6-12

top margin

1 לבכון ו[בכל נ]פ֯שכון ל[מעבד קושטא אדין י]ת֯פנה עליכון
2 ולא [יסתר אנפו]ה֯י מנכון ע֯[וד והודו]לה בכל פמכון
3 ובר[כו למרה]קושטא ור[וממו לה אנה בארעת] שביא מהודה לה
4 ומח֯[וה אנה לג]בורתה ורבו[תה קדם עם חט]אין על לבבכ֯ו֯ן
5 ק֯ו֯[שטא עבדו]ק֯דמוה[י מן] י֯ד֯[ע הן תהוה ס]ליחא[לכון [7] ולאלהי]
6 [מרומם אנה ונ]פ֯שי למ[לך שמיא]כל יומ֯[י חיי]
7 [וכ]ל[ישב]חו רבותה [8] ימללון בתהלי֯[ן]
8 [[9] ירושלם]ק֯ר֯ית קדשא י֯[כת]ש֯נ֯כ֯[י על]
9 [[10] בקו]שטא הוד[י]
10 [יתבנ]ה֯ לכ֯[י]
11 [ ]
12 [ ]
13 [[11]]
14 [מן ד]ר֯י֯ן לדרין ינתנון בכ֯י֯[ ]
15 [ו]ש֯ם רב[יהוה לד]רי עלמא [12] ארי[רין כ]ל֯ [די] ב֯י֯זין וכל די עלי[כי]
16 [ו]א֯רירין כ֯[ל שנאי]כ֯י וכל[ממ]ל֯[לין ע]ל֯י֯כי א֯ר֯י֯ר֯י֯[ן]

bottom margin

Frg. 18 Tob 13:12–14:3

Parallel: 4Q**198** 1 1–2
4Q**200 7** i
4Q**200 7** ii

top margin

1 [שורי]כ֯י֯ וכל ממגר֯י֯[ן מגדליכי]
2 [[13] אדין]חדי ובועי בב[ני קשיטיא]
3 [[14] טובי כ]ל֯ רחמיכי וטוב[י כל]
4 [ע]ל [כ]ל֯ מכתשיכי ד[י]
5 [[15] ברכי ל••••] למלכא רבא [16] ד[י]
6 [שארי]ת֯א מן זרעי ל[מחזה]
7 [תרעי ירושלם ברקת ו]ספ֯יר תתבנין [ ]
8 [מגדלי ירושלם ד]הב תתבנין ועע[יתא [17]]
9 [ ]י֯ן֯ ובאבן די י֯[[18]]
10 [י]מ֯ל[ל]ו֯ לה֯ל[לויה]
11 [בריך עד עלם]עלמיא דביכי יברכון ש֯[מה קדישא עד עלם עלמיא]
12 [[14:1] וספו מלי תודת טו]בי ומית בשלם ב֯[ר שנין מאה תרתי-עשרה וקביר]
13 [[2] והוא בר]שנין חמשין ותמ[נה הוה]
14 [חזות ע]י֯נ֯והי חי בטב ובכ֯[ל עבד]

Frg. 17 Col. ii Tob 13:6-12

1. your heart and [with all] your [s]oul to [do what is righteous. Then he] will turn to you
2. and will no lon[ger hide hi]s [face] from you. [Now acknowledge] him with all your mouth,
3. and bl[ess the Lord of] righteousness, and ex[alt him. In the land of] captivity [I] acknowledge him,
4. and [I] make kn[own] his [po]wer and [his] maj[esty before a sin]ful [people]. According to your heart
5. [do what is] right[eous] before hi[m. Who] know[s whether p]ardon[will be yours. [7]I exalt my]
6. [God, and] my [s]oul (exalts) the ki[ng of heaven]all the day[s of my life]
7. [and let al]l [prai]se his majesty. [8]Let them speak with psalm[s]
8. [[9]Jerusalem,] holy city, he will [affl]ict yo[u, concerning]
9. [[10] with righ]teousness acknowle[dge]
10. [shall be bui]lt for yo[u.]

14. [from ge]nerations to generations they will present in you [ ]
15. [and] a great name [it will be for] everlasting [gene]rations. [12]Cur[sed be al]l [who] despise (you) and all who [inveigh] against [you]
16. [and] cursed be al[l who hate] you and all [who sp]e[ak again]st you. Curs[ed be]

Frg. 18 Tob 13:12–14:3

1. [ ] your [walls], and all who overthr[ow your towers]
2. [[13]Then] rejoice and exult over the child[ren of the righteous]
3. [[14]Blessed are al]l those who love you, and bles[sed are all]
4. [a]t [al]l your afflictions, becau[se]
5. [[15] bless the **LORD**], the great king, [16]becau[se]
6. [there is] the [remna]nt of my offspring to [see]
7. [the gates of Jerusalem] will be built (with) [beryl and] sapphire,
8. [and the towers of Jerusalem] will be built (with) [g]old, and wood[[17]]
9. [ ] and with stone of [[18]]
10. [ ] and let them s[a]y, 'Halle[lujah']
11. [blessed be he forever] and ever, because in you they will bless [his holy] na[me for ever and ever.']
12. [[14:1]T]obi's [words of thanks came to an end], and he died in peace, at the ag[e of one hundred and twelve, and he was buried]
13. [[2]He was] fifty-eig[ht] years [old, when]
14. [the sight of] his [e]yes. He lived in goodness and in al[l he gave alms]

15]לברכה ל[•••• ולהודיה רב̊]ותה [3] קרא[
16]לטוביה ברה ושבע]ת בנוהי ובקדה וא̊מ̊[ר ברי [

bottom margin

Frg. 19 Tob 14:7

1] בארע אברה]ם̇ ב̊ת̇[[
2]]ר̇חמי [אלהא [
3]]ל[[

Unidentified Fragments

Frg. 20 Tob 7:?

1]ז̊[
2]להון כ[
3]סוכ[
4]ויבר◦[
5]ל̊[

Frg. 21

1]גבי ו̊[
2]◦[

Frg. 22

1]יב א[
2]ותר[

Frg. 23

1]כד[י

Frg. 24

1]לרחצנ̊[

Frg. 25

1]◦ל קום[
2]ב̊שר̊ ◦[

Frg. 26

1]◦ ארע[א

Frg. 27

1]ג מ̊ייא[
2]א̊ ̓כ̊ל[

Frg. 28

1]◦ה[
2]◦ע◦[

Frg. 29

1]◦[
2]כ̊די יפלג◦[

Frg. 30

1]ב̊ת ו◦ת[
2]ל[

Frg. 31

1]וברא לע◦[

Frg. 32

1]ע̊למיא ◦[

Frg. 33

1]א עד ד◦[

15. [to bless] the **Lord** and to acknowledge [his] majes[ty. [3] he summoned]
16. [Tobiah his son and] his [sev]en sons and ordered him, sayi[ng, ‘My son,

Frg. 19 Tob 14:7

1. [in the land of Abraha]m in [ ]
2. [ ]those who [truly] love [God]

Unidentified Fragments

Frg. 20 Tob 7:?

2.]to them [

Frg. 23

1.]whe[n

Frg. 25

1.] rise up[

Frg. 24

1.]for confiden[ce

Frg. 27

1.] the water[
2.] and all[

Frg. 26

1. the] land[

Frg. 29

2.]when he/they will divide [

Frg. 31

1.]and the son [

Frg. 33

1.] until [

Frg. 32

1.]the ages [

Frg. 34

1]י למר[

2]עׄל[

Frg. 35

1]◦בח[

Frg. 36

1]א ת[

Frg. 37

1] לם[

2]ל[

Frg. 38

1]◦א ◦◦ [

2]אׄל [

3]ל [

Frg. 39

1]לה תתו[

Frg. 40

1]שׄגיא[

Frg. 41

1]◦◦◦[

Frg. 42

1]◦[

2]◦ש [

3]ל [

Frg. 43

1]בריך[

Frg. 44

1]בחר[

Frg. 45

1]דא [

Frg. 46

1]בא[

Frg. 47

1]ל◦[

Frg. 48

1]עה ל[

Frg. 49

1]שית ל◦[

4Q**197** (4QTob[b] ar) ed. J. Fitzmyer, *DJD* XIX

Frg. 1 Tob 3:6-8

1 [מ]ןׄ די למ[חזה]

2 [7 חסדי]ןׄ מן חדה[ ]

3 [8 שדא באי]שׄא קטלׄ[אנון]

Frg. 2 Tob 4:21–5:1

1 [21 ח]יׄיׄ מסכנא[ ]

2 [5:1]◦[ ]לכׄלהון[ ]

Frg. 40

1.]much[

Frg. 43

1.]blest be[

Frg. 45

1.]this [

Frg. 44

1.]he chose[

4Q**197** (4QTob[b] ar) trans. J. Fitzmyer

Frg. 1 Tob 3:6-8

1. [th]an to se[e]
2. [[7] reproach]es from one[ ]
3. [[8]] the [ev]il [demon] killed [them]

Frg. 2 Tob 4:21–5:1

1. [[21] the li]fe of the poor[ ]
2. [[5:1]]all of them[ ]

Frg. 3 Tob 5:12-14

1 [צ]ר֯י֯ך ל֯ך֯[ ]◦[ ]

2 [ ]למנדע ◦[ ]

3 [13]אנה עזר֯[יה בר]

4 [14]ואמר ל֯ה֯[ ]

5 [ ]למנדע בק֯[שטא]

Frg. 4 Col. i Tob 5:19–6:12

Parallel: 4Q**196** 13

top margin

1 [19]א֯ל ידבק [בכס]ף ברי וכא◦[ ]

2 [20 21ו]אמר לה אל תדחלי בשלם יהך ברי

3 [בש]ל֯ם֯ א֯ל תדחלי ואל תצפי לה אחתי

4 [22]ה֯ אר[חה 6:1ושתק]ה֯ עוד ולא בכת *vacat*

5 [2 ומלא]כא עמה ו֯[ה]ך֯ [כלבא ואזלו]כ֯חדא וסדר להון

6 [לילה והכו ע]ד֯ דקלת 3ונחת עלימ֯[א ושור נו]ן֯ חד רב מן

7 [מיא למב]לע רגל עלימ[א 4 א]ת֯ק֯ף֯ נ֯[ונא וג]ב֯ר֯ עלימא

8 [לנונא ואנפ]ק֯ה ליבשא וא֯[מר לה מלאכא 5פר]ק֯הי ואנפק֯[למררתה ולבב]ה֯

9 [וכבדה שים ב]י֯דך ומעוה֯[י טרד סם הוא מררתה ולבב]ה֯ וכבדה 6ו[פרק]

10 [מררתה ול]ב֯ב֯ה֯ ו֯[כבדה מן נ]ו֯נ֯א ואכל ואף֯[ ]

11 [שארית]א אזלין תרי֯ה֯[ו]ן [כ]חדא [עד] ק֯[רבו ל]ה֯ון למדי *vacat* 7[ ]

12 [וא]מר לה עזריה אחי מה סם בלבב נונא ו֯בכ֯[בדה ובמררתה 8 הן]

13 [ת]א֯תנה קדם גבר או א֯נתא נגיעי שד או רוח[באישא]

14 [לא]י֯סחרון סחרתהו֯[ן] לעלם 9ומררתא למכחל עי֯[ני אנש]

15 [ ]◦[ ]ח֯רריא וי֯ח֯ין 10וכ֯[ד]י֯ ע֯לו לגו מדי וכבר הוא מ֯[דבק לאחמתא 11אמר
רפאל]

16 [לעלי]מ֯א ט֯[ו]ב֯י֯ה א֯חי ואמר[ ]ל֯ה֯ הא אנה ואמר לה אב֯י֯ת֯[רעואל נבית]

17 [וג]ב֯ר֯א מן בית אבונא הוא ואיתי לה ברא שפירה [12ואחרן]

18 [לא] איתי לה לה[ן] ש֯רה֯[ב]ל[חודי]ה ואנתה ק֯[רי]ב֯ לה [על כל אנש למירתה]

19 [וכול די לאבוה סבה]לך֯ ל[אנת]א֯[ו]דינא ל[ך ועלימתא]

bottom margin

Frg. 3 Tob 5:12-14

1. [ne]cessary for you[ ]
2. [ ]to know [ ]
3. [[13]]I am Azar[iah, son of]
4. [ ][14]And he said to him[ ]
5. [ ]to know in tr[uth]

Frg. 4 Col. i Tob 5:19–6:12

1. [[19]]Let my son not cling [to mon]ey, but (let it be for him) like [ ]
2. [[20] [21]And] he said to her, 'Do not fear! My son will go safely,
3. [safe]ly. Do not fear and do not become anxious about him, my sister.
4. [[22] his] journ[ey [6:1]And becoming sile]nt, she wept no more. *vacat*
5. [[2] and] the [ange]l (was) with him, and [the dog we]nt [along, and] together [they travelled.] And there followed for them
6. [a night, and they came t]o the Tigris. [3][The] youth went down [to and] a big [fis]h [leaped up] from
7. [the water to swal]low the foot of [the] youth. [[4] 'O]verpower [the] fi[sh!' And] the youth [grab]bed
8. [the fish and brou]ght it to dry land. And [the angel] s[aid to him, [5]'Sl]it it open and take out [its gall], its [heart,]
9. [and its liver. Keep them w]ith you, but [throw away] it[s] inwards. [A medicine is its gall], its [heart], and its liver.' And [he slit open]
10. [its gall,] its [he]art and [its liver. [6] some of] the [f]ish, and he ate (it). Moreover, [ ]
11. the [rest]. The two of t[h]em went along together [until they] dr[ew near] to Media. *vacat* [7][ ]
12. [and s]aid to him, 'Azariah, my brother, what medicine is in the heart of the fish, [its] liv[er, and its gall?' [8] 'If]
13. [you] smoke it in the presence of a man or a woman afflicted by a demon or an [evil] spirit,
14. [and] thei[r] encounters will [nev]er occur again. [9]And the gall is for anointing the ey[es of a human being]
15. [ ]white scales, and they will get well.' [10]When they entered Media, and he was already ap[proaching Ecbatana, [11]Raphael said]
16. to the [you]th, 'T[o]biah, my brother.' And he said to him, 'Here I am.' He said to him, 'In the house of [Raguel we shall pass the night,]
17. [and] the [m]an is from the house of our father. He has a beautiful daughter[[12]and]
18. he has [no one else] bu[t] Sarah a[lone.] You are re[lat]ed to her [more than anyone else, to inherit her]
19. [and all that belongs to her father. Take her] to yourself as [a wif]e; to [you] belongs the right. [This young girl]

Frg. 4 Col. ii Tob 6:12-18
Parallel: 4Q**196** 14 i

1 [דא היא חכימא ותקיפ]א ושׄפׄירא לחדׄא ואׄבוה רחם[לה וכל די לה יהב לה]
2 [ול]ךׄ [גזיר למירת ל]אבוהא ועליך דין קשטא [13]גזר למׄ[סבה וכען שמע לי]
3 [אחי]תׄמלל בׄעׄל[מ]תא דא בליליא דן תׄקימנה ותסבנה לך לאנתׄ[ה]
4 [נעבד לה]מׄשׄתׄוׄתא וידע אׄנה די לא יכול רעואל למכליה מנך בדיל דׄיׄ הוׄא ידע
5 [ ]וׄלמסב ברתה מן כל אנ[ש ארי ה]וא ידׄ[ע] די הן ינתננה לגבר
6 [אחרן ספר]מׄושה וכענ[נמלל בעלי]מׄתׄ[א]דא ליליא דן ונקׄימנה
7 [לך [14]אדין ענה טוביה ואמר לרפ]אל עזריהׄ אחי שׄמעת
8 [ומיתו כ]דׄיׄ עלין עליה הוו
9 [[15]וכען ד]חׄל אנה [מ]נׄ שדא די
10 [רחמה לא]בי ולאמי
11 [לקברא ובר א]חׄרן לא
12 [איתי להון די יקבר אנון [16] לפקודי אבוך]דׄי פקדך
13 [ש]דׄאׄ דן וסבׄהׄ
14 [[17]]
15 [[18]]
16 [למהוה ע]מה עׄוׄ[רו מן]
17 [וא]ל תדחלׄ[די ל]ךׄ היא חליקא ולך[דינא גזר למסבה]
18 [ ]תׄשזבׄ[ה ו]מדמה אנה די להוון לך [מנה בנין ול]הׄוון
19 [לך כאחין וכדי ש]מע טוביה מלי רפא[ל די היא ל]הׄ אחא ומן

Frg. 4 Col. iii Tob 6:18–7:10
Parallel: 4Q**196** 14 ii

top margin

1 [בית זרע אבוהי ש]גׄיא רחמה ולבהׄ <דבק> בה [לחד]א [7:1]וכדי עלו לגוא אחׄמׄ[תא אמר]
2 לה טוביה עׄזׄ[ריה אחי ד]בׄרני קשיטא לבית רעואל אחונא ודברה ואזל[ו לבית]
3 רעואל ואשכחׄ[ו ל]רׄעׄוׄאׄ[ל י]תׄב קדם תרע תׄהׄ ושאלו שלמה לקדמין ואמר לׄהון

Frg. 4 Col. ii Tob 6:12-18

1. [is wise, strong,] and very beautiful, and her father loves [her. All that he has he gives to her;]
2. [and for] you [the inheritance of] her father [is determined]; and a right decision [13]has been determined on your behalf, to t[ake her. Now listen to me,]
3. [my brother.] You will speak about this [you]ng girl tonight; you will engage her and take her for your wif[e]
4. [And we shall make] the wedding-feast [for her]. I know that Raguel will not be able to withhold her from you, becaus[e] he knows
5. [that you have more right] and to take his daughter than anyone el[se. For h]e kno[ws] that, if he were to give her to
6. [another] man, [the book of] Moses. And now [we shall speak about] this [you]ng gir[l] tonight, and we shall engage her
7. [for you. [14]Then Tobias said in reply to Raph]ael, Azariah, my brother, I have heard
8. [and they died, wh]en they went into her.
9. [[15]Now] I am [a]fraid [o]f the demon who
10. [loves her] my [fa]ther and my mother
11. [to the grave an]other [son they] do not
12. [have to bury them' [16] the commands of your father] who ordered you
13. [ ]this [de]mon, but take her
15. [18]
16. [to be w]ith her, get up [from]
17. [do no]t fear [because] she [has been destined for] you, and for you [the decision has been made to take her]
18. [ ]you will save [her, and] I am sure that there will be [children from her] for you. [And t]hey will be
19. [to you like brothers.' When] Tobiah [h]eard the words of Rapha[el that she was h]is kinswoman and of

Frg. 4 Col. iii Tob 6:18–7:10

1. [the house of relatives of his father,] he fell [ve]ry much in love with her, and his heart <clung> to her [exceeding]ly. [7:1]When they entered Ecba[tana], Tobiah [said]
2. to him, 'Aza[riah, my brother, t]ake me straight to the house of Raguel, our kinsman.' He took him, and [they] went [to the house of]
3. Raguel and foun[d]Rague[l s]itting before the gate of his dwelling. They greeted him first, and he said to them,

4 לשלם אתיתון ועלו בשל֯[ם] אחי ואעל אנון לביתה [2]ואמר לעדנא אנתתה כמא

5 דמה עלימא דן לטובי בר דדי [3]ושאלת אנון עדנא ואמרת להון מנאן אנתון אחי

6 ואמרו לה מן בני נפתלי [די] שבין בנינוה [4]ואמרא להון ידעין אנתון לטובי אחונ[א]

7 ואמרין לה די ידעין אנ֯[ח]נ֯א לה השלם הוא [5]ו֯אמרו לה֯ של[ם ואמ]ר֯ [טו]ב֯י֯ה֯

8 די אבי הוא [6]ושור רעואל נשקה ובכ֯[ה [7]]

9 טבא ע֯ל[יך ברי אנתה] ב֯[ר]ג֯ברא קשיט[א]

10 צור טוביה[בר אחוהי ובכה [8]]

11 [9]דכר די ען ט֯ב֯[ח]

12 למאכל ולמשתה [עזריה אחי אמר לרעואל די ינתן לי שרה]

13 א֯ח֯ת֯י [10]ושמ֯ע֯ [רעואל]

Frg. 5 Tob 8:17–9:4

1 [חייהון לרחמי]ן ולחד֯ו֯ה֯[ ]

2 [[18]ופקד לעבדוהי ד]י֯ יטממו[ן פחתא]

3 [[19] דבר תרי]ת֯ו֯ר֯[ין]

4 [ ]

5 [ ]

6 [[21] אוב]יל עמך לבית א֯[בוך]

7 [ ]ב֯רי אנה אבוך ועדנא א֯[מך]

8 [אל ת]ד֯חל ברי *vacat* [9:1]]

9 ואמר ל]ה֯ [2]עזריה אחי דבר עמך מן תנא אר֯[בעת עבדין]

10 [ו]ת֯אתה בי<ת> ג֯ב֯[א]ל ו֯ה֯ב לה כתב ו֯ס֯[ב כספא [4/3]אנתה]

11 [ידע די מנה]לה֯ו֯[ה אבי יו]מ֯יא והן[ ]

12 [ ]◦ מ֯ו֯מ֯ת֯[ת]

Frg. 6 Tob ?

1 ו]כ֯די מ֯פיגין[

2]◦ ו֯ה֯[

Frg. 7 Tob ?

1]כ֯להו[ן

4Q**198** (4QTob[c] ar) ed. J. Fitzmyer, *DJD* XIX

Frg. 1 Tob 14:2-6
Parallel: 4Q**196** 18 15–16

top margin

1 צדקה והוסף למדחל לאלהא ולה[ודיה רבותה [3]וקרא לטוביה ברה ושבעת]

2 ב֯נוהי ופקדה ואמר ל֯[ה [4]]

3 אלהא די מל[ל בנינוה]

4 נ֯י֯נ֯[ו]ה די מ]ל֯[לו נביאי ישראל]

4. 'In peace have you come! Enter in peac[e], my brothers,' and he brought them into his house. [2]Then he said to Edna, his wife, 'How
5. this youth resembles Tobi, the son of my uncle!' [3]Edna asked them and said to them, 'Where are you from, my brothers?'
6. They said to her, 'We are of the Naphtalites, [who] are captives in Nineveh.' [4]She said to them, 'Do you know Tobi, ou[r] kinsman?'
7. They said to her, 'W[e] do know him.' 'Is he well?' [5]They said to her, 'He is we[ll].' [And To]biah [sa]id,
8. 'He is my father.' [6]Then Raguel jumped up, kissed him, and broke into tea[rs [7]]
9. 'Blessings upon [you, my son; you are the] so[n of] a righteo[us] man. [He fell upon]
10. the neck of Tobiah, [the son of his kinsman, and wept [8]]
11. [9]He slaugh[tered] a ram of the flock [ ]
12. to eat and to drink ['Azariah, my brother, tell Raguel that he should give me Sarah]
13. my kinswoman.' [[10]Raguel] heard [ ]

Frg. 5 Tob 8:17–9:4

1. [their lives with mer]cy and with joy[ ]
2. [[18]Then he ordered his servants th]at they should fill up[the hole.]
3. [[19] take two]steer[s]

6. [[21] car]ry (it) with you to the house of [your] fa[ther]
7. [ ]my son, I am your father, and Edna [is your] mot[her.]
8. [Do not f]ear, my son. *vacat* [[9:1]]
9. [and he said to] him, [2]'Azariah, my brother, take with you from here fo[ur slaves]
10. [and] you will come (to) the hou<se of> Gaba[e]l. Give him the bond, and g[et the money. [3/4]You]
11. [know that my father] will b[e counting] the [d]ays; and if [ ]
12. [ ] oath of [ ]

Frg. 7 Tob ?

1.]all of the[m

Frg. 6 Tob ?

1. and] when they are (?) [
2.] and [

4Q**198** (4QTob[c] ar) trans. J. Fitzmyer

Frg. 1 Tob 14:2-6

1. [and gave] alms, and he continued to fear God and to ack[nowledge his majesty. [3]He summoned his son, Tobiah, and] his [seven]
2. sons, and ordered him, saying to [him. [4]]
3. God, which he utt[ered about Nineveh. and]
4. Nine[veh; what the prophets of Israel ut]ter[ed]

5 כלא יתעבד לזמ֯[ניהון [
6 בכל די אמר אלה[א כל]א יתאיית֯[א ואחינא]
7 יתבין בארע ישראל כלה֯ו֯[ן [
8 [י]ש֯ראל צ֯ו֯יה ושמ֯[רין וירושלם עד]
9 ע֯ד֯נא [5]די יתיב ב֯[רחמין אלהא אנון [
10 [ו]ל֯א֯ כקד[ם עד] עדנא [די [
11 [ויבנון]לירושלם֯ בי[קר [
12]]מללו [נב]י֯א֯[י ישראל [6] [
13] בקשטא]וירמון כ֯ל֯ אליל֯[יהן [
14]]◦[ ]ל[ ]ל[[

Frg. 2 Tob 14:10 (?)

1 לא] [
2 אנפין ל[ה [
3 ו◦ק֯ א֯◦[ונדן]
4 נפל ל֯פח [מותא ואובדה [
5 ל֯[[

4Q**199** (4QTob[d] ar) ed. J. Fitzmyer, *DJD* XIX

Frg. 1 Tob 7:11

top margin

1] ואמר טו]ב֯יה די לא אכול תנא ו֯ל[א אשתה [
2]]ל[[

Frg. 2 Tob 14:10

1] ע]ו֯ב֯די נדן[[

4Q**200** (4QTob[e]) ed. J. Fitzmyer, *DJD* XIX

Frg. 1 Col. i Tob 3:6

1]]◦
2]]◦◦◦ ע֯פר
3] מאש]ר֯ לחיות כי חרפות
4 [שקר שמעתי ועצבת]רבה עמי אמור להרויח
5 [מן עו]ל֯[מים וא]ל ת֯ס֯ת֯ר֯
6 [את פניך ממני [

Frg. 1 Col. ii Tob 3:10-11

1 יחרפו א֯[ת אבי [
2 חיה לכ֯ה֯ ב֯ת֯[יחידה [
3 עלי אין כשר לה֯[תלות לוא עוד]

5. all of those things will be done in [their] tim[es.]
6. in all that Go[d] has said. [Al]l of it will be brough[t to pass. and as for our kinsfolk]
7. dwelling in the land of Israel, all of the[m]
8. [I]srael (will become) arid; Samar[ia and Jerusalem until]
9. the time [5]when [God] will bring [them] back in [mercy]
10. [but] not as it was befo[re, until] the time [that]
11. [they rebuild] Jerusalem with hon[our]
12. [as the proph]et[s of Israel] have spoken[[6]]
13. [in truth], and they shall cast away all [their] idol[s]

Frg. 2 Tob 14:10 (?)

1. not [ ]
2. face to [him/her]
3. [and Nadin]
4. fell into the trap of [death, and it destroyed him.]

4Q**199** (4QTob[d] ar) trans. J. Fitzmyer

Frg. 1 Tob 7:11

1. [and To]biah [said], ‘I shall not eat (anything) here and I shall n[ot drink]

Frg. 2 Tob 14:10

1. [the de]eds of Nadin[ ]

4Q**200** (4QTob[e]) trans. J. Fitzmyer

Frg. 1 Col. i Tob 3:6

2. [ ] dust.
3. [tha]n to live, for [false] reproaches
4. [I have heard and] much [grief]is mine. Give command to move (me) far
5. [from for the ever]las[ting abode. Do no]t hide
6. [your face from me]

Frg. 1 Col. ii Tob 3:10-11

1. Let them [not] reproach [my father]
2. you have had alive an [only] daughter [ ]
3. For me it is not right to h[ang myself; that no longer]

4 אשמע ולוא ישמע [אבי [11] [
5 [הח]לון ות̇[ת]חנן[[

Frg. 2 Tob 4:3-9
Parallels: 4Q**196** 9
4Q**196** 10

1]]ר̇צ̇ו̇נ̇[ה ו]אל ת[וגה רוחה [4] [
2]]וסבול אותכה במע̇י̇[ה [
3] v[acat [5]וכול ימ̇ בני יכה לאלהים הי̇[ה ז]כ̇ר̇[[
4]]מ̇אמרו̇ vacat אמת היה̇[עושה כ]ול ימי ח̇[ייכה [
5 [בדרכ]י̇ שקר [6]כי בעשות ה̇[אמת יה]י̇ה עמך [7]◦[[
6]]ו̇כארך ידכה בני היה[עושה]צ̇דקות ואל תס[תר פניך מן כול[
7 [ע]נ̇ו̇ אף ממ̇כ̇ה לוא יס̇[תרו פני אלהי]ם̇ [8]אם יהיה לכה בנ[י רוב כרוב היה[
8 [עוש]ה̇ ממנו צ̇ד̇[קו]ת̇ [vacat] אם יהיה לך מעט כמעט̇[[
9] בעש]ו̇ת̇ך̇ צדקה̇ [9]שימה ט̇ו̇ב̇ה̇ [[

Frg. 3 Tob 5:2

1]]◦[[
2 והוא אי̇ן̇ [יודע אותי [
3 והאמין [[
4 ללכת̇ [שמה [

Frg. 4 Tob 10:7-9

1 [וכאשר] שלמו להמה ארבע̇[ת] עשר ימי [החתנה]
2 א̇שר נ̇שבע רעואל לעשות לשרה בתו בא [אליו]
3 ט̇ו̇[ב]י̇ה ואמור לו שלחני כבר אני יודע אשר̇[אבי איננו]
4 [מאמין ו]אף אמי איננה מאמנת אשר תראנ̇[י] ע̇וד מבק̇ש̇ ועתה
5 [אני אות]כ̇ה אבי אשר תשלחני̇ ו̇ה̇לכתי אל אבי כבר
6 ס̇פרתי לך א[י]כ̇כ̇ה ע̇ז̇ב̇תים [8]ו̇יומר רעואל לטוביה בני
7 ח̇ך אתי ואני אשלח̇ מלאכים אל טובי אב[יכ]ה̇ וה̇[מה]
8] [9]]ל̇[ ]ל̇[[

Frg. 5 Tob 11:10-14

1] ל]ק̇ר̇ת̇ בנ̇ו עד ◦[[
2] [11] ומר]ורת הדג בידו ונפוץ [בעיניו]
3] ויאמר]לו אל תירא אבי [ושם הסם]
4] ע]ל̇ ע̇יניו וחרוק [12] [
5] חוריו]ת̇ עיני̇ו [13]ויירא את̇[בנו [
6] [14]]◦ ב̇נ̇י̇[[

4. may I hear, and [my father] may not hear (them either)[[11]]
5. [the w]indow, and she [im]plored favour,[ ]

Frg. 2 Tob 4:3-9

1. [her] good pleasure, [and] do not [grieve her spirit [4]]
2. [ ]and (she) bore you in [her] womb[ ]
3. *vacat* [5]And all your days, my son, [reme]mber God [ ]
4. [ ]his command. *vacat* B[e] honest [a]ll the days of [your] li[fe]
5. [in the path]s of wickedness. [6]For in doing wh[at is honest will] be with you. [7] [ ]
6. [ ]According to your ability, my son, gi[ve] alms, and hi[de] not [your face from any]
7. [p]oor person. Then [Go]d['s face] will not be h[idden] from you. [8]If you have [much, my] son, [according to (your) bounty]
8. [giv]e al[m]s from it [*vacat*] If you have little, according to the little (you have) [ ]
9. [By] your [giv]ing alms, [9]a good deposit [you .]

Frg. 3 Tob 5:2

2. since he does not [know me]
3. and believe [ ]
4. to go [there]

Frg. 4 Tob 10:7-9

1. [and when] the four[t]een days of [the wedding] were over for them,
2. which Raguel had sworn to make for Sarah, his daughter, To[b]iah came [to him]
3. and said to him, 'Send me off; I know already that [my father does not]
4. [believe, and] also my mother does not believe that she will see m[e] again. Now [I] beg
5. you, my father, that you send me off so that I may go to my father. I have already
6. told you h[o]w I have left them behind.' [8]Raguel then said to Tobiah, 'My son,
7. stay with me, and I shall send messengers to Tobi, yo[u]r father, and th[ey]

Frg. 5 Tob 11:10-14

1. [to] meet his son as far as [ ]
2. [[11] and the g]all of the fish (was) in his hand, and he scattered (some of it) [on his eyes]
3. [and he said] to him, 'Do not be afraid, my father,' [and he put the medicine]
4. [o]n his eyes, and it smarted [[12]]
5. [the white scal]es of his eyes. [13]And he saw [his son]
6. [[14] 'my] son[ ]

Frg. 6 Tob 12:20–13:4
Parallel: 4Q**196** 17 i 1–5

top margin

1 [כתבו את כול [המעשה הזה והעלהו *vacat?* 21[ ]
2]ולוא עוד ראו[אׄ]ו[תו 22והיו המה ותומהים מברכים וׄ]מהללים את אלהים[
3] ומודים אותו על מע[שׄוׄ הגדול ותומהים איכהׄ נׄראהׄ]להמה מלאך[
4] אלהים[13:1בכן דבר טובי וכתוב תהלה בתשבוחׄתׄ וׄאׄ]מור[
5]ברוך אלהים [חׄי אשר לכול העולמים היאה מלכותו 2אשר הואהׄ] מכה[
6] והוא[הׄ מרחם מוריד עד שאולה תחתיה והואה מעלה מתהׄוׄ]ם[
7] ג[דׄוׄלׄ]ה[ומה אשר יפצה מידו 3הודו לו בני ישר]אל לפני[
8]הגוים[אשר אתמׄה נדחים בהמה 4ושמה ספרׄ]ו את גודלו ורוממו[
9]אותו לפני כו[ל חי כיא הוא אדניׄכׄ]מה[וׄהוא אלה]יכמה[
10] לכו[לׄ]עולמים [

Frg. 7 Col. i Tob 13:13-14
Parallel: 4Q**196** 18 1–11

top margin

1 [[אׄז שמחי ודוׄצי
2]על בני הצדיקים [וׄבׄרׄך את
3]אלהי עולם 14 [כוׄל
4 [ואשרי השמחים בשלומ]ךׄ

Frg. 7 Col. ii Tob 13:18–14:2
Parallel: 4Q**196** 18 11–16

top margin

1 ירושלים תהׄלׄתׄ] שמחה ישירו ברוך[
2 האלהים אשׄ]ר מרים אותך וברוך]
3 אשר] בכי יברכו את שמו הק]דוש לׄ]עולם]
4 14:1ותמׄ]ו דברי תודת טובי וימ]וׄתׄ בשלום בׄןׄ]]
5 [2והו[א בן שמונה וחמשׁ]ים]
6 [מ[רׄאׄהׄ] ו[אׄחר אׄרׄ]בע וחמשים חיה]

Unidentified Fragments

Frg. 9 Tob 3:3-4?

1 ואל]תשפׄטׄ[
2]ותטר לשׄלׄלׄ[
3]לׄ[

Frg. 8

1 [ך היום]
2 [◦ רׄה נפל גׄ]
3 [וׄבׄיׄדׄכה]
4 [לׄ]

Frg. 6 Tob 12:20–13:4

1. [‘Write down all] that has happened.’ And he ascended. *vacat*? [21][ ]
2. [and they saw] h[i]m [no more.] [22]But they were blessing and [praising God,]
3. [and acknowledging him because of] his great [de]ed and the amazing fact that [an angel of God] had appeared [to them.]
4. [13:1]Then Tobi spoke up and composed a song in praise, say[ing,]
5. [‘Blest be the] living [God], because his kingship is for all the ages; [2]because he [afflicts]
6. [and] shows mercy; he brings down to lowest Sheol, and he raises up from the [gr] eat abys[s.]
7. What is there that can snatch from his hand? [3]Acknowledge him, O children of Isra[el, before]
8. [the nations], because you are banished among them. [4]Recoun[t] there [his greatness, and exalt him]
9. [before al]l that lives. For he is your Lord; he is [your] God [ ]
10. [for al]l[ages!’]

Frg. 7 Col. i Tob 13:13-14

1. [ ]then rejoice and exult
2. [over the children of the righteous]and bless the
3. [eternal God. [14]] all
4. [and blessed are those who rejoice in] your [peace.]

Frg. 7 Col. ii Tob 13:18–14:2

1. Jerusalem [shall sing] a psalm of [exultation Blest be]
2. the God wh[o exalts you, and blest]
3. because [in you they will bless his h]oly [name] for[ever.]
4. [14:1]So [were] completed [the words of Tobi’s thanksgiving, and he d]ied in peace at the age of [ ]
5. [^{2}H]e was fif[ty]-eight years old [when]
6. his [s]ight, [and] afterwards [he lived fifty-]fo[ur years.]

Unidentified Fragments

Frg. 9 Tob 3:3-4?

1. and do not] judge[
2.]and you have kept for despoilment[

Frg. 8

1.] today[
2.] fell [
3.]and in your hand[

B. Apocalyptic Texts

1. Otherworldly Journeys

New Jerusalem

1Q**32** (1QNJ? ar) ed. J. T. Milik, *DJD* I

Frg. 1

1]◦ תשוית עמוד̇[א

2 ממע]ל לעמוד̇[א

Frg. 2

1]◦◦◦[

2]וגוא[

3]משח̇[ה

Frg. 3

1]ן̇ [

2]בחד[

Frg. 4

1]◦ ◦[

2]לתרע[א

Frg. 5

1]י̇ן ת◦[

1a עמו]ד֯ין תר[ין

2]◦ד[

Frg. 6

1]ל̇דה ◦[

2]◦◦◦ל הש[

Frg. 7

1 [כותל̇]א

2]ין/ץ ◦[

Frg. 8

1]ץ ת◦[

Frg. 9

1]◦ א◦◦[

2]ת הכ◦[

Frg. 10

Traces of letters

Frg. 11

1]◦ם[

2]ול ◦[

Frg. 12

1]◦[

2]הי ◦[

Frg. 13

1]◦ הו[

Frg. 14

1]◦ כול ◦[

2]◦◦ ג̇לגל̇[א

3 [כ̇יא גלגלא]

B. Apocalyptic Texts

1. Otherworldly Journeys

New Jerusalem

1Q**32** (1QNJ? ar) trans. E. Cook

Frg. 2

2.]and within (?)[
3.]measurement[

Frg. 4

2.]to [the] gate[

Frg. 12

2.]his [

Frg. 14

1.] all [
2. the] wheel[
3.] for the wheel [

Frg. 1

1.] base of [the] pillar[
2. abov]e [the] pillar[

Frg. 3

2.]in one[ ]

Frg. 5

1a.]two [pill]ars [

Frg. 7

1. the] wall[

Frg. 15

1]◦◦◦◦◦[

2 א]מׄיׄן תלתׄ ◦◦[

3]די לׄאׄ ◦◦[

Frg. 16

1]נׄ◦◦◦◦בׄעת[

2]◦ ותשׄעׄ[

Frg. 17

1]קׄ ◦[

2]דינׄ ◦[

3]עדׄ[

Frg. 18

1]◦ ◦[

2]◦מא נ◦[

Frg. 19

1]◦◦◦ מׄין[

Frg. 22

1]חד עׄ◦◦[

2]◦ קודם[

3]◦◦◦◦◦[

2Q**24** (2QNJ ar) ed. M. Baillet, *DJD* III

Frg. 1
Parallels: 4Q**554** 2 ii 13–16
5Q**15** 1

1] ואעלני לגוא קריתא ומשח[

2 [פרזיתא בריתא אורכא ופותיא קנין חמשין וחד ב]חמשין *vac* וׄחׄ]ד מרבעה סחור[

3 [סחור אמין תלת מאה וחמשין ושבע לכול רו]חׄ *vac* ושבק סחור סח]ור[

4 [לפרזיתא ברית שוק קנין תלתא אמין עשרין וחדא] וכדן אח]זי[נ]י [כול משחת

5 [פרזיתא בין פרזא לפרזא שוק פתה קנין שתא אמין] ארבעין ותרתין

bottom margin

Frg. 2

1]ר אמׄי[ן

2]ה ל[

Frg. 3

1]חדׄ[ ]◦◦[

2 ו]משח עד תרע ספׄי[רא

3 פתו]רׄא די קודמוהי ל[מרא

4]◦כתול תׄ[

Frg. 16

2.] and nine[

Frg. 15

2. c]ubits three [
3.]which not [

Frg. 22

1.]eleven (?)[
2.] before[

Frg. 19

1.] water[

2Q**24** (2QNJ ar) trans. E. Cook

Frg. 1

1. [he brought me into the city and measured]
2. [the outer block: length and breadth, they measured fifty-one staffs by] fifty-on[e, making a square,]
3. [three hundred and fifty-seven cubits to each sid]e. And a sidewalk aroun[d]
4. [each block, bordering the street, that is, twenty-one cubits.] And so he showed me the measurement of all
5. [the blocks. Between each block was a street six staffs in width, that is,] forty-two [cubits.]

Frg. 2

1.] cubit[s

Frg. 3

1.]one[
2. and] he measured to the gate of sapphi[re
3.] the [tab]le which was before him was for [the Lord
4.] wall [

Frg. 4
Parallel: 11Q**18** 20

1 בשרהון [… [
2 לקורבן רעוא] … [
3 [וי]עלון להיכלא] … [
4 תמנא סאין סול]תא … [
5 ויטלון לחמא ◦] … מן[
6 לקדמין על מדْ]בחא … [
7 סדרין על פת]ורא … [
8 תרי סדרי לח]מא … [
9 לחמא ויסבון לחמ]א … מן[
10 מערבה ויתפלג]ון … [
11 וחזית עד דׄי ◦ל] … [
12 רׄשמׄתא כׄ[ ] ע◦] ◦] … [
13 שביׄאׄ דׄי בהון וארבעת עשר כה]נין … [
14 כהניׄא *vac* תרתי לחמא די היׄ] … חזי[
15 הוית עד חדא מן תרתי לחמא יהיבת [ל]כׄ]הן ראשא … [
16 עמׄה ואחריתא] י]היבת לתנינה די קאם פנבד [… [
17] א◦] [*vac* חזי הוית עד די יהיב לכ]ול כהניא … [
18] ל דׄי איל ען חד לכול גבר וגבר] … [
19] ל] עד עדן די יתבו [… [
20] ח]ד בכול [… [
21] לׄ] … [

Frgs. 5–6

1] מׄיׄמׄ] [
2] אורכה ופו]תיה משחא חדא
3] ה מן כׄאן
4 [ומן כאן ◦א מן דן
5 [ומן דן ק]רן[מדבח]א
6] מא ופותיה
7] לכׄ]ו]ל
8 [רוח ◦◦[

Frg. 7

1]ופותיהון מן כאׄ]ן ומן כאן
2]וכול מדבחא]

Frg. 8

1]◦[
2 ע]שׄרא שורא ארבׄ]עא
3] כותליאׄ◦ אבן חׄוׄ]ר
4]ה אחרניא מן בר עשר]י]ן]

Frg. 4

1. their meat [ ]
2. for an offering acceptable [to the Lord]
3. then they will enter the temple[ ]
4. eight seahs, fine flou[r]
5. then they shall carry the bread [ ]
6. first upon the al[tar]
7. rows on the ta[ble]
8. two rows of br[ead]
9. of the bread, and they shall take [the] bread [ ]
10. west, and [the bread?] shall be divid[ed]
11. and while I watched [ ]
12. the marks [ ]
13. the elders among them, and fourteen pri[ests]
14. the priests. Two loaves of bread that[while watching]
15. I was, one of the two loaves was given [to the high] pr[iest]
16. with him. The other loaf was given to the second one who was standing opposite [ ]
17. [ ] While I was watching, there was given to a[ll the priests]
18. [ ] of one ram of the flock to every one [of them]
19. [ ] to the time when they sat [ ]
20. [o]ne in all [ ]

Frgs. 5–6

2. [its length and its bre]adth a single measurement
3. [ ] from one side
4. [and from the other side] from this
5. [and from that h]orn of the [altar]
6. [ ] and its breadth
7. [ ]to ev[e]ry
8. [side]

Frg. 7

1.]and their width on this sid[e and from that
2.]and all of the altar[

Frg. 8

2. -t]een, the outer wall four[teen?
3.] the inner walls white stone [
4.] the others from twenty years old [

5]בל◦[ ] ולהיון מכפרין בה עלו[הי
6]◦ ולא יתכלא עוד כול יום[ויו]ם֯[
7]ע֯זרתא [ו]אחזינ[י]◦[ ]אוחרי בר מן[
8]◦ מאה ועשר[

Frg. 9

1]◦ע֯ת[
2]אשי כול [
3]ק֯[

Frg. 10

1] אלוה[י
2]◦[

Frg. 11

1]תר֯[

4Q**554** (4QNJ[a] ar) ed. E. Cook

Frg. 1

1 תרעיא תלת]א֯ במדנחא ותלתא בדר֯[ומא
2 ותלתא במערבא ותלתא בצפונא ו]שפשין שגיאין א◦[
3 אבנין]עשרין די[

Frg. 2 Col. i

9 [ ]שתת עשר[ ]◦◦◦[ ]מא
10 [ ]ת֯ה וכלהון מכונין דן
11 [לדן מן זוית]מדנחא די בצפונא
12 [משח עד תרעא די צפונא]ראסין תלתין וחמשה ושם
13 [תרעא דן די קרין לה תרע]שמעון ומן תרעא דן ע֯[ד] ת֯רעא מציעא
14 [משח ראסין תלתין וחמשה ו]שם תרעא דן די [קר]ין לה תרע
15 [לוי ומן תרעא דן משח עד תרעא די]ד֯ר֯ומא ראסין תלתין וחמשה
16 [ושם תרעא דן די קרין לה תרע יהודה ומן]תרעא דן משח עד זוית
17 [מדנחא די בדרומא ראסין תלתין וחמשה ו]מן *vacat* זויתא דא למערבא
18 [משח עד תרע מדנחא ראסין 25 ושם תרעא דן די] קרין לה תרע יוסף
19 [ומן תרעא דן משח עד תרעא מציעא ראסי]ן 25 ושם
20 [תרעא דן די קרין לה תרע בנימין ומן ת]ר֯עא דן משח עד תרעא
21 [די מערבא ראסין 25 ושם תרעא דן די קרין לה]תרע ראובן ו[מן תר]עא דן
22 [משח עד זוית מערבא די דרומא ראסין 25 ו]מן דא זויתא משח עד

5.] and by means of it they will make atonement for [him
6.] and it shall no longer be withheld. Every day[
7.]the court [and] he showed me another outside of[
8.] hundred and ten[

Frg. 9

2.]foundations of all [

Frg. 10

1.] its pillars [

4Q554 (4QNJ^{a} ar) trans. E. Cook

Frg. 1

1. three gate]s in the east and three in (the) so[uth
2. three in the west and three in the north and] many portals [
3.]twenty [stones] that[

Frg. 2 Col. i

9. [ ]sixteen[ ]
10. [ ] and all of them facing each
11. [other he measured from the] northeastern [corner]
12. [to the north gate], thirty-five stades, and the name
13. [of this gate is called the gate of] Simeon. From this gate t[o] the middle gate
14. [he measured thirty-five stades a]nd the name of this gate is [call]ed the gate of
15. [Levi. From this gate he measured to the] south [gate], thirty-five stades,
16. [and the name of this gate is called the gate of Judah. And from] this gate he measured to the
17. [southeastern] corner, [and 35 stades f]rom *vacat* this corner westwards
18. [he measured to the east gate 25 stades and the name of this gate] is called the gate of Joseph.
19. [He measured from this gate to the middle gate,] 25 [stades] and the name
20. [of this gate is called the gate of Benjamin. From thi]s gate he measured to the [west] gate
21. [25 stades and the name of this gate is called] the gate of Reuben. And [from] this [ga]te
22. [he measured to the southwestern corner 25 stades and] from this corner he measured to

Frg. 2 Col. ii
Parallels: 2Q**24** 1
5Q**15**

1 [תרעא די דרומא ראסין תלתין וחמשה ושם תרעא דן די קרין לה]
2 [תרע יששכר ומן תרעא דן משח עד תרעא מציעא ראסין]
3 [תלתין וחמשה ושם תרעא] דן די קרין לה תרע זבולון ומן תרעא
4 [דן משח עד תרעא די צפונא ראסין תלתין וחמשה ושם תרעא דן די]
5 [קרין לה תרע גד ומן תרעא דן משח עד זוית מערבא די בצפונא ראסין]
6 [תלתין וחמשה ומן זויתא דא למדנחא] מׄשׄח [עד תרעא מערבא ראסין]
7 25 ושם[תרעא דן די קרין לה תרע דן] ומן תרעא דן [משח עד תרעא]
8 מציעיא רסין[25 ושם תרעא] דׄן ק[רי]ן לה תרע נפתלי [ו]מן דׄן֯
9 תרעא משח עׄד תרעא[די מדנחא ר]סין 25 ושם תרעא דן קרין
10 לה תרע *vacat* אשר ומש[ח מן תר]עׄא דן עד זוית די מדנחא רסין
11 25 *vacat*
12 ואעלני לגוא קריתא ומ[שח כל פר]זיתא [ ]◦ אורכא ופתיא קנין
13 51 ב51 מרבעה ס[וחר סחור] אמין 350
14 7 ולכל רוח ושבק סחר סחו[ר] לפרזיתא ברית שוק קנין
15 תלתה אמין 21 וכדן אחזיני מש[ח]ת פרזיא כלהן בין פרזא לפרזא
16 שוק פתה קנין שתה [אמי]ן 42 ושקיא רברביא די נפקין
17 מן מדנחא למערׄב[א קנין] עשרה פתי שוקא אמין
18 70 2 מנהון ות[לי]תיא *vacat* די על ש[מא]ל מקדשא משח
19 קנין ~~אמין~~ 18 פתיה [א]מין 6[2]1 ופתי
20 שוקיא די נפקין מן דרו[מא לצפונא קנין 9
21 ואמין 4 לשוק חד לאמי[ן] 67 ומציעיא די במצ]יעת
22 קריתא משח פתיה קני[ן] 13 ואמה ולאמין 40 +] 52
23 וכל שוקא וקריתא [רציפין באבן חור]

bottom margin

Frg. 2 Col. iii
Parallel: 5Q**15** 1 i, ii

1–11 [ ]
12 [ואחזיני משחת תרעי פרזיא פתי]הׄ[ו]ןׄ [ ]קׄנׄיׄןׄ[2 אמין 14]
13 ופתי ◦[ ]יא משחתא אמין[ ] פות[יה די כל אספא]
14 קני[ן] ת[רין א]מין 14 וית טלולה אמה חדה [ומשח]א ב[ ]
15 יתׄ דש[י]ן לה ומשח בגוא אספא ארכה א<מין> 13 ופתיה אמין עשר[ ]
16 ואׄעלני לגוא אספא והא אסוף אחרן ותרעה ליד כתלא גויא די ליד ימינא

Frg. 2 Col. ii

1. [the south gate, 35 stades, and the name of this gate is called]
2. [the gate of Issachar. He measured from this gate to the middle gate,]
3. [35 stades, and the name] of this [gate] is called the gate of Zebulun. And from this gate
4. [he measured to the third gate, 35 stades, and the name of this gate]
5. [is called the gate of Gad. And from this gate he measured to the northwestern corner]
6. [35 stades and from this corner] he measured [until the western gate]
7. 25 [stades], and the name [of this gate they called the gate of Dan.] And from this gate [he measured to the middle gate]
8. [25] stades [and the name of] this [gate is called] the gate of Naphtali. And from this
9. gate he measured to the [east] gate, 25 [s]tades, and the name of this gate is called
10. the gate *vacat* of Asher. And he measur[ed from] this [ga]te to the eastern corner
11. 25 stades. *vacat*
12. Then he brought me into the city, and mea[sured ci]ty blocks, length and breadth,
13. 51 staffs by 51 staffs, making a square a[ll around], 350+
14. 7 cubits to each side. Each block had a sidewalk around it, bordering the street,
15. three staffs, that is, 21 cubits. So he showed me the mea[su]rement of all the blocks: between each block was
16. a street six staffs in width, that is, 42 cu[bits.] The main streets that passed
17. from east to west were ten [staffs.] The width of the street was
18. 70 cubits, for 2 of them. A third street, *vacat* which was on the [left] of the temple, he measured at
19. 18 staffs ~~cubits~~ in width, that is, [126] cubits. And the width of
20. the streets that go from sou[th to north, for two of them,] 9 staffs,
21. and 4 cubits to each street, making [sixty-seven] cubits. He measured [the middle street in the] middle
22. of the city. Its width was [13 s]taffs and one cubit, that is 92 cubits.]
23. And every street and the city itself [was paved in white stone.]

Frg. 2 Col. iii

12. [He then showed me the measurements of the gates of the city-blocks.] Th[eir width was two] staffs, [fourteen cubits,]
13. and the width of the [ ]s, the measurement cubits. [ ] the wid[th of each atrium:]
14. [tw]o staff[s,] 14 [c]ubits, and the ceiling, one cubit. [Then he measured]
15. its doors. Then he measured inside the atrium: its length was 13 cubits, and its width [ten] cubits.
16. He brought me into the atrium and there was another atrium. And the gate by the inner wall on the right side

17 כמש[ח]ת תרעא בריא פתיה אמין ארבעֹ רומה אמין 7 ודשין לה תרין וק[ודם]
18 ת[ר]עא דן אסף עללה פתיה קנה חד̊ אמין שבע וארכה עלל קנין תרין א[מין]
19 14 ורומה קנין תרין א<מין> 14 ותרע לקבל תרעא פתיח לגואֹ פרזית[א]
20 כמשחת תרעא בריא   ועל שמאל מעלה דן אחזיני בית דרג סח[ר וס]לק פ[תיה]
21 וארכה משחה חדה קנין תרין בתרין אמין ארבע עשרא ות[רעין לקבל תרעין]
22 כמשחה ועמוד [בגוא]גוהֹ די דרגא סחר וסלק עלוהי פתי[ה ואורכה]

bottom margin

Frg. 3 Col. i

1–13 [ ]
14 [קני]ן תרין
15 [ ]א̊ ואמין
16 [ ]○○ משחת
17 [תח]ו̊מי קריתא

Frg. 3 Col. ii

13 [ ] [ ]ן ○○○○○ן ○○תא יסודה פ̊[תיה] קנין תרין א̊[מי]ן
14 ארבע ע[ש]רא ורומה קנין שבעה אמין ארבעין ותשע וכלה
15 בניה בחש[מל] וספיר וכדכוד ועעיתה דהב ומגדליה אלף
16 [וארבע מא]ה ות̊לתין ותרין ופתיהון וארכהון משחה חדה
17 [ ] ו̇רמהון קנין עשרה
18 [ ] 14
19 [ ]תרין
20 [ ]תרעיא אמין
21 [ ]תרין לתרעא
22 [ ]חיא תלת תלת ומגדליא נפקין

bottom margin

Frg. 3 Col. iii

1–13 [ ]
14 ○○○○ לק̊[
15 באתרה ומלכות מ[
16 כתיא באתרה כלהון בסוף כלהון[
17 אחרין שגיאן וישון עמהון מ[
18 עמהון אדום ומואב בני עמון[
19 די בבל ארעא כלה די לא ישר̊[
20 ויבאשון לזרעך עד עדן די י[

17. had the same measurements as the outer gate. And its width was four cubits. Its height was seven cubits. It had two doors, and in fro[nt of]
18. this [ga]te was an entrance way. Its width was one staff, seven cubits, and its length, passing inward, two staffs,
19. 14 cu[bits;] and its height, two staffs, 14 cubits. Now a gate opposite the gate opened into the bloc[k]
20. and its measurements were like those of the outer gate. On the left of this entrance he showed me a spiral staircase go[ing u]p: its w[idth]
21. and its length was a single measurement, two staffs by two, fourteen cubits; and g[ates opposite the gates]
22. were of a like measurement. There was a pillar [in the very center] that the stairs went around and up. Its wi[dth and its length]

Frg. 3 Col. i

14. [ ] two [sta]ffs
15. [ ] cubits
16. [ ] measurement of
17. [bound]aries of the city

Frg. 3 Col. ii

13. [ ] its foundation. It was two staffs [wid]e,
14. four[teen] cu[bi]ts, and it was seven staffs high, forty-nine cubits. All of it was
15. built of elec[trum] and sapphire and chalcedony; and its beams were of gold, and its towers numbered one thousand
16. [four hun]dred and thirty-two. Their length and width were the same measurement
17. [ ] and their height was ten staffs,
18. [ ] 14 [ ]
19. [ ] two
20. [ ] the gates, cubits
21. [ ]two [ ] to the gate
22. [ ] three by three, and the towers project

Frg. 3 Col. iii

15. in place of it, and the kingdom of M[
16. the Kittim in place of it. All these kingdoms shall appear one after another[
17. many others, and they will station their people[
18. with them Edom and Moab and the Ammonites[
19. of the whole land of Babylon, which not [
20. and they shall do evil to your descendants until the time of [

21 בכל עמ◦[ ]מלכות[ ] די ◦ל[
22 ויעב[דון] בהון עממין[

bottom margin

4Q**554a** (4QNJ[b] ar) ed. E. Cook

Frg. 1 Col. i

1 [ ]קנין
2 [ ]בׄע

Frg. 1 Col. ii
Parallel: 5Q**15** ii 5–15

top margin

1 עׄלׄ[והי פתיה וארכה] אׄמׄ[ין 6 ב6 מרבע]ודרגא די [סלק] פתיה אמין ארבע וסחר
2 [וסלק רום קנין ארבע עשר עד רמת אגר] *vacat*
3 [ואעלני בגוא פרזיתא ואחזויאני בתיא מן תרע] לתרע חמשת עשר תמניה בחדה רוח עד זויתא
4 [ושבע מן זויתא עד תרעא אחרנא פתי]הן ארך בתיא קנין תלתה ארכין 21 ופתיהון
5 [קנין תרין אמין ארבע עשר וכדן כל תוניא ו]רומהון קנין תרין אמין 14 ותרעהון במצעתא
6 [פתי קנין תרין אמין 14 אמין] ארבע ארך ורום קנה חד אמין שבע
7 [ואחזויני משחת גוא בתיא דכא אמין תשע עשרא]אׄרכהון ופתיהון אמין 12 בית
8 [ערשין ותרתין ערשין וחדה עשרה כוין אטימן עלא מן ערשין ו]לידה אמה בריתא
9 [ומשח פתי כותא רומה אמין תרתין ארכה אמה חדה ועובי פתי כות]לא קדמיתא אמין
10 [ואחרנתא אמין ומשח תחומי דוכניא ארכהון אמין תשע עש]רא ופתיהון אמין
11 [תרתי עשרה ורום פתיחן]קנין תרין אמין ארבע
12 [עשרה ופתיהון אמין תלת וארכין עשר א]מה חדה ופלג ורומה בגו
13 [ ]ין ורום כותא יתׄ טלולא די עליהון
14 [ ]◦[ ]◦◦[ ]

4Q**555** (4QNJ[c] ar) ed. E. Cook

Frg. 1

1 ב]דיל די ד[
2 [ ] במשח רבות[א
3]לה על פתור[א

21. among all the peoples[ ] the kingdom[
22. and in them the peoples sha[ll d]o[

4Q554a (4QNJ[b] ar) trans. E. Cook

Frg. 1 Col. i

1. [ ]staffs

Frg. 1 Col. ii

1. up[on it. Its width and its length were 6 by 6 cu[bits, square.] And the stairway that [went up] was four cubits wide and spiralled
2. [and went up fourteen staffs high to the (*or*: . . .went up to the height of fourteen staffs to the)] *vacat*
3. [and he brought me into the block and he showed me the houses. From gate] to gate there were fifteen, eight in one direction to the corner
4. [and seven from the corner to the other gate; such was] their [width]. The length of the houses was three staffs, 21 (cubits) long, and their width was
5. [two staffs, fourteen cubits. All the rooms were likewise and] their height was two staffs, 14 cubits and their gate in the middle was
6. [in width two staffs, 14 cubits cubits] four in length and in height one staff, seven cubits.
7. [And he showed me the measurement of the house's interior, a place nineteen cubits]in length, and their width was 12 cubits. A house of
8. twenty-two beds and eleven closed windows above the beds; and] beside it the outer gutter
9. [and he measured the width of the window: its height was two cubits, its length one cubit; and the thickness of the width of] the first [wa]ll
10. [and the other, cubits and he measured the boundaries of the platforms; their length was ninete]en [cubits], and their width was [twelve] cubits
11. [and their height opened] two staffs, four[teen] cubits
12. [and their width was three cubits, and their length ten] one and a half [c]ubits and its height within
13. [ ] and the height of the window. The roof that was over them

4Q555 (4QNJ[c] ar) trans. E. Cook

Frg. 1

1. be]cause [
2.] with the oil of anointi[ng
3.] on [the] table[

Frg. 2

1 [◦◦◦]
2 [רומׄא ד]י[לעלׄא וׄלׄא]
3 [פתורא וביומא שב]יעיא
4 [◦יא אלין ושתה]

Frg. 3

1 [הוא]
2 [למתא ל◦]

5Q15 (5QNJ ar) ed. J. T. Milik, *DJD* III

Frg. 1 Col. i
Parallels: 2Q**24** 1 i
4Q**554** 2 ii, iii
4Q**554a**

1]סחור א[מׄין]תלת מאה ו[חׄמשין ושבע לכל]רו[ח ושבק סוחר סחור לפרזׄתא
בׄרית שוקׄ] קנין תלתה א[מׄין עשרין
2]וחדה[*vac* וכדן]אחזיאני מ[שחת פׄרׄ]זיא כלהן בין פרזה לפרזה שוק[פׄתׄהׄ
קנין שׄתׄ]ה[אמין ארבעין ותרתין
3]ושוק[יׄאׄ רברביא]די[נפקיׄ]ן[מן מדנחׄא]למערבא[קׄנין עשרה פׄותׄ]י שוקא
אמין[שׄב]עין תרי[ןׄ מנהון ותליתיׄאׄ
4]די על[שׄ]מא[ל מקׄ]דשא מ[שׄח קנין תמנית עשׄ]ר[פותי אמין מאׄ]ה ועשרי[ןׄ
]ו[שׄתׄ וׄפׄוׄ]תי שוקיא[די נפקין מן דרומׄ]א[
5]לצפונא תרי[ןׄ מׄ]נהון[קניןׄ תשׄ]ע[הׄ ואמין א]ר[בׄע לשוק חד אמי]ן[שתין ושבע
]ו[מצׄ]יעא די במצ[יעת קריתא
6]משח פותי[הׄ קנׄ]ין תל[תׄת עשר ואמׄה חדה לאמין תשעׄ]י[ן ותׄ]רתין[וׄכׄל
]שוק['א וקריתא ר[צׄיפין באבן חור
7] [◦◦] [ב◦] [◦ ◦רׄגׄ]י[אׄ וא] [שש ויהלם
vacat
8]ואחזיאני משחת שפשיא ת[מׄנׄין פוׄתׄ]יהון די[שפשיא קנין תרין]אמין ארבע
עשרה [
9] ע[ל כׄל תׄרע ותׄרׄע דׄשין תרין די אבׄןׄ פותיה דיׄ] דשי[אׄ
קנׄהׄ] חד אמין שבע *vacat*]
10]ואחזיאני משחת [יא תרי עשר פותי תרעיהון קׄנין תלתה אמי]ן עשרין
וחדה על כל[
11]תרע ותרע דשין תר[יׄןׄ פותי דׄשׄיׄ]א[קנא חד ופלג אׄמׄיׄ]ן ע[שר ופלגׄ]
]
12]וליד כל תרע תרי מגד[לׄיןׄ חׄדׄ מׄ]ן י[מׄיׄנא וחד מן שמׄ]אל[אׄ פותיהון וׄאורׄכׄהון
]משחה חדה קנין חמשה בחמשה[
13]אמין תלתין וחמש ודרגא די סלק ליד [תׄרעא בגוא על]ימי[ן מגדליא ברׄום
מׄגׄ]דליא פתיה אמין חמש מגדליא[

Frg. 2

2.]height which i[s] above and not (?)[
3.] the table and on the sev[enth] day[
4.] these and six[

Frg. 3

1.]he [
2.]to come to [

5Q**15** (5QNJ ar) trans. E. Cook

Frg. 1 Col. i

1. [around three hundred and] fifty-seven [c]ubits to each [si]de. Each block had a sidewalk around it, bordering the street, [three staffs, that is,] twenty [c]ubits
2. [and one.] *vac* And so [he showed me the mea]surement of [all the] blo[cks: between each block was a street] si[x] staffs in width, that is, forty-two cubits.
3. [And] the main st[reets that] pass from east [to west] were ten staffs. The widt[h of the street was] seve[nty cubits, for tw]o of them. A third street,
4. [which was on] the l[ef]t of the tem[ple he m]easured at eightee[n] staffs in width, that is, on[e hundred twen]ty-six cubits. And the wid[th of the streets] that pass from sout[h]
5. [to north, for tw]o o[f them,] ni[n]e staffs, with f[o]ur cubits to each street, making sixty-seven [c]ubits. [And the] mid[dle street in the mid]dle of the city
6. [he measured. Its widt]h was [th]irteen sta[ffs] and one cubit, that is, ninety-t[wo] cubits. And all [the streets and the city itself were p]aved with white stone.
7. [ ] marble and onyx. *vacat*
8. [and he showed me the measurements of the ei]ghty portals. [Their] width was two staffs, [fourteen cubits]
9. [ ] Every gate had two doors of stone. Their width was [one] staff, [seven cubits *vacat*]
10. [He showed me the measurements of] the twelve [ ]. The width of their gates was three staf[fs, twenty-one cubits. Every]
11. [gate had tw]o [doors.] The width of the door[s] was one-and-a-half sta[ffs, t]en-and-a-half cubit[s]
12. [Two tow]ers [flanked each gate,] one on the right and one on the l[ef]t. Their breadth and length [was the same, five by five staffs,]
13. [that is, thirty-five cubits. The stairs that went up next to] the gate on the inner side, [to the rig]ht of the towers, is of the same height as the to[wers. Their width is five cubits. The towers]

14 [ודרגיא קנין חמשה בחמשה ואמ]ין חמש ל[אמין א]רבעין בכל רוח תרע]א
vacat]

15 [ואחזיאני משחת תרעי פרזיא פתיהון]קנין תרין אמין ארב[ע] עש[רה ופו]ת[י
יא משחתא אמין]

16 [ומשח]פות[יה די כל א]ספא קנין תרין אמין ארבע עשרה [וית
טלולה אמה חדה]

17 [ומשח על כל] אספא ית ד[שין ל]ה ומשח בגוא א[ס]פא אורכה אמין [תלת
עשרה ופותיה אמין עשר *vacat*]

18 [*vacat* ואע]לני ל[גוא אספא [והא] אסף אוחרן ותרעא ליד כותלא גויה
[די ליד ימינא כמשחת תרעא]

19 [בריא פותיה אמ]ין ארבע רומ[ה אמין] שבע ודשין לה תרין וקודם [ת]רעא דן
[אסף עללה פתיה קנה חד אמין]

Col. ii
Parallel: 4Q**554a** 1 ii, iii

1 שבע ואו[ר]כה עלל קנין תרין אמין א[ר]בע עשרה ורומה קנין תרין אמין
ארבע ע[שרה ותרע]

2 ל[קבל תר]ע פתיח לגוא פרזיתא כמשחת תרעא בריא ועל שמאל מעלה דן
אחזיא[ני בית דרג]

3 סחר[וסלק] פותיה ואורכה משחה חדה קנין תרין בתר[י]ן אמין ארבע עשרה
ותר[עין לקבל]

4 תרעין כמשחה ועמוד בגוא גוא די דרגא סח[ר ו]סל[ק] עלוהי פתיה ואו[רכה
אמין שת בשת]

5 מרבע ודרגא די סלק לידה פתיה אמין ארבע וסחר [וס]ל[ק]רום ק[נין תרי]ן
עד] *vacat*]

6 ואעלני [לגוא] פרזיתא ואחזיאני בה באתין מן תרע לתר[ע חמשת עשר
תמני]ה בחד[ה רוח עד זויתא]

7 [וש]בעה מן ז[ו]יתא עד תרעא אחרנא פותאהון ארוך בת[י]א קנין תלתה אמין]
עשרי[ן וחדה ופתיהון]

8 [קני]ן תרין אמין ארבע עשרה וכדן כל תוניא [ורומהון קנין ת]רין א[מי]ן ארבע
ע[שרה ותרעהון]

9 [במציעתא פות]י קנין ת[רי]ן אמין ארבע עש[רה ומשח פותי מצי]עת ביתא
וגוהון די ת[וניא אמין]

10 [ארבע ארוך ורום קנה חד אמין שבע ואחזיאני משחת בתי]מכלא דכא אמין
תשע ע[שרה ארכהון]

11 [ופתיהון אמין תר]תי עשרה בית [ע]שרין ות[ר]תין ערש[ין וחדה] עשרה כוין
אטימן עלא מ[ן ערשין]

12 [ולידה אמה בריתא ומשח]◦◦י כותא רומה [אמ]ין תרתין [פתיה אמין]ועובי
פותי כותלא[רום קדמיתא]

13 [אמין ואחרנתא אמין ומשח ת]ח[ו]מי דוכנ[יא אורכהון אמין] תשע עשרה
ופות[יהון אמין תרתי עשרה]

14. [and the stairs were five by five staffs, plus] five [cubi]ts, [f]orty [cubits] for each side of the doo[r. *vacat*]
15. [He then showed me the measurements of the gates of the city-blocks. Their width was] two staffs, [fou]rteen cubits, [and the width of the the measurement in cubits.]
16. [He then measured the] width[of each at]rium: two staffs, fourteen cubits, [and the ceiling, one cubit.]
17. [Then he measured over each] atrium i[ts doors.] Then he measured inside the at[riu]m: its length was [thirteen] cubits, [and its width ten cubits. *vacat*]
18. [*vacat* He brough]t m[e i]nto the atrium [and there was] another atrium and the gate alongside the inner wall [on the right side had the same measurements as]
19. [the outer gate. Its width was] four cub[its. Its]height was seven [cubits.] It had two doors, and in front of this [g]ate was an entrance [way. Its width was one staff, seven cubits,]

Col. ii

1. and its le[ng]th, passing inward, two staffs, fourteen cubits; and its height, two staffs, fourteen cubits. [Now a gate]
2. o[pposite the gat]e opened into the block and its measurements were like those of the outer gate. On the left of this entrance he showed [me a staircase]
3. going around[and up:] its width and length were a single measurement, two staffs by t[w]o, fourteen cubits; and gat[es opposite]
4. the gates were of a like measurement. There was a pillar in the very center (?) that the stairs spira[lled upwards a]roun[d.] Its width and [its] len[gth were, six cubits by six,]
5. square. The stairs that went up around it were four cubits wide and they spiralled up[wards]height of t[wo staf]fs until [*vacat*]
6. Then he brought me [within] the city-block and showed me the houses in it. From gate to ga[te there were fifteen houses, eigh]t in on[e direction to the corner]
7. [and se]ven from the c[o]rner to the other gate. Such was their width. The of [the] hous[es was three staffs, twenty-[one cubits, and their width]
8. was two [staff]s, fourteen cubits. The rooms likewise were [t]wo [staffs high,] fourteen c[ubit]s, [and their gate]
9. [in the middle gate] was t[w]o staffs, fourte[en] cubits [wide. And he measured the width of the mid]dle of the house and the interior of [the] r[ooms; four]
10. [cubits. It was one staff, seven cubits, in length and height. And he showed me the measurement of the houses of] dining. The site was [ninet]een cubits [long]
11. and twe[lve cubits wide.] A house of [t]wenty-t[w]o beds [and el]even closed windows above the [beds]
12. [and next to it an outer gutter. And he measured] the window two [cu]bits high [its width cubits] and the thickness of width of the wall [the height of the first]
13. [? cubits, and the other one? cubits. And he measured the bord]ers of [the] platforms. Their length was] nineteen [cubits] and [their] width [twelve cubits]

14] ◦[ ]◦ ורו̇[מהון] פתיחן ב̇◦[
קנין תרין אמין]

15 [ארבע עשרה ופותיהון אמ]ין ת̇ל[ת] וא̇ר̇כ̇ין [ע]שר̇[אמה
חדה ופלג ורומה בגוא]

Frg. 2

1]◦א̇ כ̇וין [

2] כל בתיא די בגוא ◦[

3 תר]ע̇א כולה ואספיא פת[יהון

4 ע]מודיא אמין תרתי עשרה̇ [

5]◦ עמוד לעמ̇ו̇ד [

Frg. 3

1] ◦◦◦ [

2 תר]ע̇יא רבר̇[ביא

3 קנין] שתה בשת[ה אמין ארבעין ותרתין

4] *vacat* [

5] ו̇פ̇◦[

Frg. 4

1]◦[

2]ב וע◦◦[

3 מש]חה ק̇נ̇ין [

Frg. 5

1] ◦◦ [

2]כל ת◦◦[

3]עשר̇[

Frg. 6

1] ותרתי̇[

2]◦שק̇[

3]◦[

Frg. 7

1]◦◦[

2 אמ]י̇ן̇ תרתין ◦[

Frg. 8

1] ופותי[

Frg. 9

1 פ]ותי ◦[

2 תר]ע̇יא די [

Frg. 10

1]◦◦◦[

2] ו̇מ̇שח

Frg. 11

1]◦ ותר̇ת̇[י

2]◦◦◦[

Frg. 12

1]א̇מין [

2 ת]רע[

Frg. 13

1]מש[ח

14. [ ] open [windows, two staffs,]
15. [fourteen cubits, and their width] thr[ee cub]its, and length [t]en one-and-a-half cubits, and its height within.

Frg. 2

1.] windows [
2.] all the houses that were within [
3.] the whole [ga]te and the atria, [their] width [
4.] the p]illars, twelve cubits [
5.] pillar to pillar [

Frg. 3

2.]the mai[n ga]tes[
3.] six by si[x staffs, forty-two cubits
4.] *vacat* [

Frg. 5

2.]all [
3.]ten[

Frg. 4

3. meas]urement, staffs [

Frg. 7

2. cu]bits two [

Frg. 6

1.] and two[

Frg. 9

1. wi]dth [
2. ga]tes that [

Frg. 8

1.] and (the) width[

Frg. 11

1.] and two[

Frg. 10

2.] and he measured

Frg. 13

1.]measu[re

Frg. 12

1.]cubits [
2. g]ate[

Frg. 14

1 א[מין ◦[

2]◦◦ת ◦[

Frg. 15

ק]נ֯[ין

1 ת]ר֯יׄן[

Frg. 16

1]◦[

2 ד[י ליׄ[ד

Frgs. 17–21

traces of letters

11Q**18** (11QNJ ar) ed. F. García Martínez, E. J. C. Tigchelaar, and A. S. van der Woude, *DJD* XXIII

Frg. 1

top margin

1]י֯ן֯ סר֯◦[

2] אר֯עיׄ [

3]כ֯ו֯[

Frg. 2

[top margin]

1]◦ה֯יא א◦[

2]◦ח֯תא כ[

3]רתא ◦[

4]◦◦◦[

Frg. 3

top margin

1]◦פׄ◦[

2]◦יא֯[

3]◦מ◦[

4]◦[

Frg. 4

top margin

1]מׄ◦ ◦◦◦◦ ◦◦◦◦ [

2]◦◦ ◦◦ בׄע֯[

3]◦◦◦◦ [

4] ע֯ד֯ [

5] ע֯ו֯ב֯ ב֯ [

6] מׄר֯ ל◦◦◦ [

Frg. 5

3]◦נׄ[

5]מׄפ֯◦[

Frg. 6

top margin

1] מאתין ותמנין אמ֯[ין

2 א[לן֯ פרזיא ליד שור֯[א

3] ד֯רומא ופלג[

4]פׄרזיא[ ]ח֯[

5]ל[

Frg. 7

top margin

1] על כול זרע בנ֯י [

2]◦א די להוון אכלׄין[

3]ב להון סחור [

4]תׄ מאה וחמש[ין

5]לע֯ל[

Frg. 15

s]t[affs
1. t]wo[

Frg. 14

1. c]ubits [

Frg. 16

2. whi]ch is b[y

11Q**18** (11QNJ ar) trans. F. García Martínez, E. J. C. Tigchelaar, and A. S. van der Woude

Frg. 1

2.] below [

Frg. 6

1.] two hundred and eighty cub[its
2. the]se blocks alongside [the] city wall[
3.] the south and half (?)[
4.]the blocks[

Frg. 7

1.] on all the seed of the children of [
2.] which shall eat[
3.] for them around [
4.] hundred and fif[ty
5.]on[

Frg. 8

top margin

דהב]טב כולה ארבע רגלו֯ה֯[י
פ]ותיה אמה ותרתי עשר֯[ה
פתו]רא ועלוי לחמא שוי֯ן֯[
]פו֯תי תרע֯[ ]ו֯רו֯מ֯◦◦[
]◦ ◦◦[

Frg. 9

top margin

] סחור לעליתא ד[
]אמין עמודין שבעה ת֯[
אורכיהון ופו]ת֯יהון אמין שת בשת [
]בא ובנא בנין עלוי עמ[
]ב֯א וכול בנינא דן [
]מ֯קד֯שא ו֯ל◦ל֯[

Frg. 10 Col. i

top margin

]י מין חיין
]ורא דן דהב טב
]ין מיא מן
] *vacat*
]◦בן כול אבניהון
]◦וך חפא דהב
]◦אה ועש[ר]
]◦[ ]◦[

Frg. 10 Col. ii

top margin

ארב[עה
מ֯◦[
◦[
ומ◦[
הל◦[
מ֯ו֯◦[
וא[
ור◦ח֯[
חד[

Frg. 11

top margin

]ת֯והי ארבעא רמין אמין א֯[רבע
]י֯נא ליד כותלא די סחר ל◦[

Frg. 8

1.] pure [gold,] all of it, i[ts] four legs [
2.] its [w]idth is a cubit. And the twel[ve
3.] the [tab]le, and they had placed the bread upon it [
4.]the width of the door and its height [

Frg. 9

1.] around the upper room [
2.]cubits, seven columns [
3. their length and] their [wid]th are six by six cubits [
4.]and a construction built on it [
5.] and this whole construction [
6.]the Temple and [

Frg. 10 Col. i

1.] living water
2.] this [ ] of pure gold
3.] water from
4.] *vacat*
5.] all their stones
6.] overlaid with gold
7.] and te[n]

Frg. 10 Col. ii

1. fo[ur

4. and [

7. and [
8. and [

Frg. 11

1.] its four [ ] were f[our] cubits high [
2.]the [ ] near the wall which surrounds [

3 פותיה אמי]ן֯ תרתין ורומה אמין תרתי[ן

4]נ֯אמה וכולה דהב טב די֯[

5 [*vacat*]

6 ד]י עמודין סחר מן תרע לת֯[רע

7]מן תרע לתרע בשורתא֯[

8]ל֯[ ]ן בכיו֯ר ◦ [ ]◦[

Frg. 12 Col. i

top margin

1]◦ מן אלן וערבליא די

2]יא פרישא ודי מעשריא

3]הון פרישא וסכנתא

4 [*vacat*

5]כ֯ול רוח מערב

6]◦ שורא

7]ב֯ן֯ הובן

8]בימי֯ן֯

9]◦◦[

Frg. 12 Col. ii

[top margin]

1]

2]

3 ב֯[

4 מ֯[

5 רו◦[

6 ט◦[

7 ועלא֯[

8 די֯ ◦[

Frg. 13

top margin

1]בארבע רגלוהי ונשט תורא ◦[

2 ר]ח֯ע רגלוהי וקרבוהי ומלח כולה[

3 ו]ש֯ויה על נורא ואיתי קמח סולת[

4 ר]ו֯ב֯ע סתא ואסקה למדבחא כולה[

5 רו]ב֯ע סתא ונסך לגוא מורכי֯[ותא

6]א ובשרא מתערב בחדא[

7 [ר֯יחא *vacat*]

8]מרפסתא ליד יס◦[

9]◦א֯ ו֯מ֯ב֯ ◦מ◦◦[

10]◦ורנ֯[

11]◦[

3. its width is] two [cubit]s and its height is two cubits[
4.] and all is of pure gold that[
5.] *vacat* [
6. o]f columns, turning from door to d[oor
7.]from door to door in the city wall[
8.] with panels [

Frg. 12 Col. i

1.] from these and the sieves which
2.] dedicated and of the tithes
3.] dedicated and arranged
4.] *vacat*
5.]each side, west
6.] the wall

8.]at the right side

Frg. 12 Col. ii

7. and above[

Frg. 13

1.]by its four legs, and stripped the bull [
2. he wa]shed its legs and its intestines, and salted all of it[
3. and] placed it on the fire, and brought fine sifted flour[
4. a fo]urth of [a seah], and he brought all of it to the altar[
5. a fou]rth of a seah, and he poured it into [the] troughs [
6.] the [ ] and the flesh were mixed together[
7.] the smell. *vacat* [
8.]the gallery near [

Frg. 14 Col. i

top margin

1]◦

Frg. 14 Col. ii

top margin

1 גפן כדי פרש מן לולביׄ[א
2 מנצבהון וכלילא חמיׄ[שיא
3 גוא כפרה וכלילא שתיתיׄ[א
4 שביעיא כדמות נצ ורד[
5 להוה לבש כהנא רבא[
6 [   ]יׄם וׄבׄכול עׄל[
7 [   ]לכול עׄ[
8 [   ]◦◦[

Frg. 15

top margin

1]משרתא עוד להן די להוה[
2]א וכול די להוון משצין שבעתיהוׄ[ן
3]אחיהון עללין חלפהון ארבע מאהׄ צׄ[
4]אׄ ואמר לי לעשרין ושת ◦[
5 קד]ישי קדישיא וׄלאׄ[
6 ע]לל[י]ן עׄ[

Frg. 16 Col. i

top margin

1]◦ני הובן כולהון
2]ל בׄוׄצׄ
3 כ]תׄפׄן
4]◦תׄ

Frgs. 16 Col. ii + 17 Col. i

top margin

1 ברכה תניניׄ[   ]ל ותודתהון
2 ופסחיהון ל◦[כ]הׄניא מקבלין
3 מן ידהון דפׄשׄ[טו   ]תׄא ל◦[ו]ל[א]
4 עלל לה כול א[נש
5 ידוהי כול ◦[

Frg. 17 Col. ii

top margin

1 שבעא בשבעא וא[
2 קנין תלתא ורום תרעׄ[יא
3 לכול תרי עשר תרעיׄ[ן

Frg. 14 Col. ii

1. grape, when it comes out from [the] sprouts[
2. from their shoot. And the fif[th] crown[
3. the inside of a cypress flower. And the sixth crown[
4. the seventh (crown) is like the bud of a rose[
5. the high priest will be clothed[
6. [ ] and in all [
7. [ ]for all [

Frg. 15

1.]any more, except who is (?)[
2.] and all who will have completed their weeks[
3.]their brothers will enter in their place, four hundred [
4.] and he said to me: 'For twenty six [
5.]the [Ho]ly of Holies, and [
6.] they will [en]ter [

Frg. 16 Col. i

1.] all of them
2.] linen
3. shoulder-]pieces

Frgs. 16 Col. ii + 17 Col. i

1. second blessing[ ] and their thank-offerings
2. and their Passover sacrifices [ ] the [pr]iests receiving
3. from their hand which [they] stre[tch out] [and] n[o]
4. per[son] shall enter it [
5. his hands, everything [

Frg. 17 Col. ii

1. seven by seven. And [
2. three reeds, and the height of [the] door[s
3. to all twelve doors[

4 תרתׄין ועובי פותי כות[לא
5 קדמהׄןׄ קנין מאה[
6 [ ]◦[ ]ל[

Frg. 18

top margin

1 כסין שבעה וספלין למרח שׄתׄהׄ[
2 ◦י ועליא שבעא דודין תפין על אבׄנׄיׄ[
3 [וכ]ולהון תלתין ותרין אלפין ותשע מאה[
4 [ ] *vacat* [ ]
5 [ ]אׄמר לי חזא אנתה דׄי
6 [ ] לבתי חדוא ול[
7 [ ]לׄ[ ]ן[ ]לל[ ]ןׄ ◦◦ל[

Frg. 19

top margin

1]ה תרעיא די לקובל היכלא ל[
2]ביׄומא שביעיא וביום ראשי ח[דשא
3 ק]דׄיש הוא היכלא ויקרא רבׄ[א
4]לכול עלמין *vacat* [
5]שרי למקרא לי בכתׄ[ב
6]מחזא לי כתב כ[
7]מׄ[ ]ל[ ]ל[

Frg. 20
Parallel: 2Q**24** 4 9–16 (underline)

top margin

1 כו]ל יום שביעי קודם אל דכרׄ[נא
2 לחמא ויסבון לחמא]לברא מן היכלא לימין מערבהׄ[ויתפלג
3 וחזית עד די פ]ליׄג לתמנין וארבעה כהנין שׄ[
3a]מן כול שבעת פלוגת פתורי
4 שביא די בה[ון וארבעת עשר כה[נין
5 כהניא תרתי לחמ]א די הות לבונתא [עליהון
6 חזא הוית עד חדא מן תרתי לחמא י]היבת לכׄהנא רׄ[בא
7 עמה ואחריתא יהיבת לתנינה די קא[םׄ פנבד ◦[

Frg. 21

top margin

1 [*vacat*
2]◦ר ותרעין תרין
3]ד לתרתי עליתא
4]◦ןׄ[ק]נא חד פותי

4. two, and the thickness is the width of [the] wal[l
5. the first of them, one hundred reeds[

Frg. 18

1. seven cups, and six bowls to smell [
2. and above are seven cauldrons, placed (for cooking) on stones[
3. [and a]ll of them are thirty two thousand and nine hundred[
4. [ ] *vacat* [
5. [ ]he said to me: 'You are seeing th[at
6. [ ] to the rooms of the joy and to[

Frg. 19

1.] the doors which are before the Temple [
2.]on the seventh day, and on the first day of the m[onth
3. h]oly is the Temple and the great glory [
4.]for all ages. *vacat* [
5.] he began to read to me from [a] wri[ting
6.]to show me a (*or*: the) writing [

Frg. 20

1. eve]ry seventh day before God, a memori[al offering
2. bread. And they shall take the bread] outside the Temple, to the right of its west side, [and it shall be divided
3. And while I was watching, it was distrib]uted to the eighty-four priests [
3a.]with everything was satiated the division of the tables of
4. the eldest among th]em and fourteen prie[sts
5. the priests; two bread]s [upon] which was the incense [
6. and while I was watching, one of the two breads was g]iven to the h[igh] priest [
7. with him; and the other was given to his deputy who was stan]ding close to him [

Frg. 21

1.] *vacat*
2.] and two doors
3.] for the two upper rooms
4.] one [re]ed; the width of

5]א *vac* וכדן
6]◦ דרגא

Frg. 22

top margin

1]◦על ארבע קרנת מדבחׄ[א
2]יׄן מנה כול תרבה
3]◦ תרתין כוליתה
4 נ]שיפה פיל
5 מד]בחא לריח
6]לקדמין
7] *vacat*
8]◦עיׄן

Frg. 23 Col. i

top margin

1]◦יׄן ומן
2]פׄא

Frg. 23 Col. ii

top margin

1 עליהון ל[
2 וׄדשלם ◦[
3 נכסיהון [
4 ומברכין בׄ◦[
5 כולה סגׄי[
6 הׄן כולהׄ[
7 [י]שראל[

Frg. 24

top margin

1 מע]ל שמשא אר[
2]ה דין מן כול ש◦[
3]◦א די ארבעת[
4]על כול זרעׄא[
5]בכול שנא לׄ[
6]כה עללין [
7]כׄול די ל[

Frg. 25

top margin

1]מן קודשי ישראל[
2]ור ובלילה הׄ[
3]ריתא ויקרא[

5.] *vacat* And likewise
6.] the stairs

Frg. 22

1.] on the four corners of [the] altar
2.] from it all its fat
3.] both its kidneys
4.] the [wh]eat flour soaked
5.] the [al]tar for a smell
6.]first
7.] *vacat*

Frg. 23 Col. i

1.] and from

Frg. 23 Col. ii

1. upon them [
2. and [
3. their sacrifices [
4. and blessing [
5. it all [
6. if it all[
7. [I]srael[

Frg. 24

1.] the [su]nset [
2.] judgement (?) from all [
3.] of four[
4.]on all the seed[
5.]in each year [
6.] entering [
7.]all who/which [

Frg. 25

1.]from the sacrifices of Israel[
2.] and in the night [
3.] the [ ] and the glory[

4]◦בי בשרה די◦[
5]◦לון עמה ומן[
6]ון ויכלון ויש]תון
7]◦◦ ומ֯[

Frg. 26

top margin

1]וכול אנשא די יחׄ[
2]יתמנון עלוהיׄ[
3]א עד תדנח שמ֯]שא
4]הי כחדא *vacat*[
5]*vacat* שבעה֯[
6]להוון שב[
7] להו֯]ון

Frg. 27

top margin

1 כו]ל ישראל חׄ[
2] *vac* וכדי יש◦[
3]לׄיׄ פסחיא חפ◦[
4 עד ת]ד֯נׄח שמשא וכו֯]ל
5]שי שלמיהון[
6]לׄא לרויו ◦[

Frg. 28

top margin

1]לה֯וון דברין בׄ[
2]◦בר שבעתׄ[
3]אׄ עד מעל ש]משא
4]קורבני א[
5]יׄ{ן} תורין תר֯]ין
6]◦ין וכו[

Frg. 29

top margin

1]ןׄ קודם מד]בחא
2]בו֯ן עם עו֯◦[
3]ר֯בון לה [
4]משח וחמ]ר
5]קודמוהיׄ[
6 רי]ח ניחׄ]וח

4.] its flesh which [
5.] with it and from[
6.] they will eat and dr[ink
7.] and [

Frg. 26

1.]and all the men who [
2.]they will be appointed over it[
3.] till [the] su[n] sets [
4.] together. *vacat* [
5.] *vacat* Seven[
6.](to) be [
7.] (to) b[e

Frg. 27

1. al]l of Israel [
2.] *vacat* And as soon as [
3.] Passover offerings [
4. until] the sun sets, and al[l
5.] their peace-offerings[
6.]not (?) for saturation (?) [

Frg. 28

1.]they will take [
2.] seven[
3.] until s[un]set[
4.]offerings of [
5.] tw[o] bulls[

Frg. 29

1.] in front of [the] alt[ar
2.] with [
3.] for him/it [
4.]oil; and win[e
5.]in front of him[
6.]a pleas[ant aro]ma[

Frg. 30

top margin

1]◦[ ]ין ככול ד◦[
2]ון עוד לויא דבחׄ[ין
3] ולהוה להון ◦[
4]◦◦ מן מועדי אלׄ[
5]ןׄ מא די לׄ[
6]תרוהׄ◦[

Frg. 31 Col. i

top margin

1]תׄ
2]נׄון
3]לא

Frg. 31 Col. ii

top margin

1 ד◦[
2 כורסׄיׄ[א
3 מנה בׄ◦[
4 ידא ח◦[
5 ועל שׄ◦[
6 היכלאׄ[
7 ויק◦[

Frg. 32

top margin

1]כורסיא [
2]וׄכׄתא וישוורׄ[
3]א היכלא ומן דמׄ[
4 ש]בעת קניה [
5]על ארבע שׄ[
6]ן מן היכלא
6a]וׄיׄד אבן דמא◦[ומני[
7]ויקדשנה עליׄהׄ[
8]לארבע
9]◦יׄןׄ ויסוד

Frg. 33

1]לׄריח ניחוח[
2]◦יא ואיליא ג[
3]פרישא עלׄ[
4]ןׄ כ◦[

Frg. 30

1.] like all [
2.] while the Levites sacrifice[
3.] and it will be for them [
4.] from the festivals of G[od (?)
5.] what is for [

Frg. 31 Col. ii

2. [the] throne[
3. from it [
4. the hand [
5. and on [
6. the Temple[
7. and [

Frg. 32

1.]the throne [
2.] the [ ] and he hastens[
3.] the Temple and from [
4.] its [s]even (*or*: [f]our) reeds [
5.] on four [
6.] from the Temple

6a.] stone of [

7.]and he will sanctify it
8.] to four
9.] and the foundation of (?)

Frg. 33

1.]for a pleasant aroma[
2.] and the rams [
3.]dedicated [

Frg. 34

top margin?

1]◦ אלן [

2]◦ורח֯[

3]◦◦[

Frg. 35

1]א מן כול֯[

2] רוחי֯ ע[

Frg. 36

top margin?

1]◦רין[

2]ש֯[

Frg. 37

1]עלון ◦[

2]◦י מ◦[

3]י֯א פחתא֯ ל֯[

4]די ישר֯[

2. SYMBOLIC APOCALYPSES

4Q**246** (4QapocrDan ar) ed. É. Puech, *DJD* XXII (corrected, 2004)

Col. i

1 ע]לוהי שרת נפל קדם כרסיא

2 מ]לכא {<ל>}<ב>עלמא אתה רגז ושניך

3 אפש]ר֯א חזוך וכלא אתה עד עלמא

4 ר]ב֯רבין עקה תתא על ארעא

5]ונחשירין רב ב֯מ֯דינתא

6]מלך אתור[ומ]צרין

7] רב להוה על֯ א֯רעא

8 י]ע֯בדון וכלא ישמ֯שון

9 ר]ב֯א יתקרא ובשמה יתכנה

Col. ii

1 ברה די אל יתאמר ובר עליון יקרונה כזיקיא

2 די חזו֯תא כן מלכותהן תהוה שני[ן] ימלכון על

3 ארעא וכלא ידשון עם לעם ידוש ומדינה למדי֯[נ]ה

4 *vacat* עד יקו/ים עם אל וכלא ינו/יח מן חרב

5 מלכותה מלכות עלם וכל ארחתה בקשוט ידי֯[ן]

6 ארעא בקש֯ט וכלא יעבד שלם חרב מן ארעא יסף

7 וכל מדינתא לה יסגדון אל רבא באילה

8 הוא ו֯עבד לה קרב עממין ינתן בידה וכלהן

9 ירמה קדמוהי שלטנה שלטן עלם וכל תהומי

Frg. 35

1.] from all[
2.] spirits of [

Frg. 37

3.] governor? (*or*: curse?) [

2. Symbolic Apocalypses

4Q**246** (4QapocrDan ar) trans. E. Cook

Col. i

1. [ ] rested upon him, he fell before the throne.
2. [O ki]ng, wrath is coming to the world, and your years
3. [ ] is your vision, and all of it is about to come unto the world.
4. [Amid] great [signs], tribulation is coming upon the land.
5. [After much killing] and slaughter, a prince of nations
6. [will arise]the king of Assyria[and E]gypt
7. [ ] he will be ruler over the land
8. [ ] will do and all will serve
9. [him.]will be called The Great, and be designated by his name.

Col. ii

1. He will be called the Son of God, they will call him the son of the Most High. But like the meteors
2. that you saw, so will be their kingdom. They will reign only a few years over
3. the land, and all will tramplepeople will trample people and nation [will trample] nation, .
4. *vacat* until the people of God arise; then all will have rest from warfare.
5. Their kingdom will be an eternal kingdom, and all their paths will be righteous. They will judge
6. the land justly, and all (nations) will make peace. Warfare will cease from the land,
7. and all the nations shall do homage to them. The great God will be their help,
8. He Himself will fight for them, putting peoples into their power, all of them
9. he will overthrow before them. God's rule will be an eternal rule and all the depths of

4Q**552** (4QFour Kingdoms[a] ar) ed. E. Cook

Frg. 1

1]◦ מן
2]רׄחם
3]◦◦◦◦

Frg. 2 Col. i

5 [נ]הור מׄלׄאׄכׄיׄאׄ די הׄוׄו
6 [ ]אמר להון להוא כולה
7 מ]דׄיׄנתא דימין הוא דן
8]*vacat* ואמר לי מלכא בדיל כדן
9]◦נך איך כלא עביד הוו קאמין
10]אמר להו'ן ומפקא להון בפרוש
11]מראיהון ו◦◦ חד מנהון

Frg. 2 Col. ii
Parallel: 4Q**553** 6 ii 2–6

1 נוגהא קאם וארבעה אילניׄא[ ]
2 וקאם אילנא ורחקו מנה ואמרׄ[ ]
3 צורתא ואמרת אן אחזא ואתב[ונ]ן ב[ה וחזית]
4 אילנא די *vacat* אשים ב◦[ ]
5 ושאלתה מן שמך ואמר לי בבלׄ[ואמרת לה]
6 [אנ]תׄהׄ הוא די שליט בפרס ו[חזית אי]לנא
7 [ ]חׄזׄיׄת למערבא ל[ ] ואמר
8 למש◦[ ]ושאלתה מן שׄמׄ[ך ואמר לי]ל
9 ואמרת לה אנתה הוא דׄ[י שליט ועל]
10 תקפי ימא ועל מחוזא [ ]
11 אילנא תליׄתיׄ[א ו]אׄמׄרׄתׄ ל[ה מן שמך]
12 [ ]

Frg. 2 Col. iii

1]◦חי ואמרת לה היא דא מן ◦[
2]ת לעלמׄ[ ]ת וחזי[ת
3]ל נ[
4]◦ חיל◦[

Frg. 3

9]מרא[
10]ין אל עליון לאׄ [
11]◦קא די עליהון ית◦[
12]◦יא די כול מותבה דינין[

4Q552 (4QFour Kingdoms[a] ar) trans. E. Cook

Frg. 2 Col. i

5.] angels that were
6.] to them all of it will be
7.] the land of the south is this
8.] *vacat* and the king said to me, because of this
9.] your [ ] how everything is made. They were standing
10.]he said they will be (*or*: to them) and explaining to them openly (?)
11.]their lords and one of them

Frg. 2 Col. ii

1. brightness standing, and four trees[ ]
2. and the tree standing, and they moved far away from it, and he said[ ]
3. the form, and I said, 'Where should I look that I may understand [And I saw]
4. the tree which *vacat* I shall place in [ ]
5. and I asked him, 'What is your name?' and he said to me, 'Babylon [and I said to him]
6. [Y]ou are he who rules over Persia and [I saw a t]ree
7. [ ] I looked to the west [ ] and he said
8. [ ]and I asked him, 'What is [your] name?' [and he said to me]
9. and I said to him, 'You are he who [rules and over]
10. the strongholds of the sea and over the harbour [ ]
11. the third tree and I said to hi[m 'What is your name?']

Frg. 2 Col. iii

1.] and I said to him, 'She/it is that from [
2.] forever[ ] and I saw [

4.] might (?)[

Frg. 3

9.]lord[
10.] God most high not [
11.] which is upon them will [
12.] of all his seat/dwelling, judges [

Frg. 4

8]ה[ ]
9]יחדון
10] חזוה
11]הם מללתא
12]א די יפלט

4Q**553** (4QFour Kingdoms^b ar) ed. E. Cook

Frg. 1

3 רב[

Frg. 2 Col. ii

1 מלאכיא קד[שיא
2 לי מלאכא ◦◦[
3 מץ נעיצין ו֯ד֯[
4 מע֯מרין סמ◦[

Frg. 3 Col. i

1]◦ה
2]◦ת
3]ן ריש

Frg. 3 Col. ii

2 שמ טמרו כול שלי[ט
3 מחטה ב[ ]ל[

Frg. 4

1]רימ[
2]ב֯רתא ◦◦י֯נ֯יא [

Frg. 5

1 מ֯לכא֯ בד֯[י

Frg. 6 Col. i

2]◦◦◦נא ידי
3]◦ די אהך
4]◦א ואף֯ ל֯י֯ במלכות
5]◦ין למ֯חדה יב֯ד֯ו֯ ארו

Frg. 6 Col. ii
Parallel: 4Q**552** 2 ii 1–10

1] [*vacat* וחזית[ ]
2 די עלוה[י נוגהא קאם] *vacat* וארב֯[עא אלניא]ן לה וקמו אלניא
3 ורחקו[מנה] *vacat* ואמ֯^ר^ת אן אחזה ואתבונן
4 בה וחזית [אלנא]ושאלתה מן שמך ואמר לי בבל ואמר^ת^ לה אנתה
5 הוא ד[י שליט בפרס וחזית א]לנא אחרנא ושאלתה ואמרת לה מן
6 שמך [וא]מר לי צ֯[ר ואמרת אנתה הוא די שליט ע]ל [מחוזוא וע]ל תק[פי ימא]

Frg. 4

9.]they will seize (*or*: rejoice)
10.] the vision
11.] you spoke
12.] who will escape

4Q553 (4QFour Kingdoms[b] ar) trans. E. Cook

Frg. 2 Col. ii

1. ho[ly] angels [
2. to me the angel [
3. [of] chaff inserted (?) and [
4. dwelling [

Frg. 3 Col. ii

2. name, they hid every rul[er
3. to sin [

Frg. 3 Col. i

3.] head

Frg. 5

1. the king [

Frg. 6 Col. i

2.] hands of
3.] that I shall go
4.] and also to me in the kingdom
5.] to rejoice (*or*: to seize it), he will scatter, because

Frg. 6 Col. ii

1. [ ] *vacat* and I saw[ ]
2. upon which [brightness was standing] *vacat* And four [trees] and the trees stood
3. and moved far off [from him] *vacat* and I said, 'Where should I look that I may see and understand
4. it?' And I saw [the tree] (and) I asked him 'What is your name?' and he said to me, 'Babylon,' and I said to him, 'You
5. are the one who [rules over Persia,' and I saw] the other tree and I asked him and I said to him 'What is
6. your name?' And he said to me, [ ]. And I said, You are the one who rules o]ver [the harbours and o]ver [the] strong[holds of the sea]

Frg. 8 Col. i

1] בלחדוהי
2]מן מושה
3]◦רא אתר די
4]טנה לאתקריה
5]ה בשמה די [

Frg. 8 Col. ii

1 מחזוהי וע̇[ל
2 תקיף חיל[
3 מביניהון [
4 לי תלתי[א
5 [ ]ל̇[ ]

Frg. 9

1 ש̊פרא בשמיא למשל[ט
2 [ ]ל[

Frg. 10

1 אזל באר[ע
2 לה רב איל[ניא
3 ו̊איל[נא

Frg. 11

2 [ ]א אשר[י

Frg. 12

2 [ ]הוא [
3 [ ]ן לנ̊א ותת̇[

Frg. 13

1 [א]תר מלא
2 [ ]ועגלין וא̇מרין
3 [א]תר[

Frg. 14

1 [ ]לטורא̊[

3. Non-Symbolic Apocalypses

4Q**248** (4QHistorical Text A) ed. M. Broshi and E. Eshel, *DJD* XXXVI (corrected, 2004)

1]◦◦[
2]מ̊צ̊רים וב̊יון ו[
3 [ ]ם̇ ה̇גד̊י̊[ל]ב̊כן יאכלו [
4 [בנ]י̊ה̇ם ובנותי̇[ה]ם במצור ב[
5 [וה]ע̊בר ״״״ רוח[ ]א̊צ̇רותיהם וש̊[
6 [ו]ב̊א למצרים ומכר את עפרה ואת[ה
7 אל עיר המקדש ותפשה עם כ[ל
8 וה̇פך בארצות גוים ושב למצר̇י̊[ם וככלות
9 נ̊פץ יד עם הק̇[דש תכלינה
10 כל אלה̊ י̊שו̊ב̊ו̊ ב̊נ̊י̊[ישראל

bottom margin

Frg. 8 Col. ii

1. his seeing and up[on
2. mighty of power[
3. from among them [
4. to me the third[

Frg. 8 Col. i

1.] by himself
2.]from Moses
3.] the place where
4.]to be called
5.]in the name of [

Frg. 10

1. he went in the lan[d
2. to him ruler of the tre[es
3. and the tre[es

Frg. 9

1. the beautiful [tree?] in heaven to ru[le

Frg. 12

2.]he [
3.] to us and [

Frg. 11

2.] he caused to dwell [

Frg. 14

1.]to the mountain[

Frg. 13

1. p]lace full
2.]and calves and lambs
3. p]lace[

3. Non-Symbolic Apocalypses

4Q**248** (4QHistorical Text A) trans. M. Broshi and E. Eshel

2.]Egypt and in Greece and[
3.] he shall magni[fy (himself)]thus they shall eat [
4. [of] their [son]s and daughters in the siege in[
5. [and] the **Lord** shall cau[se] a spirit to go [ ]their lands and [
6. [And] he shall come to Egypt and sell its land. And he shall come
7. to the Temple City and seize it and al[l
8. and he shall overthrow lands of (foreign) nations and (then) return to Egyp[t]
9. And when the shattering of the power of the ho[ly] people [comes to an end]
10. [then shall] all these things [be fulfilled] the children of[Israel] shall return [

Apocryphon of Jeremiah

4Q**383** (4QapocrJer A) ed. D. Dimant, *DJD* XXX (corrected, 2004)

Frg. 1

1 [   ]פ֯ן ◦[
2 ואני ירמיה בכו אב[כה
3 יענה בארץ לוא נוש֯[בת
4 על א֯שר הערותי[
5 אליהם וא֯ש֯[ר

Frg. 2 (formerly 4Q**387** 10)

1]◦שב מאׄחׄרׄי[
2 ולא שמ[עו לדברי ירמי[ה
3]עה וׄי◦[

Frg. 3 (formerly 4Q**389** 13)

1]◦ הׄי◦[
2]תׄים ושלוה כי כׄי◦[
3]◦◦◦ ויבוא עד א[

bottom margin

Frg. 4 (formerly 4Q**389** 16)

1]◦ב֯◦ ◦[
2 וי[אמר ברוך עמׄ[
3]ה ו֯ל֯א ◦[

Frg. 5

1]◦◦ פ֯[
2]גׄבול גדולה[
3 ה[מטה להובי[ל
4]ם מ◦ך ל[

Frg. 6 (formerly 4Q**389** 15)

1 הנב[יא
2 למצ[רים
3 תו◦[
4 בח[

Apocryphon of Jeremiah

4Q**383** (4QapocrJer A) trans. D. Dimant

Frg. 1

2. And I Jeremiah bitterly we[ep
3. will answer in an unin[habited]land[
4. because I have provoked/aroused[
5. unto them and becau[se

Frg. 2

1.] from after[
2. and]they[did not lis]ten to the words of Jeremia[h

Frg. 3

2.] and peace, for [
3.] and he/it will come until [

Frg. 4

2. and he]said, 'Blessed be the people[
3.] and not [

Frg. 5

2.]boundary large[
3. the]staff to lea[d

Frg. 6

1. the pro[phet
2. to Eg[ypt

Unidentified Fragments

Frg. A

1]◦ב֯גו ה֯[

2]ש֯ה מחללי הברית מט[מאי

3]א֯בות֯ם בוזי֯ אמותם הפוחזים [

bottom margin

Frg. B (formerly 4Q**383** 2)

1]ם במלוא ידיהם֯[ ]בחמוץ ונ֯[

2]תנו המכה֯[ ]לוה◦[

Frg. C (formerly 4Q**383** 3)

1]כי כח֯יו[

2]ד֯ כך כף ו֯◦[

3 ירו]שלים *vac* [

4Q**384** (4Qpap apocrJer B?) ed. M. Smith, *DJD* XIX

Frg. 1

top margin?

1 [וחדש֯]

Frg. 2

1]ת֯ אדוני֯[

2 [ל֯]

Frg. 3

1]◦ ואל ר֯[

2]ה֯ עם איש[

3]ע֯ד֯ אש[ר

Frg. 4

1]◦ ◦[

2]ג֯ילי גיל א֯[

3]ישיב לו ◦[ ]ל[

4]ל֯[

Frg. 5

top margin

1 [יספרו֯ [

2]ל֯[

Frg. 6

1 [נ֯פ֯ש֯ [

Frg. 7

1]◦ ה֯מ֯◦[

2]א֯ל תחפנ[ס

3]סוע כי֯[

4 [◦◦תס◦[

5]ל בש◦[

6]ל֯◦[

Frg. 8

1]מ֯ע֯שיהם֯[

2]כאשר כתוב[

3]מ֯ע֯שיהם למינ֯י֯[הם

4]ל֯מ֯שפחותם עד֯[

5 [ס֯ו֯ת֯ עד[

6]ק֯ו֯ר֯ [ ]לשון [

7]ת֯ם לד◦[

Unidentified Fragments

Frg. A

2.] those who profane the covenant, who de[file
3.]their fathers, despoilers of their mothers, the reckless [

Frg. B

1.] as/when their hands are filled[ ]with oppression and [

Frg. C

2.] thus a palm [
3. Jeru]salem *vac* [

4Q**384** (4Qpap apocrJer B?) trans. M. Smith

Frg. 2

1.] Lord[

Frg. 4

2.] rejoice greatly [
3.]he will return (?) to him [

Frg. 3

1.] and to (?) [
2.] with a man (?)[
3.] unti[l

Frg. 5

1.] they will recount [

Frg. 8

1.]their deeds[
2.]just as it is written[
3.]their deeds according to [their] kinds[
4.]their families until (?)[

6.] [ ]tongue [

Frg. 7

2.]to Taḥpane[s

Frg. 9

1]ת ומ[
2 בספר מ]חלקות העת[ים
3]העונות לדו[
4]לברית ש[

Frg. 10

1]◦◦יים להול[
2]את חלקות[
3]ים לחולי◦[
4]ול [ ]ש◦[
5]דר מהם ו◦ [
6 א]שמת כול הע[ם

Frg. 11

top margin

	Col. ii	Col. i
1	◦[	]כיא

Frg. 12

top margin

	Col. ii	Col. i
1	ק[	]כה
2	ח[	]
3	◦[	]

Frg. 13

1 ◦◦◦◦[
2 אם גמל על[
3 אל תימו[
4 שופט את[
5]לי ו[

Frg. 14

1]◦ וב[

Frg. 15

1 כאשר כ]תוב[
2]ה י[

Frg. 16

1]עמי[
2]◦◦[

Frg. 17

1]ת ישלחני ו[
2]ואתה אל ת[
3]תקוה כיא ר[
4]ול צו ◦◦◦[
5]נעדר מ◦[

bottom margin

Frg. 18

	Col. ii	Col. i
1	ו ◦[	]
2	א[	]ו

Frg. 19

	Col. ii	Col. i
1	ת◦[	]◦
2	תו[	]
3		]ל[

Frg. 20

1 ל]פניו וישבו[
2] *vacat* [
3]אל השבים[
4]בנצובים *vacat*[

Frg. 21

1 נ]בונות ע]ינים
2]קושי [לב

Frg. 9

2. In the book of the di]visions of the tim[es
3.]the transgressions [
4.]for the covenant [

Frg. 11 Cols. i–ii

1.]because

Frg. 10

1.] to [
2.] portions of[

5.] from them and [
6. the g]uilt of all the peo[ple

Frg. 13

2. if he repays [
3. to/do not [
4. judges [
5.]to me and[

Frg. 15

1. as it is w]ritten[

Frg. 17

1.] he will send me [
2.]and you, do not [
3.]hope, because [

4.] command [
5.]be missing (?) [

Frg. 21

1. i]nsightf[ul
2.] hard of [heart

Frg. 20

1. b]efore him and they returned/sat[
2.] *vacat* [
3.]to the returnees[
4.]with those stationed *vacat*[

Frg. 22

1]י֯רשׁים

Frg. 23

1]שׁ֯ר [
2]ל֯[

Frg. 24

1]כשׁי֯ל [
2]◦[ ]ל֯[

Frg. 25

1]◦◦[
2]◦עד֯[
3]◦◦◦[

Frg. 26

1]◦רו֯◦ *vacat* [

Frg. 27

1]◦רי֯◦ם֯[

4Q**385a** (4QapocrJer C[a]). ed. D. Dimant, *DJD* XXX

Frg. 1a–b Cols. i–ii (formerly frgs. 43 + 13)

	Col. i	Col. ii
1		וא]ק֯ימה לב֯[
2		]את איבו [
3		]א֯ איבו ואסי֯]רה
4	[	ב֯שחרו פני ולא רם לבבו ממני ש֯[
5	[	וישלמו ימיו וישב שלמה ◦◦◦[
6	[	ואתנה נפש איביו בכפ֯ו[
7	]◦ע	ואקחה מידו עול]ה
8	]◦ה֯	ל[ ]ל[

Frg. 2 (formerly frg. 15)

1]◦[ ]◦[
2]◦ב֯ים וישב֯חו]
3]◦ו֯◦[ ]◦ לה֯ לא]

Frg. 3a–c (formerly frgs. 42 + 14)
Parallels: 4Q**388a** 3 2–7 (underline)
4Q**387** 1 1–6 (dotted underline)

1]]ד֯ א[[
2] בהתה]ל֯כ֯כם ב֯]שגגה מלפני [
3] ק]ר֯יאי השם ◦[[
4] כא]שר֯ אמרתי ליע]קוב [
5]]א ו]תאמרו]עזבתנ֯]ו אלהינו ותמאסו את חקותי[
6]ותשכחו את]מ֯ועדי בריתי ותח֯]ללו את שמי ואת קדשי[
7]ותטמאו את] מקדשי ותזבחו[את זבחיכם ל]שעירים ו]ת[
8]]את ש[ ]◦א֯◦[ ]ב֯רו֯ז[[

4Q**385a** (4QapocrJer C[a]) trans. D. Dimant

Frg. 1a–b Col. ii

1. [and I]raised up for [
2.]his enemy [
3. [ ] his enemy and I remo[ved
4.] when he sought me, and his heart did not grow haughty towards me [
5.] and his days were completed and Solomon sat [
6.] and I have delivered the life of his enemies into his hand[
7.] and I took sacrifi[ce] from his hand [

Frg. 2

2.] and they praised [
3.] [ ] not [

Frg. 3a–c

2. [while]you[were wal]king in[error before me]
3. [th]ose called by name [ ]
4. [a]s I told Jac[ob]
5. [ ] and[you said,] 'You have left u[s, our God,' and you spurned my statutes]
6. [and you forgot] the festivals of my covenant and you pro[faned my name and my consecrated things]
7. [and you defiled] my Temple and you sacrificed[your sacrifices to the]goat-demons and[ ]
8. [ ]the [ ] [ ]in the secret[ ]

9] ר]ותפרו הכל ביד
10]רמה ואבקש אמונה ו]לא
11]מצאתי [

Frg. 4 (formerly frg. 41)
Parallels: 4Q**387** 2 ii 3–11 (underline)
4Q**389** 8 ii 1–3 (dotted underline)

1]שלמות עשרה יבלי שנים ו]התה[לכתם בשגעון[
2]ובעורון ותמהון הלבב ומתם]הדור[ההוא אקרע[
3]את הממלכה מיד ה]מחזיקים אות[ה והקימותי[
4]עליה אחרים מעם[אחר ומשל הז]דון בכל הארץ[
5] ומ]מלכת[ישרא]ל תא]בד בימים ההמה יהיה[
6]מלך והוא גד]פן וע]שה תעבות וקרעתי את ממלכתו[
7]וגם המלך]ההוא למלכים ופני[מסתרים מישראל[
8] והממלכה]תשוב לגוים רבים ו]בני ישראל[
9]זעקים מפני על כבד ב]ארצות ש]בים ואין משיע[

Frg. 5a–b (formerly frgs. 40 + 44)
Parallel: 4Q**387** 3 2–7 (underline)

1]] אלהים[[
2]]מנין כהנים[[
3]]°א אחרים [[
4]]המזבח[[
5] הנופ]ל[ים בחרב [
6] חנ]פה[[
7]]אשר לא יתהלכו בד[רכי הכהנים על שם אלהי[
8]יש]ראל יקראו והורד [בימיהם גאון מרשיעי[
9]ברי]ת[וע]בדי נכר ו]יתקרע ישראל בדור ההוא[

Frg. 6 (formerly frg. 39)

1]ם ומ°[
2 ויר]או בעיניהם °[
3]משמים ומעל חו[
4]°° ירושלים ה[

Frg. 7 (formerly frg. 23)

1]°בת ה°[ ]אה °[
2 וע]שה חסד[

9. [ ]and you violated everything delib-
10. [erately and I looked for faith and I] did not
11. [find]

Frg. 4

1. [the completion of ten jubilees of years and you]will be wa[lking in madness]
2. [and in blindness and bewilderment of heart. And that] generation[comes to end, I shall tear away]
3. [the kingdom from the hand of those who] seize i[t and I shall raise]
4. [over it others from] another [people], and the in[solence]will rule[over all the land]
5. [and the k]ingdom[of Israe]l will be lo[st. In those days there will be]
6. [a king and he will be a blas]phemer and he will co[mmit abominations, and I shall tear away his kingdom]
7. [and]that[king too] (will be) to kings (?). And my face[will be hidden from Israel]
8. [and the kingdom]will return to many nations. And[the children of Israel]
9. [will be crying out because of the heavy yoke in the]lands of [their] cap[tivity and there will be none to deliver]

Frg. 5a–b

1. [ ] God[ ]
2. [ ]a number of priests[ ]
3. [ ] others [ ]
4. [ ]the altar[ ]
5. [those ki]ll[ed by the sword]
6. [be pollu]ted[ ]
7. [ ]who will not walk in the w[ays of the priests who by the name of the God of]
8. [Is]rael were called. And [in their days] will be brought down [the pride of those who act wickedly against]
9. [the cove]nant[and of sla]ves of foreign things and[Israel will be rent asunder in that generation]

Frg. 6

2. and they sa]w with their eyes [
3.]from the heavens and above [
4.] Jerusalem [

Frg. 7

2. and to a]ct in kindness[

Frg. 8 (formerly frg. 21)

1]◦תׄון ◦[ ]◦◦[
2]לׄבבו לדעת[
3]◦[ ]ל֯[

Frg. 9 (formerly frg. 20)

1]◦רשים אׄ[
2 א]בׄרהם אביכם ול֯[
3]יׄרׄש י֯[

Frg. 10 (formerly frg. 18)

	Col. i	Col. ii
1		]◦ר◦[
2	[	בבׄ[
3	]◦הם	לכה[
4	]אׄל ◦אׄישׁׄתׄ	]
5	]לוׄךׄ ◦◦י֯	אשׄ[
6	]םׄ	◦[

Frg. 11 (formerly frg. 17)

	Col. i	Col. ii
1		]יׄגעו בית[בבית
2	[	ומעשיהםׄ[
3	]וכהשלם	ובׄלי נשע[נו
4	]◦ שבעים יחלקו	לבלתׄיׄ[
5	]ל֯[ ]אׄת הדרך	לכׄןׄ[
6	]◦[	]◦[

Frg. 12 (formerly frg. 10)

1]◦[ ]◦[
2]שׁׄבע מאו[ת
3]קאה את תעׄ[בות
4 או]תׄם אל בית לא [בנו
5 י]שראל שנתים י֯[מים
6]ל֯[ ]וׄבני ישרא[ל

Frg. 13a–b (formerly frg. 11)

1]◦[ ]אׄבׄ[
2]הנה גת [
3]שערי מצרים[
4]יׄ אל אש[ר]יש◦[
5]ל◦[ ]◦קׄו ואׄ[ ]אׄ[
6]◦◦ל השוׄעפים[
7]ל֯[

Frg. 8

2.]his heart to know[

Frg. 9

2. A]braham your father and [
3.]inherited [

Frg. 11

	Col. i	Col. ii
1.		]they will join house[to house
2.		and their deeds[
3.	]and when will be completed	and without lea[ning
4.	] seventy will be split	so as not to[
5.	] [ ] the way	therefore[

Frg. 12

2.]seven hundre[ds
3.]spew out the abo[minations
4. th]em to a house [they had] not [built
5. I]srael a pe[riod of] two years [
6.] [ ]and the sons of Israe[l

Frg. 13a–b

2.]here Gath [
3.]the gates of Egypt[
4.] to that whi[ch] [

6.] disquieting thoughts[

Frg. 14 (formerly frg. 8)

1]חלב וד֯בש
2]◦בׄי

Frg. 15 (formerly frg. 7)

	Col. ii	Col. i
1	מזרת֯]	]ו
2	את]	אלי]הׄם אשׄר לא הקשיבו
3	ואי֯]	]ת֯לוי על העץ ועוף
4	]	]השמים]ו֯ אׄמת אל תותירו
5	]	]◦[ ]ל[ ]ו֯אמרה[א]ת֯
6	]	]לשון נפ֯שׄם
		vacat

Frg. 16a–b (formerly frg. 9)

1 המ]ה יׄתר֯[
2]ב֯ר עם לעדרי עׄ[
3]ע֯ם וזרע ויסב ◦עמו ויׄ[
4 וה]ורשתי את יון[
5 והשלחת]י֯ החיה בכן ה◦◦[
6 הה]ר והלבנון ירשו֯[
7 ידר]ו֯שון ליהוה לאמר֯[
8]י֯עקוב ורׄ[
9]◦[ ]◦[

Frg. 17a–e (formerly frg. 6)

	Col. ii	Col. i
1	]הבתר וא[ ]	
2	]◦◦◦[ ]◦◦ ימי חייהם[ ]	
3	ב֯ע֯פׄי עׄץ החיים *va[ca]t*	]םׄ
4	היכן חלקך אמון ה[ש]כׄנה ביארי[ם]	]מת נהרי
5	מים סביב לך חׄ[ילך] ים ומים חמ[תך]	]תׄכבש
6	כוש מצריׄ[ם עצמה ו]אין קץ לבריח[יך]	]◦[ ]
7	לוב בסעדך והיא בגולה תלך בש֯[בי]	]שׄן
8	]ו֯עלליה יׄ[רטש]ו֯[ ]בׄראש֯[הר]ים ועל	
9	נכבדיה ידו]גׄורל וכל [גדול]יה בזק֯[ים]	

Frg. 14

1.]milk and honey

Frg. 15

Col. i

2. to th]em because they did not listen
3.]hung upon the tree and the birds
4. [of heaven] truth. Do not leave over
5.] [ ] [ ]and I said [t]he
6.]the tongue of their throat

vacat

Col. ii

2. the[
3. and [

Frg. 16a–b

1. th]ey (are) the remaining(?)[
2.] people to the flocks of [
3.]people(?) and seed and he will turn [unto] his people and [
4. and]I[will dis]possess Greece[
5. and]I[will loose] wild beasts against you [
6. the mount]ain and Lebanon they will inherit[
7.]they[shall see]k the Lord saying[
8.]Jacob will [

Frg. 17a–e Col. i

4.] the rivers of
5.]will be subdued

Frg. 17a–e Col. ii

1.]the cleft and [ ]
2.] [ ] the days of their life[ ]
3. in the foliage of the Tree of Life *va*[*ca*]*t*
4. Where is your portion, O Amon, which [d]wells by the Nile[s]
5. waters surround you, [your]ra[mpart] is the sea, and waters (are) [your]wall.
6. Cush, Egyp[t (is) her might, and]there is no end to [your] bar[s].
7. Libya is your help, yet she shall go in exile, into cap[tivity]
8.]and her babes shall be da[she]d at the head[of mount]ains and for
9. [her honoured ones]lots[will be cast] and all her [great one]s in chain[s]

Frg. 18a–b Col. i (formerly frg. 16)

1 *va[c]at*
2 [ויצא]ירמיה הנביא מלפני יהוה
3 [וילך עם ה]שבאים אשר נשבו מארץ ירושלים ויבאו
4 [לרבלה אל]מלך בבל[ ]בׄהכות נבוזרדן רב הטבחים
5 [ ]עׄים ויקח אׄת כלי בית אלהים את הכהנים
6 [החרים]וׄבני ישראל ויביאם בבל וילך ירמיה הנביא
7 [עמהם עד]הנהר ויצום את אשר יעשו בארץ שביא[ם]
8 [וישמעו] בקול ירמיה לדברים אשר צוהו אלהים
9 [לעשות]ושמרו את ברית אלהי אבותיהם בארץׄ
10 [בבל ולא יעשו]כׄאשר עשו הם ומלכיהם כהניהם
11 [ושריהם]°°°[וי]חׄללׄ[ו ש]םׄ אלהים ל[טמא]

Frg. 18a–b Col. ii (formerly frg. 16)

1 בתחפנס א[שר בארץ מצרים]
2 ויאמרו לו דרוש[נא בעדנו לאל]הׄיׄם[ולא שמע]
3 להם ירמיׄ[ה ל]בׄלׄתי דרוש להם לאלה[ים ושאת בעדם]
4 רנה ותפלה ויהי ירמיה מקונן °[קינות]
5 [ע]ל ירושלים *vacat* [ויהי דבר יהוה אל]
6 ירמיה בארץ תחפנס אשר בארץ מצ[רים לאמר דבר אל]
7 בני ישראל ואל בני יהודה ובנימים °[כה תאמר אליהם]
8 יום יום דרשו את חקותי ואת מצותי שמׄ[רו ואל תלכו]
9 אחרי פ[ס]ילי הגוים אשר הׄלׄ[כו אחריהם אבותיכם כי]
10 לא יושׄי[עו] לׄ[כם]° לא °[ ]

Unidentified Fragments

Frg. A (formerly frg. 22)

1 שבת]שבתון הוא [
2]°צׄרׄ°[

Frg. B (formerly frg. 28)

1 יר]מיהו הנב[יא
2]°° וׄבׄאׄ°[

Frg. 18a–b Col. i

1. *va[c]at*
2. [and] Jeremiah the prophet [went out] from before the Lord
3. [and he went with the] captives who were led captive from the land of Jerusalem and they came
4. [to Riblah to] the king of Babylon, when Nebuzaradan, the commander of the body-guard, smote
5. [ ] and he took the vessels of the House of God, the priests,
6. [the nobles] and the Children of Israel and brought them to Babylon. And Jeremiah the prophet went
7. [with them until] the river. And he commanded them what they should do in the land of [their] captivity,
8. [(that) they should listen] to the voice of Jeremiah concerning the things which God had commanded him
9. [to do]and they should keep the covenant of the God of their fathers in the land
10. [of Babylon and they shall not do] as they had done, they themselves and their kings and their priests
11. [and their princes] [(namely, that) they]defiled[the na]me of God to[desecrate]

Frg. 18a–b Col. ii

1. in Tahpanes wh[ich is in the land of Egypt]
2. and they told him, 'Please inquire [of Go]d [on our behalf' but] Jeremia[h did not listen]
3. to them, [n]ot inquiring of Go[d] on their behalf [nor offering up on their behalf]
4. supplication and prayer. And Jeremiah was lamenting [laments]
5. [ov]er Jerusalem *vacat* [And the word of the Lord came to]
6. Jeremiah in the land of Tahpanes, which is in the land of E[gypt as follows, 'Speak to]
7. the Children of Israel and to the Children of Judah and Benjamin; [thus shall you say unto them]
8. 'Every day seek my statutes, and ke[ep] my commandments [and do not go]
9. after the i[d]ols of the gentiles, [after] which [your fathers] we[nt, because]
10. [t]he[y] will not sa[ve] y[ou] not [ ]

Unidentified Fragments

Frg. A

1. it is a[sabbath]of sabbatical observance [

Frg. B

1. Jere]miah the pro[phet

Frg. D (formerly frg. 31)

Col. ii Col. i

1 [בל̇ב̇]

2 ◦[ו]

Frg. C (formerly frg. 30)

1]◦

2 יהו̊◦]

3] [ל̇ו̊]

Frg. F (formerly frg. 36)

1]אם נלחם̊[

2] אצחך א◦[

Frg. E (formerly frg. 35)

1] שלמ̇[

2]ע בעמ[

Frg. H (formerly frg. 47)

1]◦ים רג[

2]ויה[

Frg. G (formerly frg. 45)

1]◦לת בלו̊[

2]ל ופ̊ק̇[

Frg. J

1]ואם ישוב ה◦[

2]ש̇או̊י ה◦[

Frg. I

1 ו̇בית ◦[

2 שלמה[

3 ה̊◦ו̊[

Frg. K

1]◦ם̊ ק̊◦[

2] ו̇הנ̊ו̇ט̇[ם̇

4Q**387** (4QapocrJer C^{b}) ed. D. Dimant, *DJD* XXX (corrected, 2004)

Frg. 1

Parallels: 4Q**385a** 3 4–11 (underline)
4Q**388a** 3 3–7 (overbar)
4Q**389** 6 1–2 (broken underline)
4Q**389** 7 2 (dotted underline)

1 [ ]ר̊תי̊[כ]ם כ[אשר]

2 [ותא]מרו עזב[תנו אלהינו ותמאסו]

3]את חקותי ותשכחו את מועדי בריתי]ותחלל̇[ו]א̊ת [שמי ואת קדשי[

4]ותטמאו מקדשי ותזבחו את זבחיכ[ם̇ לשעירים ות[ ]

5 [ ]ר ותפרו הכ̊ל ב̇[י]ד[ ]רמה]

6 [ואב]קש אמונה[ו]ל̇א מצאתי̊[ ]

7 [ואתנה את]כ̇ם ביד אי[ב]כם ואשמה̊[ ]את[ארצכם]

8 [והארץ]ר̊צ̊תה את ש[ב]ת̇[ו]תי[ה בהשמה[ ]

9 [ ]ם בארצ[ות] איבי̊[כ]ם̇[ ]עד שנת[ ]

10 [א]ל̇ א̊דמתכם [לפ[קוד ◦[ ]

Frg. D
Col. ii
1. with heart[

Frg. J
1.]and if the [ ] returns

Frg. I
1. and a house [

4Q387 (4QapocrJer C^{b}) trans. D. Dimant

Frg. 1

1. [ ] [ ] a[s]
2. [and you sa]id, [‘You]have left[us, our God’ and you spurned]
3. [my statutes and you forgot the festivals of my covenant], and [you] profaned [my name and my consecrated things]
4. [and you defiled my Temple, and you sacrificed yo]ur[sacrifices] to the goat-demons, and you[ ]
5. [ ] , and you violated everything de[li]be[rately]
6. [and I loo]ked for faith, [but] I did not find[ ]
7. [and I delivered]you into the hand of your enem[y], and I made desolate [your land]
8. [and the land]paid off its sa[bba]th[s] by being desolate[ ]
9. [ ] in the land[s] of [yo]ur enemies until the year of[ ]
10. [t]o your land [to re]visit [ ]

Frg. 2 (formerly frg. 3)
Parallels: 4Q**385a** 4 1–9 (underline)
4Q**389** 8 ii 1–4 (dotted overbar)

Col. ii — Col. i

top margin

1 [ ]יע[ ]◦[ ]כם[ ]ותחזקו לעבדני בכל לבבכם
2 ובכ֯[ל נפשכם ובק]ש[ו] פ֯[נ]י֯ בצר להם ולא֯ אדרש להם
3 בעבור מעל֯ם [א]ש֯ר֯ מעל[ו]ב֯[י]עד שלמות עשרה
4]תי — יבלי שנים וה֯ת֯ה֯[ל]כתם ב֯ש֯[געון]ובעורון ותמהן
5 הלבב ומתם֯ הדור֯[ ]ההוא א[קרע]את הממלכה מיד המחזיקים
6 אתה ו֯[ה]קימותי ע֯ליה אחרים מעם אחר ומשל
7 [הז]דון בכ֯ל֯[הא]רץ וממלכת ישראל תאבד בימים
8 ההמה[י]ה֯[יה מלך וה]וא גדפן ועשה תעבות וקרעתי
9 [את] ממלכ֯[תו והמלך ה]הוא למכל[י]ם ופני מסתרים מישראל
10 [ ]לל[ ]תשוב [ל֯]גוים רבים וב֯נ֯י֯ ישראל זעקים
11 [מפני על כבד בארצות שבי]ם֯ ו֯[אין משי]ע֯ להם
12 [יען ביען חקתי מאסו ותרתי געלה נפשם ע]ל֯[ ]כן

Frg. 2 Col. iii (formerly frg. 3)
Parallels: 4Q**388a** 7 ii 4–7 (underline)
4Q**389** 8 ii 10–11 (dotted underline)

top margin

אשבר
1 [את ישרא]ל מעם בי֯מ֯ו֯ את ממלכת [מצרים]
2 [את מצרי]ם֯ ואת ישראל אשבר ונ[תתו לחרב]
3 [והש]מותי א[ת]ה֯[א]ר֯ץ ורחקתי את האד֯ם֯[ ]ועזבתי[
4 [ ]את ה֯א֯רץ ביד מלא֯כי המשטמות והסתרתי [פני]
5 [מיש]ר֯אל וזה להם האות ביום עזבי את הארץ[ ]בהשמה[
6 [ושב]ו֯ כהני ירושלים לעבוד אלהים אחרים[ ]ולעשות[
7 [כתע]בות ה֯[ג]וים [ ]ל[ ]ל[ ]

Frg. 3 (formerly frg. 2)
Parallel: 4Q**385a** 5 4–9

1 [ ]◦המז֯[ב]ח[ ]
2 [ ]ם֯[ ]הנו[פ]לים בח֯[ר]ב[ ]
3 [ ]ב֯ו[ ]ב חנפה אח◦[ ]
4 [ ]י֯ם כהנ֯ים שלושה אשר לא יתהלכו בדרכ֯י

Frg. 2 Col. ii

1. [ ] [ ] your[ ]and be resolute to serve me with all your heart
2. and with al[l your soul.' And they will se]e[k] my pre[s]ence in their affliction, but I shall not respond to their inquiry,
3. because of the trespass [wh]ich they have trespassed [against] m[e], until the completion of ten
4. jubilees of years; and you will be wa[l]king in ma[dness] and in blindness and bewilderment
5. of heart. And after that generation comes to end, I shall [tear away] the kingdom from the hand of those who sei$_{\text{ze}}$
6. it, and [I sha]ll raise up over it others from another people, and the insolence will rule
7. over all[the l]and, and the kingdom of Israel will be lost. In those days
8. there[will]b[e a king and h]e (will) be a blasphemer and he will commit abominations, and I shall tear away
9. his]king[dom, and th]at [king] (will be) to the destroy[e]rs. And my face shall be hidden from Israel
10. [ ] [will return]to many nations. And the Children of Israel will be crying out
11. [because of the heavy yoke in the lands of]their[captivity] and [there will be none to deliv]er them
12. [because they have spurned my statutes and abhorred my Torah. There]fo[re]

Frg. 2 Col. iii

1. [Israe]l from (being) a people. In his days $^{\text{I shall break}}$ the kingdom of[Egypt]
2. [Egyp]t, and I shall break Israel and de[liver her up to the sword]
3. [And]I[shall lay wa]ste the [l]and and I shall drive man away[and I shall abandon]
4. [ ]the land in the hand of the angels of Mastemot, and I shall hide [my face]
5. [from Is]rael. And this shall be the sign for them: in the day when I abandon the land[in desolation]
6. the priests of Jerusalem [will retur]n to worship other gods[and to act]
7. [according to the abo]minations of the[Gentiles] [ ] [ ]

Frg. 3

1. [ ] the al[tar]
2. [ ] [those ki]lled by the sw[ord]
3. [ ] [ ] be polluted [ ]
4. [ ] three priests who will not walk in the ways of

5 [הכהנים ה]ראשנים על שם אלהי ישראל יקראו
6 [והורד]בימיהם גאון מרישיעי ברית ועבדי נאכר
7 ויתקרע ישראל בדור הה[וא] להלחם א[י]ש ברעהו
8 על התורה ועל הברית ושלחתי רעב ב[אר]ץ ולא
9 לל[ח]ם וצמא ול[א] למ[ים כי] אם ל[שמוע את דברי]

bottom margin

Frg. 4

Col. i — Col. ii

top margin

1]א בגורל למטותיה[ם]◦ [
2]ל[ ]מלכי הצפון שנים[
3]ה ו[ז]עקו[ ]בני ישראל לאלהים[ ]◦◦[ ]מ [
4 וגשם שוטף וא]בנ[י א]ל[גב]יש אש וגפרית [ ]◦[
5]תש[ ]ם [ ]עם הח[
6]ש א[ ]◦[

Unidentified Fragment

Frg. A (formerly 4Q**387** 5)

top margin

1]המה במעלם אשר[מעלו] לחלל את ש[ם קדשי
2]בערותם לקרוב איש אל שאר בשרו[
3 אנוכי]ק[ר]אתי לבכי ולמספד והמה אמר[ו
4]אשמות לא הבינו על כן יללו ביום [
5]ביום שמור ויום ◦[

4Q**388a** (4QapocrJer C^c) ed. D. Dimant, *DJD* XXX (corrected, 2004)

Frg. 1 (formerly frg. 5)

1]בים י[
2 הצ]דיקים ל[
3]ים שמים[
4]ל[ ] ◦[

Frg. 2 (formerly frg. 17)

1]ק להם [
2] ביריעות עזי[ם
3 ארב]עים שנה ויה[י
4 וי]פנו אחרי י[
5]ה אתם כ[

5. [the]former[priests] will be called by the name of the God of Israel
6. [And] in their days [will be brought down] the pride of those who act wickedly against the covenant and of the slaves of foreign things
7. and Israel will be rent asunder in th[at] generation, each m[a]n fighting against his neighbour
8. over the Torah and over the covenant. And I will send hunger upon the [lan]d, but not
9. for br[ea]d, and a thirst, but no[t] for water;[ra]ther, for [hearing the words]

Frg. 4

Col. i

1.] by lot according to the[ir] tribes[
2.] [ ]the kings of the North for years[
3.] and the Children of Israel [will c]ry out to God[ ] [ ] [
4. and torrential rain and h]a[i]l st[on]es, fire, and brimstone [
5.] [ ] [ ]with [

Unidentified Fragment

Frg. A

1.]they in their trespass which[they have trespassed], defiling [my holy na]me[
2.]in their nakedness, each drawing near to his close kin[
3.]I sum[mo]ned for weeping and lament, but they said[
4.]offences they did not understand. Therefore they wailed on the day [
5.]in the day of keeping and the day [

4Q**388a** (4QapocrJer C[c]) trans. D. Dimant

Frg. 1

2. the ri]ghteous [
3.] heavens[

Frg. 2

1.] for them [
2.] in curtains of goat[s' hair
3. for]ty years; and it came[to pass
4. and t]hey turned after [
5.] them [

Frg. 3 (formerly frgs. 2 + 3)
Parallels: 4Q**385a** 3 2–9 (underline)
4Q**387** 1 3–5 (overbar)

1] ב]עׄת ה]היא [
בשג]גה
2] בהתהלככם מלפ]ני [
3] כא]שר אמרתי ליעק]וב [
4] ותאמרו עזבתנו אלהינו ותמאסו] את חקותיׄ] ותשכחו את]
5 מועדי ברי]תי ותחל]לו את שמי ואת קדשי ותטמאו מקדשי ותזבחו את]
6 זבחיכם ל]שׂעירים ו]ת ר]
7 ותפרו הכ]לׄ ביד רׄ]מה [

Frg. 4

1] יׄ◦[
2 שבתות השׁ]נים[
3 אׄ הׄ[

Frg. 5 (formerly frgs. 15 + 7)

1] עזׄבוניׄ[

Frg. 6

1 יׄהו א[
פני]
2 א]סתיר מׄ]הם[
3 כ]ול הנת[
4] רעוׄ]ת[

Frg. 7 (formerly frg. 1)
Parallel: 4Q**389** 8 ii 7–11

Col. i	Col. ii
	top margin
1	מאׄ[ס]תים ושבו[ועשו רעה ורבה הר]עה מ[ן הראשונה והפרו את]
2]ד	הברית אשר כׄ[רתי ע]ם אברהם ועם יצחקׄ[ועם יעקוב בימים]
3	ההמה יקום מלך [לגו]יםׄ גדפן ועשה רעות ובימׄ[ו אעביר]
4	את ישראל מעם בימו אשבור את מלכות מצרים[ ]
5]תׄי	את מצרים ואת ישראל אשבור ונתתו לחרב [והשמותי את הארץ]
6]ה	ורחקתי את האדםׄ[ו]עׄזבתי את הארץ בה[שמה ושבו כהני ירושלים]
7	לעבוד אלהים אח]רים ולעשו]תׄ כתועׄבותׄ[הגוים]

Frg. 3

1. [at] t[hat] time[ ]
2. [ ]when you were walking in err[or] befor[e me]
3. [a]s I told Jac[ob]
4. [and you said: 'You have left us, our God,' and you spurned] my statutes[and you forgot]
5. [the festivals of]my[covena]nt and you profa[ned my name and my consecrated things and you defiled my Temple and you sacrificed]
6. [your sacrifices to the]goat-demons and[ ]
7. [and you have violated every]thing delibe[rately]

Frg. 4

2.]sabbaths of the y[ears

Frg. 5

1. [ ] they forsook me[ ]

Frg. 6

2. I will]hide my face from[them
3. a]ll [
4.] evil[s

Frg. 7 Col. ii

1. I have sp[ur]ned them and they will once again[do evil, and the ev]il[will be greater] tha[n the former (evil), and they will violate]
2. the covenant which [I]ma[de wi]th Abraham and with Isaac[and with Jacob. In] those[days]
3. will arise a king [of the Genti]les, a blasphemer and a doer of evils. And in [his]day[s I shall remove]
4. Israel from (being) a people. In his days I shall break the kingdom of Egypt[ ]
5. Egypt, and I shall break Israel and deliver her up to the sword. [And I shall lay waste the land]
6. and I shall drive man away,[and] I shall abandon the land in des[olation, and the priests of Jerusalem will return]
7. to worship oth[er]gods[and to ac]t according to the abominations[of the Gentiles]

8 שלשה אשר ימלכ֯ו[ ]ל֯[ ]
9]ו[ק֯דש הקדשי]ם[ ]
10]]ר והמצדקי]ם[ ]
11]]◦[ ]

Unidentified Fragments

Frg. A (formerly 4Q**388** 16)

1 בנ֯ך֯[
2 ויאמ[ר
3 מש֯[

bottom margin

Frg. B (formerly 4Q**388** 18)

1 מבו◦[
2 מוש[

Frg. C (formerly 4Q**388** 20)

1]ו֯ת
2]צרה
3]היא
4 א]שר

Frg. D (formerly 4Q**388** 21)

1]ברנה כי[
2 ומלאך יה]וה הלך לפני מ֯[חנה ישראל
3 בה]ושע ב[

Frg. E (formerly 4Q**388** 22)

1]ח֯שך כ[
2]◦[

Frg. F (formerly 4Q**388** 19)

1 א]ת שני המ[
2]ץ אמר֯[
3]כ֯ת ג[

Frg. G (formerly 4Q**388** 23)

1]ש֯[
2 א]יך תש[
3]שמי֯ם֯ [◦ש֯[

Frg. H

1 לפנ[י
2 ואמר[
3 קש[
4]ל[

Frg. I (formerly 4Q**388** 24)

1]מ֯◦◦ ל֯◦[
2]◦ את ש[
3]ויאמ[ר

8. three who will rule[ ] [ ]
9. [and]the holy of holie[s]
10. [ ] and thos[e]who lead to righteous[ness]

Unidentified Fragments

Frg. A

1. your son[
2. and he sai[d

Frg. C

2.]distress
3.]she/it
4. wh]ich

Frg. D

1.]with cries of joy, for[
2. and the angel of Go]d marching before the c[amp of Israel
3. when is s]aved [

Frg. F

1. t]he two [
2.] said[

Frg. H

1. befo[re (me?)
2. and he said[

Frg. E

1.]darkness [

Frg. G

2. h]ow [
3.]heavens/sky[

Frg. I

2.] the [
3.]and he sa[id

4Q**389** (4QapocrJer C^{d}) ed. D. Dimant, *DJD* XXX

Frg. 1 (formerly frg. 6)

1 [ ]צׄ ∘∘[ ]
2 [ ]ה בארץ יׄ[הודה]
3 [ ]ובקשו על כ[ל]
4 [ו]כׄל הנשאר בארץ מצׄ[רים]
5 [י]רמיה בן חלקיה מארץ מצר[ים]
6 [שלו]שים ושש שנה לגלות ישראל קׄראׄו הדברים[האלה לפני]
7 כׄ[ל בני י]שראל על נהר סור במעמד ד[ ]

bottom margin

Frg. 2

top margin

1 [ת]דרשני הייתי[ ]
2 [וא]רׄים ראשיכם בהוציאׄי אׄ[תכם מארץ מצרים]
3 [ ] להם ואת אשר גמלוני ואשאםׄ[כאשר ישא איש את בנו עד]
4 [בואם אל]קׄדש ברנע ואמרה להם [ ]לׄ[ ]
5 [ ]תם עליהם ואשבעה ב∘[ ]
6 [ ] ואת בניהם הבאתי אל ה[ארץ]
7 [ ]תׄם ואתהלכה עמהם ב∘[ ]
8 [ ]ארבעים שנה ויהי [ ]
9 [ ]לׄ[ ]

Frg. 3

1 [םׄ אחרי]
2 [ש]

Frg. 4 (formerly frg. 7)

1 [י ותב]או
2 [הׄארצׄ]

Frg. 5 (formerly frg. 4)

1 [יׄ] [תׄה אׄ∘] [אחׄ]
2 כאשר [אׄמרו תנה לנו מלך אשר]
3 שמוא[ל] בן א[לקנה לדׄ]

Frg. 6 (formerly frg. 9)
Parallel: 4Q**387** 1 7–8 (underline)

1 [ ] ואתנכם ב[יׄדׄ איביכם ואשמה] את ארצכם
2 [והארץ רצתה את שבתותי]ה בהשמה]

4Q389 (4QapocrJer C^d) trans. D. Dimant

Frg. 1

2. [ ] in the land of J[udaea]
3. [ ]and they prayed for a[ll]
4. [and]all who remained in the Land of Egyp[t]
5. [Je]remiah son of Helkiah from the Land of Egyp[t]
6. [the thi]rty-sixth year of the exile of Israel they read [these] things[before]
7. a[ll the Children of I]srael upon the river Sour in the presence [ ]

Frg. 2

1. [you]have/will inquire/d me, I have been[ ]
2. [and I]raised your heads when I brought y[ou out of the land of Egypt]
3. [ ] to them and what they repaid me, and I carried them[as a man carries his son until]
4. [they came to]Kadesh Barnea, and I said to them [ ] [ ]
5. [ ] upon them and I swore in [ ]
6. [ ] and their children I brought to the[land]
7. [ ] and I walked with them [ ]
8. [ ]forty years; and it came to pass [ ]

Frg. 3

1.] after[

Frg. 4

1.] and you ca[me
2.]the land[

Frg. 5

2. when]they said, 'give us a king who[
3. Samue]l[son of E]lkanah [

Frg. 6

1. [I delivered you into]the hand of your enemies and I made desolate[your land]
2. and the land paid off]its[sabbaths] by being desolate[

Frg. 7 (formerly frg. 8)
Parallel: 4Q**387** 1 10 (underline)

1	[ ] ∘∘[
2	אדמתכם]
3	ר֯שו בׄו]

Frg. 8 (formerly frg. 1)
Parallels: 4Q**385a** 4 6–9 (underline)
4Q**387** 2 ii 8–12 (lower underline)
4Q**387** 2 iii 1–2 (dotted underline)
4Q**388a** 7 ii 1–5 (overbar)

	Col. i	Col. ii
1		[גדפן ועשה תעבות וקרע]תי את מׄ[מלכתו וגם הוא למכלים]
2		[ופני מסתרים מישרא]ל והממלכה תשוב לגוים ר֯בים ובני ישראל
3		[זעקים מפ]ני על כבד בארצות שבים ואין משיע להם
4		יען ביען חקתי מאסו ותרתי געלה נפשם על כן הסתרתי
5		פני מ[הם עד] אשר ישלימו עונם *vacat* וזה להם האות בשלם
6	∘]	עונם [כי] עזבתי את הארץ ברום לבבם ממני ולא ידעו
7	מ]צרים	[כ]י֯ מאסתים ו]שבו ועשו רעה ר֯[ב]הׄ מן הרע֯[ה] ה֯ראשנה
8		[והפרו את הברית אשר כרתי]ע֯ם אברה֯[ם] וע֯[ם י]צחק ועם
9		[יעקוב בימים ההמה י]קום מלך לגוים גדפן [וע]שׄה רעות ו[ ]
10		[ובימו אעביר את ישרא]ל מעׄםׄ[בימו] אׄשבור אׄ[ת מ]מׄלכת
11		[מצרים את מצרים ואת ישרא]ל֯[אשבור ונתתו לחרב]

bottom margin

Frg. 9 (formerly frg. 10)

1	]ת∘[
2	]ת֯י אלהם ויאמר֯[ו
3	]לדרות ש∘[

Frg. 7

2.]your land
3.] in it / him

Frg. 8

	Col. i	Col. ii
1.		[a blasphemer and he will commit abominations and]I[shall tear away his]k[ingdom and he too (will be) to the destroyers.]
2.		[And my face will be hidden from Israe]l and the kingdom will return to many nations. And the Children of Israel
3.		[will be crying out be]cause of the heavy yoke in the lands of their captivity, and there will be none to deliver them
4.		because they had spurned my statutes and abhorred my Torah. Therefore I have hidden
5.		my face from[them until] they accomplish their iniquity. *vacat* And this is the sign to them of the requital of
6.		their iniquity [for] I shall leave the land because of their haughtiness towards me, and they will not know
7.	E]gypt	[tha]t[I have spurned them and]they will once again do evil, and the evil will be gr[eat]er than the former (ev[il),]
8.		and they will violate the covenant which I made]with Abraha[m] and wi[th I]saac and with
9.		[Jacob. In those days will]arise a king of the Gentiles, a blasphemer, [and a do]er of evils and[ ]
10.		[And in his days I shall remove Israe]l from (being) a people.[In his days] I shall break th[e k]ingdom
11.		[of Egypt Egypt, and I shall break Israe]l[and deliver her up to the sword]

Frg. 9

2.] to them and [t]he[y] said[
3.]for generations [

Unidentified Fragments

Frg. A (formerly frg. 5)

1]תׄי להׄ[ ]כׄ◦ ◦[
2]כדמן אשר נשפ[ך על פני השדה
3] ויביאם בשער כב◦[
4]◦[

Frg. B (formerly frg. 11)

1]םׄ ממש◦[
2]מות[

Frg. C (formerly frg. 12)

1] אש[
2]מדבר◦[

Frg. D (formerly frg. 14)

1]תׄ כי אב לשכׄ[
2]אׄ◦ ◦◦◦◦[ ]לׄ[

Frg. E (formerly frg. 17)

1]בׄונם לכול קׄ[
2]ביום ולילה ללי[לה

4Q**390** (4QapocrJer C^{e}) ed. D. Dimant, *DJD* XXX

Frg. 1

1]]◦[ ]◦◦[[
2 [ו]מפ[ני וא]שוב[ונתתים]ביד בני אהר[ון]שבעים שנה [ ]
3 ומשלו בני אהרון בהמהׄ ולא יתהלכו[בדר]כי אשר אנוכי מצׄוׄך אשר
4 תעיד בהם ויעשו גם הם את הרע בעיני ככל אשר עשו ישראל
5 בימי ממלכתו הרישונים מלבד העולים רישונה מארץ שבים לבנות
6 את המקדש ואדברה בהמה ואשלחה אליהם מצוה ויבינו בכול אשר
7 עזבו הם ואבותיהם ומתום הדור ההׄוא ביובל השביעי
8 לחרבן הארץ ישכחו חוק ומועד ושבׄת וברית ויפרו הכול ויעשו
9 הרע בעיני והסתרתי פני מהמה ונתתים ביד איביהם והסגרתׄ[ים]

Unidentified Fragments

Frg. A

2.]as dung that is spil[led upon the field
3.]and he brought them into the gate [

Frg. D

1.] for a father to [

Frg. E

1.] to all [
2.]by day and night to nig[ht

4Q**390** (4QapocrJer C^{e}) trans. D. Dimant

Frg. 1

2. [and]be[fore me and a]gain I shall [deliver them]into the hand of the sons of Aar[on] seventy years [ ]
3. And the sons of Aaron will rule over them, and they will not walk [in]my[wa]ys, which I command you so that
4. you may warn them. And they too will do what is evil in my eyes, like all that which the Israelites had done
5. in the former days of their kingdom, except for those who will come first from the land of their captivity to build
6. the Temple. And I shall speak to them and I shall send them commandments, and they will understand everything which
7. they and their fathers had abandoned. And from (the time) when that generation comes to an end, in the seventh jubilee
8. of the devastation of the land, they will forget statute and festival and Sabbath and covenant. And they will violate everything and they will do
9. what is evil in my eyes. Therefore I shall hide my face from them and deliver them into the hands of their enemies; and [I] shall deliver [them up]

10 לחרב והשארתי ‏(מהם) פׄליטים למע[ן] אשר לא יׄ[כ]ל[ו]בחמתי [ו]בׄהסתר פׄ[ני]
11 מהם ומשלו בהמה מלאכי המשׂ[ט]מות ומׄ[אסתים ו]ישובׄ[ו]
12 וׄיעשו [את] הרׄעׄ בׄעינׄ[י] ויתהלכו בשרׄ[ירות לבם]
13 [ ]ת[ ]◦◦[ ]

Frg. 2 Col. i

1 [ ]◦[ ]◦[ ]
2 [וא]תׄ[ ]ביתׄ[י ומזבחי וא]ת מקדש הקדׄ[ש]
3 נעשה כן ◦[ ]◦ כי אלה יבואו עליהם[ ]ן וׄ[ת]הי
4 ממשלת בליעל בהם להסגירם לחרב שבועׄ שניםׄ[ו]בׄיׄובל ההוא יהיו
5 מפרים את כול חקותי ואת כל מצותי אשר אצוה אׄ[ותם ואשלח בי]דׄ עבדי הנביאים
6 וי[ח]ל[ו] להריב אלה באלה שנים שבעים מיום הפר ה[אלה וה]ברית אשר יפרו ונתתים
7 [ביד מל]אכי המשטמות ומשלו בהם ולא ידעו ולא יבינו כי קצפתי עליהם במועלם
8 [אשר עז]בוני ויעשו הרע בעיני ובאשר לא חפצתי בחרו להתגבר להון ולבצע
9 [ולחמס ואי]שׂ אשרׄ לרׄ[ע]הו יגזולו ויעשוקו איש את רעהו את מקדשי יטמאו
10 [את שבתותי יחללו]את[מו]עדי ישׂ[כח]וׄ ובבני[נכר]יׄחׄלׄלׄ[ו]אׄת זר[ע]ם כוהניהם ‏(יחמסו)
11 [ ]◦יה◦[ ]הׄם ואת
12 [ ]בׄניהם

Frg. 2 Col. ii

1 [
2 [
3 בׄ[
4 מעליה[
5 ובדברׄ[
6 אנחנו שוׄ◦[
7 ידעו ואשלחׄ[ה
8 וברמחים לבק[ש
9 בקרב הארץ על א◦[
10 [א]חׄוזתם ויזבחו בה[
11 [יח]ללו בה וׄ[א]תׄ מזׄבׄח

10. to the sword. But I shall leave $^{\text{among them}}$ refugees, s[o] that [t]he[y] should not be an-[nihi]lated in my wrath[and] when [my]fa[ce]is hidden
11. from them. And the Angels of *Mas*[*te*]*mot* will rule over them, and[I shall]sp[urn them and they] will return
12. to do [wh]at is evil in[my]eyes, and they will walk in the will[fulness of their heart]

Frg. 2 Col. i

2. [and my]house[and my altar and th]e Holy of Ho[lies]
3. so it was done [ ] for these things will befall them[ ] and[there]will be
4. the rule of Belial over them so as to deliver them to the sword for a week of years[and]in that jubilee they will be
5. violating all my statues and all my commandments which I shall have commanded th[em and sent in the ha]nd of my servants, the prophets.
6. And[t]he[y]will be[gi]n to quarrel among themselves for seventy years, from the day of the violation of the[oath and the]covenant which they will have violated. So I shall deliver them
7. [into the hand of the An]gels of Mastemot, and they will rule over them. And they will not know and they will not understand that I was angry with them because of their trespass,
8. [by which they will have for]saken me, and will have done what is evil in my eyes, and what I did not want they will have chosen: to pursue wealth and gain
9. [and violence, ea]ch robbing that which belongs to his neigh[b]our, and oppressing each other. They will defile my Temple,
10. [they will profane my sabbaths,] they will for[ge]t my[fes]tivals, and with fo[reign]ers [t]he[y]will profane their offspr[ing]. Their priests will commit violence
11. [ ] [ ] and the
12. [ ]their sons

Frg. 2 Col. ii

4. from upon it[/ the[m
5. and with the word (?)[
6. we [
7. they will know. And I shall send[
8. and with spears to see[k
9. in the land on [
10. their [pos]session and they will sacrifice in [
11. they[will pro]fane in it and[t]he alt[ar

Frg. 3

1]◦[
2]בם א[
3]◦ בעיני וא[
4 כ]ל[ ]א֯שר ו֯נ֯[

Frg. 4

1]הי֯ בקו֯[
2]בא֯רץ[
3]◦◦[

Frg. 5

1]ה ישכ]בו
2]◦ ◦ל[

Frg. 6

1]כמשפח֯]ות
2]◦◦[

Frg. 7

1] שלו]ם
2]מות [

Frg. 8

1]ת֯ו֯[
2]שקר ופש֯]ע

4Q**387a** (4QapocrJer $\mathrm{C^f}$) ed. D. Dimant, *DJD* XXX

Frg. 1 (formerly frg. 6)

1]שוב[
2]ול◦[
3]בכל ◦[
4]י֯ו֯[

Frg. 2 (formerly frg. 7)

1]◦למ֯[
2]לגו◦[
3]◦המ[

Frg. 3 (formerly frg. 8)

1]מים וידי[
2]בהוציאי[
3]◦ לפ֯שע[

Frg. 4 (formerly frg. 9)

1]בי אם ◦[
2]ו֯אתננה להם[
3]אשר להתה֯ל]ך
4]◦ם מאיביהם[
5 [ ]◦[ ]ולא֯ ◦[
6]ויאמרו ת[
7]ואל בן֯ נ֯]כר

Frg. 3

3.] in my eyes(?) and [
4. every]thing which [

Frg. 4

2.]in the land[

Frg. 5
1.] [t]he[y]will li[e

Frg. 6
1.]as famil[ies

Frg. 7
1.] pea[ce

Frg. 8

2.]a lie and a cri[me

4Q387a (4QapocrJer C^{f}) trans. D. Dimant

Frg. 1

3.]in all [

Frg. 3

2.]when I took out[
3.] to iniquity[

Frg. 4
1.] if [
2.]and I gave it to them[
3.]which to wa[lk
4.] of their enemies[
5.] [ ] and not [
6.]and they said [
7.]and unto a fo[reigner

Frg. 5 (formerly frg. 11)

1] בנימ֯ין ◦[
2] מעליׄו ◦[
3] בשחרו [
4 [◦◦]

Frg. 6 (formerly frg. 12)

1]קׄללׄתם
2 א]ת הנהר
3]◦[

Frg. 7 (formerly frg. 13)

1 ביו]ם ההואׄ[
2] ה[ ]סׄ[

Frg. 8 (formerly frg. 14)

1]ת֯◦סׄ [
2]◦רׄוח באו[

Frg. 9 (formerly frg. 15)

1]◦◦[
2]ם לגוי וגוי עם ועם [
3]ם זורע לחם לפי תבא]תו
4 ל]פי חטאתם[
5]◦ה֯מׄ◦ למׄי[ ]◦◦[

Pseudo-Daniel

4Q**243** (4QpsDan[a] ar) ed. J. Collins and P. Flint, *DJD* XXII

Frg. 1

top margin

1 שאיל דניאל לממר בד[י]ל [
2 𐤀𐤋𐤄𐤊𐤄 ומׄנין֯ ◦[ ]ל[
3 יצלה ינ֯[
4 עׄ[

Frg. 2

top margin

1]דניאל קוד֯ם
2]בלשצ֯ר[

Frg. 3

top margin?

1]איתי[
2]מלכא [

Frg. 5

1.] Benjamin [
2.] from him [
3.] while he was seeking [

Frg. 6

1.]their curse
2.] the river

Frg. 7

1. on]that [da]y [

Frg. 9

2.] to every people, every nation [
3.] he who sows wheat according to [its] produc[e
4. acc]ording to their iniquity[

Pseudo-Daniel

4Q**243** (4QpsDan[a] ar) trans. J. Collins and P. Flint

Frg. 1

1. He asked Daniel saying 'On ac[count] of [
2. **YOUR GOD,** and a number '[
3. he will pray [

Frg. 3

1.]there is[
2.]O King (or: the king) [

Frg. 2

1.]Daniel befo[re
2.]Belshazzar[

Frg. 4

top margin

1 [מ]ל[כ]אׄ יתרמ֯הׄ ל[

Frg. 5

1]דניאלׄ[

2] ◦◦◦ [

Frg. 6

1]◦[

2]ובה כתיב◦[

3]דׄניאל די י◦[

4]◦[א]שׄתכח כתי[ב

Frg. 7

1]◦ חׄ[

2]כשדיא הׄאׄ בׄני[

3]אוׄרחת ק[ושטא

Frg. 8

1 כר]סׄא

2 מן י]שראל גברין

3]די לא לשניה

4]◦◦[ ]◦[

Frg. 9

1] לחנוךׄ[

2]ל◦ל[

Frg. 10

1]לׄאׄ ◦[

2 ע]ל מגדלא ושלחׄ[

3 ל]בׄקרה בבנין [

4 כ]רׄסאׄ[

Frg. 11 Col. i

1]

2]תׄוׄן

3]◦

Frg. 11 Col. ii

1 וחכׄ[מי]ן ויאׄ[מר

2 מצרין ביד ◦[

3 שלטן באר[עא

Frg. 12

1 שנין אר]בׄעׄ מאה ומן

2]סׄהון ויתון מן גוא

3] מעברהון ירדנא יובל[א

4]ובניהון [

5]דיתׄוׄ[

Frg. 13

Parallel: 4Q**244** 12 1–3

1 ב]חׄרו בני ישראל אנפיהׄ[ון

2 דב]חׄיןׄ לבניהון לשידי [

3] למנתן אנון ביד נׄבׄ[כדנצר

4 ארעה]וׄןׄ מנה[וׄן   ]שׄ[

Frg. 5

1.]Daniel[

Frg. 4

1. [O K]i[n]g, he shall be cast in[to

Frg. 6

2.]and in it was written [
3.]Daniel, who [
4. it] was writte[n

Frg. 7

2.]the Chaldaeans, indeed the children of[
3.]the way of t[ruth

Frg. 9

1.] to Enoch[

Frg. 8

1. thr]one
2. from I]srael, men
3.]which is not to be changed

Frg. 10

2. o]n the tower, and he sent (?)[
3. to]inspect a building [
4. th]rone (?)[

Frg. 12

1. fo]ur hundred [years,] and from
2.]their [ ] and they will come out of
3.] their crossing the rive[r] Jordan
4.]and their children [

Frg. 11 Col. ii

1. and wis[e me]n, and he sa[id
2. Egypt, by the hand of [
3. rule/dominion in the la[nd

Frg. 13

1.] The Israelites [ch]ose [their] presence[
2. they were sacri]ficing their children to the demons of [
3.] to give them into the hand of Neb[uchadnezzar
4. th]eir [land] from the[m

Frg. 14

1 בתר]דׄנה יתעב[ד
2]◦ מאהׄ מלכׄ[ין
3]אנון בגו ע[ממיא

Frg. 15

top margin

1]רׄ בשלר◦[

Frg. 16

1]]איׄןׄ ◦◦עׄין שנין[ ]כׄ[
2] בי]דה רבתא ויושע אנ[ון
3]]חסינין ומלכות עממׄ[יא
4]]הׄיא מלכותא קדׄ[ישתא

Frg. 17 Col. i

top margin?

1]מד
2] מלכותא
3]◦◦
4]◦◦א ובני
5]◦◦

Frg. 17 Col. ii

top margin?

1 יכ[
2 לה מׄ[
3 למל[
4 ◦◦[
5 [

Frg. 18 Col. i

1]◦
2]◦

Frg. 18 Col. ii

2 ומלכיׄ[
3 ומׄלׄ[כי

Frg. 19

1]שניׄןׄ ◦◦[
2]רהׄוס בוׄ[
3]וס שנין ת[לתין
4]ימללוׄןׄ [

Frg. 20

1]ס בׄרׄ מׄלׄכׄ[
2 שנ]ין עשרין[
3]די מל[ ]ל[

Frg. 21

1 י]מׄלׄך שׄניׄן ◦[
2]אׄןׄ בלכרוס
3]◦[ ]◦תׄהׄ[

Frg. 22

1 ב]ר ושמהׄ תׄ[
2]ל◦◦◦ן להוׄן תרין[
3]מלל[

Frg. 23

1]◦[
2]ברח כ◦[
3]מׄעל[
4]◦[

Frg. 14

1. After]this it will be don[e/be mad[e
2.] hundred king[s
3.]them in the midst of [the] p[eoples

Frg. 16

1.]oppressed(?) for [seven]ty (?) years[
2. with] his great [ha]nd and he will save th[em
3.]powerful[ ]and the kingdoms of [the] peoples[
4.]It is the h[oly] kingdom[

Frg. 17 Col. ii

2. to her/its/his[
3. to [

Frg. 17 Col. i

2.] the kingdom

4.] and sons of

Frg. 18 Col. ii

2. and kings of[
3. and kin[gs of

Frg. 19

1. y]ears [

3.] for thir[ty (*or*: three/thirteen) years
4.]they will speak [

Frg. 21

1. shall] rule for years [
2.] Balakros

Frg. 20

1.] son of [the] king[
2.]twenty [yea]rs[
3.]which [

Frg. 23

2.]he fled [
3.]faithlessness (*or:* entrance)[

Frg. 22

1. so]n and his name [
2.] to them two[
3.]spoke/speak[

Frg. 24

1 בני רש]ע֯א א֯ט֯עו [
2 בתר]ד֯נה יתכנשון קריאי֯]ן
3]ע֯ממיא ולהוה מן יום [
4]ש֯ין ומלכי עממיא]
5]ע֯בדין עד יומא] דנה

Frg. 25

1]◦◦◦[ ]◦◦[
2]ל֯הו עד יש]
3]ותתמלא א]רעא
4]כ֯ו֯ל שלדיה֯ו֯ן]
5]◦ל]]ל֯]

Frg. 26

1]◦ו֯ף מניניה֯ו֯]ן
2]די לא מנין]
3 יש]ר֯אל]

Frg. 27

1 מן בני]
2 יהב ר֯◦]
3]ל כ֯◦]

Frg. 28

1]◦אל וק◦]
2 פינח]ס אביש]וע
3]ש֯] ◦ ◦י ◦]

Frg. 29

1]ב ע֯]

Frg. 30

1]◦◦◦א]
2]ם מן

Frg. 31

1]ן ◦]
2 [צ֯למי֯ן]

Frg. 32

1 א]להי֯ן]
2]◦]

Frg. 33

1 ש]בק֯ו א֯ו֯]חת
2]◦◦]

Frg. 34

top margin

1]מן משכנ֯א]
2]◦ק◦◦]

Frg. 35

]כ֯◦]
1]◦ן אגרה [
2 ד]י֯ ארעא [

Frg. 36

1]◦]
2]נ֯אור]
3]◦ל]

Frg. 37

1]ד מ֯]
2]◦ למ֯]
3]◦]

Frg. 38

1 [א֯ו֯ר֯ ◦◦]
2]◦שי֯ ה֯ת֯]

Frg. 24

1. the sons of ev]il have led astray [
2. after]this the elect shall be assembled[
3.]the peoples, and there will be from [that] day [
4.] and the kings of the peoples[
5.]are doing until [this] day[

Frg. 26

1.] the[ir] numbers[
2.] without number [
3. Is]rael[

Frg. 25

2.] until [
3.]and [the] la[nd] will be filled[
4.]all their decayed carcasses [

Frg. 28

1.]*el* and Qo[hath
2. Phineha]s, Abish[ua

Frg. 27

1. from the sons of[
2. he gave [

Frg. 30

2.] from

Frg. 32

1. G]od (*or*: to them[)

Frg. 31

2.] images[

Frg. 34

1.]from the tabernacle[

Frg. 33

1.]they [l]eft the wa[y of

Frg. 36

2.]shine[

Frg. 35

1.] his reward [
2. o]f the land [

Frg. 38

1.] light [

Frg. 39

1]◦[
2]א סנא◦[

Frg. 40

1]◦[
2] ת[
3]קימא [
4]ליכ◦[

4Q**244** (4QpsDan[b] ar) ed. J. Collins and P. Flint, *DJD* XXII

Frgs. 1–3

top margin

1 קודם רבב{ר}ני מלכא ואשׁריא ע◦[ ]ד̇י מל[כא
2 [ ]ר̊[ ]אקימ̊[ ]◦י̊◦[
3 [ ]ו̊כמה ו◦◦[
4 [ ]מ̊לכא מס◦[
5 [ ]◦[

Frg. 4

1]◦ קדים א◦[
(above line 2:)]אמר
2]ד̇ניאל[
3]◦◦[

Frg. 5 Col. i

3]סגד
4]◦א̊

Frg. 5 Col. ii

1 ו̊ע̊ר̇[
2 ב◦[
3 פלג נט̊◦[
4 ואת̊וא ע̊ד̇[
5 [ ]א̊לוה[ין
6 [ ]◦ שנ◦[

Frg. 6

1]די י[

Frg. 7

1]ו̊לשמי[

bottom margin

Frg. 8

1]◦◦◦[ ]ן[
2]מן בתר מבולא [
3]נ̊וח מן לובר [טורא
4]◦ ק̊ר̇יה[

Frg. 9

1]◦◦[ ]◦[
2]א̊ מגדלא רו̊[מה
3] *vacat* [

Frg. 10

1] קמוא מ̇ן[
2] *vacat* [

Frg. 11

1 די ר[
2 דאני̊[ן

Frg. 40

3.]treaty/covenant [

Frg. 39

2.] hate [

4Q**244** (4QpsDan[b] ar) trans. J. Collins and P. Flint

Frgs. 1–3

1. Before the nobles of the king and the Assyrians [ ] of [the] ki[ng
2.]He appointed[
3.]and how [
4.]O (*or*: the) king [

Frg. 5 Col. i

3.]worship

Frg. 4

1.] east [
2.]Daniel said[

Frg. 6

1.]which/of [

Frg. 5 Col. ii

3. he divided [
4. and they came to[
5. [ ]Go[d

Frg. 8

2.]from after the Flood [
3.]Noah from [Mount] Lubar [
4.] a city [

Frg. 10

1.] they arose from[
2.] *vacat* [

Frg. 9

2.] the tower, [whose] heig[ht
3.] *vacat* [

Frg. 11

1. who [
2. judgi[ng

Frg. 12
Parallel: 4Q**243** 13 1–4

top margin

1]בׄחׄרו בני ישראל אנפיהׄון מׄן [
2 ל]שׄידי טעותא ורגז עליהון אלוהיןׄ וא[מר
3 ב]כל ולאחרבׄא ארעׄ˹ה˺ון מנהון מןׄ די [
4]◦◦אׄשׄתׄאׄ[ ]◦ בני גלותא ◦[

Frg. 13

top margin

1] ובדר אנון[

Frg. 14

1]יחין

4Q**245** (4QpsDan[c] ar) ed. J. Collins and P. Flint, *DJD* XXII

Frg. 1

top margin?

	Col. i	Col. ii
1	]יא	
2	]◦◦ ומה די	
3	] דניאל	
4	]כׄתב די יהיב	
5	לו]יׄ קהת	
6	]בׄוקי עוזיׄ	
7	צדו]קׄ אבׄיׄתר	
8	חׄ[ל]קיה	
9	]◦[ ] וׄחוניׄה	דיׄ]
10	יונ]תׄן שמעון	ד]
11	]וׄדויׄד שלומוׄה	
12	]אחזיׄ[ה יוא]שׄ	
13	]◦[ ]	

Frg. 2

1]◦◦[
2]לׄמסף רשׄעׄא
3]אׄלן בעור וׄטעו
4 א]לׄןׄ אדׄין יקומון
5 ק]דׄיש[ת]א ויתוׄבון
6]◦ רשעא

Frg. 12

1.]The Israelites chose their presence rather than [the presence of God,
2. and they were sacrificing their children to] the demons of error, and God became angry at them and sa[id
3. into the hand of Nebuchadnezzar king of Babyl]on, and to make their land desolate of them, because [
4.]   the exiles   [

Frg. 13

1.] and he scattered them[

4Q**245** (4QpsDan^{c} ar) trans. J. Collins and P. Flint

Frg. 1

	Col. i	Col. ii
2.	] and what	
3.	] Daniel	
4.	]a book/writing that was given	
5.	Lev]i, Qohath	
6.	]Bukki, Uzzi	
7.	Zado]k, Abiathar	
8.	Hi[l]kiah	
9.	] [ ] and Onias	who [
10.	Jona]than, Simon	
11.	]and David, Solomon	
12.	]Ahazia[h, Joa]sh	

Frg. 2

2.]to exterminate wickedness
3.]these in blindness, and they have gone astray
4. th]ese then will arise
5.]the [h]oly [   ], and they will return
6.] wickedness

Frg. 3

1]◦◦[

2]◦ תלתין וחׄמׄשׄ[ה

Frg. 4

1]◦[

2]דין

4Q**529** (4QWords of Michael ar) ed. É. Puech, *DJD* XXXI

Frg. 1

top margin

1 מלי כתבא די אמר מיכאל למׄלאכיא עׄ[ל חזוא די]

2 אׄמר די גדודי נורא תמה השכח[ת תמה]

3 [חזית]תשעה טורין תרין למדנ[חא ותרין למערבא ותרין לצפונא ותרין]

4 [לדר]ומא תמה חזית לגבריאל מלאכאׄ[די]

5 כׄחׄזוא וׄהחזיתה חזוה ואמר לי ד[י]

6 בספרי די רבי מרא עלמא כתיב הׄאׄ[בין]

7 בני חם לבני שם והא רבי מרא עלמא[ ]

8 כדי כשבין דמעא מן אנׄדרא {מׄןׄ ◦[}

9 והא מתבניה קריה לשמה די רבי מׄ[רא עלמא בדי]

10 יתעבד כׄל די באיש קודם רבי מר[א עלמא]

11 וידכר רבי מרא עלמא לבריתה ◦[ויעבד]

12 רׄבי מרא עלמא לה רחמיןׄ ולה אׄ[די]

13 במדינתא רחיקתא להוא גבר לׄ[מה]

14 הוא ולהוא אמר לה הא דן הוׄ[א]

15 לי כספא ודהבא דׄ[̇]◦ׄ ◦ ׄאר[

16 ב]צׄדיקאׄ[

Frg. 2

1]הׄאׄ דׄנח שמשאׄ[

2]וׄאמר ל◦[

4. REVELATORY TEXTS TOO FRAGMENTARY FOR FURTHER CLASSIFICATION

4Q**410** (4QVision and Interpretation) ed. A. Steudel, *DJD* XXXVI

Frg. 1

1 [ ]עה אשׁרׄ[ ]

2 [ ]א תעבור לכול ע◦[ ]

Frg. 3

2.] thirty-five[

4Q**529** (4QWords of Michael ar) trans. E. Cook

Frg. 1

1. The words of the book that Michael said to the angels re[garding the vision of]
2. he said, I found there fiery troops [there]
3. [I saw] nine mountains, two to the east, [two to the west, two to the north and two to
4. [the] south. There I saw the angel Gabriel [ ]
5. I showed him a vision and he said to me th[at]
6. in my book of the Great One, Eternal Lord it is written [ ]
7. the children of Ham and the children of Shem, and behold, the Great One, Eternal Lord [ ]
8. when sap flows (?) from the ? [ ]
9. and, behold, a city is to be built to the name of the Great One, [Eternal Lord]
10. evil shall be done before the Great One, [Eternal] Lord [ ]
11. and the Great One, Eternal Lord, will call His creation to mind [ ]
12. and the Great One, Eternal Lord will [show] mercy to him and to him [who]
13. in the distant lands there will be a man
14. is he, and he will say to him, This one is [ ]
15. to me silver and gold [ ]
16. concerning] the righteous one[

Frg. 2

1.]behold the sun has shined[
2.]and he said to [

4. Revelatory Texts Too Fragmentary for Further Classification

4Q**410** (4QVision and Interpretation) trans. A. Steudel

Frg. 1

1. [ ] which[ ]
2. [ ] cross over all [ ]

3]]ת אשר ר֯מות לוא י֯◦[ ]◦[[
4]]◦ ל֯כה וארר֯ה על א֯ר[ר]ה֯ תדבק [ב]כה
5]]ע֯לי֯כ֯ה֯ ואין לכה שמה שלו֯ם [ ]◦◦
6]] מה מ֯ׄאמת טוב ומה מ֯ׄה ◦◦[ ]רע
7] כ]ו֯ל ימי עד *vac* ועתה אני את א[דני]ב֯רוח
8]ראיתי כאשר יבוא עליה]מה ולוא יכזב המ[שא ו]לוא [הח]ר֯י֯ש
9]החזון *vacat* על]ד֯ המשא ועל בית י֯[ה]חזון כ֯[י ר]איתי
10]]ר֯ים ו֯ה[וא]ה֯פר ת[ורת אל]◦וה
11] [ ]]א֯ת֯ [[

Frg. 2

1]◦ לכול ע֯בודה֯[
2]◦ לאמ◦[
3]עב[ ] להמה֯[
4]ל[

Frg. 3

1]ה֯◦[
2]תה[
3]לא֯[

Frg. 4

top margin?

1] הודו [

4Q**458** (4QNarrative A) ed. E. Larson, *DJD* XXXVI

Frg. 1

top margin

1]ב לידיד מׄ[
2]הׄ הידיד הׄ[
3]ד֯ באהל [
4]ל֯וא ידעו את֯[
5]שרופות אש [
6]ו֯ע֯מדו עמו מ◦[
7 א]מ֯ר לרישון לאמורׄ[
8]ל֯חיים ושלך המלאך הריש֯[ו]ןׄ
9 חר]ב מחרבת ויך את עצ הרשע
10]ל[ ]ה֯צרים לבזה
11]◦◦ר֯ כי[

3. [ ] which are lifted (?), not [ ] [ ]
4. [ ] for you, and curse upon curse will cleave [to] you
5. [ ]upon you, and you will not have there peace [ ]
6. [ ] what is good in truth and what is bad in [ ]
7. [a]ll days of eternity. *vacat* And now I with (the help of) the L[ord] in spirit
8. [saw what will come upon t]hem, and it will not lie, the or[acle, and it will] not [be s]ilent
9. [the vision. *vacat* Concerning] is the oracle and concerning the house of [is the vision, f[or] I [s]aw
10. [ ] and h[e] defied the T[orah of God]

Frg. 2

1.] for every deed[

3.] to them[

Frg. 4

1.] Give thanks [

4Q**458** (4QNarrative A) trans. E. Larson

Frg. 1

1.] to the beloved [
2.] the beloved [
3.] in the tent [
4.]they did not know the[
5.]burned with fire [
6.]and they stood with him [
7.]he [sp]oke to the first saying[
8.]for life and the first angel cast down
9. a] destroying swor[d], and he struck the tree of evil
10.] [ ]the oppressors for spoil (*or*: to plunder it)
11.] for[

Frg. 2

Col. i

1]◦◦לׄםׄ
2 היר]ח והכוכבים
3]הׄשנית
4]וׄברח בקרׄ[י]הׄ
5]ות הטמאהׄ
6]אׄ הזנות

Col. ii

2 את מ◦[
3 ויאבדהו ואת חׄיׄלׄוׄ[
4 ותבלע את כל הערלים ותק◦◦[
5 ויצדקו והלך על הרׄוׄםׄ הׄ[
6 משיח בשמן מלכות ה[

Frg. 3

1]לׄים שמעׄ[י]םׄ
2]רׄא
3]וׄרׄ

Frg. 4

1]הׄמׄהׄ[
2]בׄנפח בם[
3 שנ]ים עשר וי[
4]לׄ[

Frg. 5

1]ת[

Frg. 6

1]ת את[

Frg. 7

1]מׄים אׄתׄ [
2] וׄהׄ◦◦[

Frg. 8

1]◦ה◦[
2] זאבׄ[
3]לׄ[

Frg. 9

1] על הימׄ[
2] ממזרח וׄ◦[

Frg. 10

1a]י◦[
1]ישראׄ[ל
2]לׄ[

Frg. 11

1]◦תוׄת
2] כאשר
3]לׄח מרעהו

Frg. 12

1]ח◦◦◦[
2]נׄ◦◦◦ ל◦[
3] יׄהׄודה נׄ[ ]◦[
4] געל ראובן[
5]יהוסף[

Frg. 13

1]נׄרדם [
2]נׄרדם ◦[
3]הׄנבו[
4]לׄ[

Frg. 14

1]ת המ[

Frg. 2

Col. i		Col. ii
1.	] them	
2.	the moo]n and the stars	the [
3.	]the second	and he will destroy him and his army[
4.	]and he will flee, in the to[w]n	and it will devour all the uncircumcised and it will [
5.	] of uncleanness	and they will be justified and he ascended (will ascend) the height [
6.	] fornication	anointed with the oil of kingship [

Frg. 4

2.]by blowing into them[
3. tw]elve and [

Frg. 3

1.] ones hear[i]ng

Frg. 8

2.] wolf[

Frg. 7

1.] the [
2.] and [

Frg. 10

1.] Israe[l

Frg. 9

1.] on the [
2.] from the east and [

Frg. 12

2.] to [
3.] Judah [ ] [
4.] Reuben abhorred[
5.]Joseph[

Frg. 11

2.] as
3.] from his neighbour

Frg. 13

1.]he fell asleep [
2.]he fell asleep [

Frg. 15

]בכורי[
]הנבואה א[
]תא ◦השו◦[

Frg. 16

]יתך ל֯כ֯[
]◦◦[

Frg. 17

]משך֯ [
]◦ו֯א[

Frg. 18

]ד֯ מן [

Frg. 19

]רך [
]◦[

4Q**489** (4QpapApocalypse ar) ed. M. Baillet, *DJD* VII

Frg. 1

[וחזו֯תה ז֯◦]
[ו֯חזי֯תה מ֯]

Frg. 2

י֯חא [

Frg. 3

]ע֯ם֯[
]שמ[

Frg. 4

]ל֯כ◦[
[ו֯[

Frg. 5

]◦◦זי֯[
]◦ [

Frg. 6

[ו֯יא◦]
bottom margin?

Frg. 7

]◦ מא֯[

Frg. 8

]◦יאו֯[

4Q**556** (4QVision[a] ar) ed. E. Cook

Frg. 1

י]ע֯ר֯קון[
]לטור סיני [
]משרית֯[א י]שוא אנפוהי[
]◦ ויקד בנו[הי] נורא באישה [
]וקדמוה ויציד֯[ ]יפו ויחדנה *vacat* [
]מ֯דינתא חרתא די שבה כל די הוא ב[
]◦ על דנה אמר נביאא די יח◦[
]א֯ מן קדם זונא ארו להוא[

Frg. 15

1.]my firstborn
2.]the prophecy [

Frg. 16

1.] to [

Frg. 17

1.]he drew [

Frg. 18

1.] from [

4Q489 (4QpapApocalypse ar) trans. E. Cook

Frg. 1

1.] and his appearance [
2.] and I saw [

Frg. 2

1. he shall live [

4Q556 (4QVision[a] ar) trans. E. Cook

Frg. 1

1.]they will flee[
2.]to Mount Sinai [
3.]the camp, he will set his face[
4.] and he burned/will burn [his] sons [ ] the bad fire [
5.]and before him, and he will catch [ ] and he will seize him. *vacat* [
6.]the free land that he took captive. All that he [
7.] because of this the prophet said that [
8.] from before the food (?), for it/he will be[

9]∘∘ מן יפוא עד טור[
10]מלא[

Frg. 2

1] די ∘[
2]∘ מלל[
3]∘∘ מע∘[
4]∘תר על ע∘[

Frg. 3

1]∘ ח∘[
2]והמין בא[להא
3]עמ֯מין די ספר [
4]יא ומואביא ע֯מלק[יא
5]∘∘ נהובד אנון [
6]∘∘∘∘ צ֯דיקיא [
7]ממר הא אלין [
8]ה הח֯דא היא חפ[
9]אדין ירדף חד א֯[לף
10]לא ישבקון[

Frg. 4

1]צ֯ל ∘[
2]∘שתא∘[
3]∘ דא[
4]ארו מן[
5]א [
6]הא[

Frg. 5

1]ורד[
2] אדין [
3]∘ור יל[

Frg. 6

1]צ∘[
2]∘נא [ ]∘י[ ]דן∘[
3]∘∘∘∘ כמא [
4]ולא ידון [
5] ואבד מן [
6]∘[ ]ן ∘ס∘∘∘∘לון[

9.] from Jaffa to Mount[
10.]full[

Frg. 2

1.] which [
2.] spoke[

4.] upon [

Frg. 3

2.]and he believed in G[od
3.]peoples which the book of [
4.]the [Edomites?] and the Moabites, the Amalek[ites
5.] we shall destroy them [
6.] the righteous [
7.]saying, Behold these [
8.] is this one [
9.]then one shall pursue a th[ousand
10.]they will not leave[

Frg. 4

3.] this (?)[
4.] for from[

6.]behold[

Frg. 5

2.] then [

Frg. 6

2.] this [
3.] as [
4.]and he will not judge [
5.] and perished from [

Frg. 7

1 ח[

2 א◦[

Frg. 8

1]ן֯ למך[

Frg. 9

1]מ ◦[

2]ס֯ יח◦[

3]מ ◦[

Frg. 10

1]א֯ נ[

Frg. 11

1]רא אנ֯ה ה◦[

2]ן מן מצרים מ[

3]◦ מ◦[

Frg. 12

1]◦◦ מצ[רים

2]◦◦ ◦[

3]ד֯ל֯[

4] ו֯ד[

Frg. 13

1] א[

2]א ד[

Frg. 14

1 י]שמעון עממיא

2] די הוא֯ פתכר וישרון

3] מלך֯ מצרים

4] מרא אנון

5] *vacat*

6]ית בתגמא ל֯א

7]ין די משתארין

8 י]אכלון בשר חזירא

9]מלכותה ואף

10] מן קודם רשעיא

11] לאר[ע]צ֯ד֯ותא

12] סיני ומלכא דך

13]◦◦ה◦

4Q557 (4QVision^{c} ar) ed. E. Cook

1]◦◦[

2] גבריאל מל[אכא

3]ה ושאר כול [

4]למכלא מלי פמנא מ[ן

5] אטמ֯תון כלא ל◦[

6]◦◦ינא לב֯ק◦[

Frg. 8

1.] Lamech (?)[

Frg. 12

1.] Egypt[

Frg. 11

2.] from Egypt [

Frg. 14

1.]the peoples will hear
2.] which is an idol, and they will dwell
3.] the king of Egypt
4.] lord, they
5.] *vacat*
6.] by decree not
7.] which are left
8.]they shall eat the flesh of swine
9.]his kingdom and also
10.] from before the wicked
11.] to the lan[d] of desolation
12.] Sinai and that king

4Q**557** (4QVision^{c} ar) trans. E. Cook

2.] Gabriel [the] an[gel [
3.] and the rest of all [
4.]to restrain the words of our mouth fr[om
5.] you have defiled all [

7 [ר֯חמין ^מן קדם ∘]
8 [∘ת עקתא ∘]
9 [ם לטב]

4Q**558** (4QpapVision^b ar) ed. E. Cook

Frg. 1

1 [∘לי וה∘∘∘]
2 [ת מלאכיא א]
3 [∘∘]

Frg. 2

1 [מלאכא ∘]

Frg. 3

1 א]נתה ∘[
2 [שלט]
3 [י֯ ואנ֯]

Frg. 4

1 [ו֯אמׄר֯ו֯ לי ∘]
2 [ומני]
3 [∘מׄי֯א די כ]
4 [ל∘]

Frg. 5

1 ב]ריכין דח֯[
2 [ז֯ל [ ]ל]

Frg. 6

1 [∘לה הי דא מׄן]
2 [יקר]
3 [∘ א∘]

Frg. 7

1 [∘א די ח∘]

Frg. 9

1 [∘ ארזא]
2 [נ֯י מלא]

Frg. 10

1 [∘ה ארעא]

Frg. 11

1 [באיש]

Frg. 12

1 [לרבי֯]

Frg. 13

1 [∘]
2 [כתב אח֯]
3 [י֯ן מש]

Frg. 14

1 [∘ין וחמׄש֯]

Frg. 15

1 [ה
2 [ו֯ב∘]

Frg. 16

1 [מיא֯]

Frg. 17

1 [טה]
2 [∘ *vacat*

7.]mercy ^{from} before [
8.] distress [
9.] for good [

4Q**558** (4QpapVision^{b} ar) trans. E. Cook

Frg. 1

1.] to me (?) and [
2.] the angels [

Frg. 2

1.] the angel [

Frg. 3

1.]you [
2.]rule(s) [

Frg. 4

1.]and they said to me [
2.] and he appointed [
3.] the (?) which [

Frg. 5

1. b]lessed [

Frg. 6

1.] which one from[
2.] glory [

Frg. 7

1.] which [

Frg. 9

1.] the cedar [
2.] (is) full [

Frg. 10

1.] the land [

Frg. 11

1.]bad[

Frg. 12

1.] to [

Frg. 13

2.](he) wrote [

Frg. 14

1.] and five[

Frg. 16

1.] water (?)[

Frg. 18

1]אא [

Frg. 19

1]◦ *vacat*

2]◦דא [

Frg. 20

1]◦מס◦[

2 שרשין אבד [

3 מלכותה חס]ינה

Frg. 22

1 י]הׄודה ◦◦[

2 א]בד לנשר [

3 שלי]טין במלכותׄ[

4]◦◦ וׄיׄ◦[

Frg. 23

1]◦[

2]לעלם[

Frg. 24

1]◦מ◦[

2]לני לל[

Frg. 25

1]בגו עממין הא מלוׄ[

2]◦וׄלא מערב עמ]הן

3]וׄמׄ◦[ ]ל[

Frg. 26

1] חׄכים[

2]◦ר ◦[

Frg. 27

1] אנה [

2] מנ[

Frg. 28

1] בעדן קץ זנ◦יין עם שרשׄ[

2]ל◦◦◦◦ל◦◦[

Frg. 29

1]דבשאׄ[

Frg. 30

1]◦ יכפרוׄ]ן

2]ל[

Frg. 31 Col. i

1]שני

2]◦שר

3]◦נין

Frg. 31 Col. ii

1 ש◦[

2 כ[

Frg. 32 Col. i

1]◦ *vacat*

2]ומיׄן

Frg. 32 Col. ii

1 כ[

Frg. 22

1. J]udah [
2. pe]rished (?) for the eagle [
3. ru]ling the kingdom of[

Frg. 20

2. roots he perished/destroyed [
3. his kingdom (is) str[ong

Frg. 24

2.] me/my to ? [

Frg. 23

2.]forever[

Frg. 26

1.] wise[

Frg. 25

1.]in the midst of peoples, behold [
2.] and not mingled with[them

Frg. 27

1.] I [

Frg. 28

1.] in the time of the end they with the root[

Frg. 30

1.] they will atone[

Frg. 29

1.]honey[

Frg. 33

] ◦מ֯ה ה֯◦◦ [

] עדן *vacat*]

[*vacat*]

] יתותר במלכות עוזיה]

]ח֯רה בחורב ואמר]

[◦◦◦ ◦] [א֯ ב◦]

Frg. 34

]◦ סיאפא]

]זרע֯] [◦◦◦]

]ל֯ולבין ◦◦]

Frg. 35

] עדן]

Frg. 36

]ת֯◦ף֯ ומן ◦◦]

]◦ניא די מניו מ]

Frg. 37 Col. i

]י

]בוס

]

]ת֯ר֯י ◦

]

]◦[ ]לא

]◦ חוי֯א

]◦ מן

]ש֯לם

Frg. 37 Col. ii

ומטלין]

רשעא ◦◦]

שיחוהי מתקצצי֯ן֯]

ומלאו כן לארעא֯]

]ל]

]◦◦]

מרי]

Frg. 38

] מצ֯ו֯]ין

Frg. 33

2.] time. *vacat* [
3.] *vacat* [
4.] will be left in the kingdom of Uzziah[
5.] in Horeb and he said [

Frg. 34

1.] the end [
2.]seed[
3.]palm branches [

Frg. 35

1.] time [

Frg. 36

1.] and from/who [
2.] the [ ] who appointed/were appointed [

Frg. 37 Col. i

4.]two

6.]not
7.] the serpent (?)
8.] from
9.]peace/well

Frg. 37 Col. ii

1. and shelters [
2. wickedness [
3. his/its branches are cut off [
4. and they filled thus the land[

Frg. 38

1.] Egyp[t

Frg. 39

1]דא[
2]סׄא בגוא כסלא [
3] לׄמחלפ◦[

Frg. 40

1]בׄ◦ר◦ותא יכ[
2]◦◦◦ש◦[

Frg. 41

1]◦◦◦[
2]*vacat* נפלו עמׄיׄ[
3]נה[

Frg. 42

1] ובמשרי כ[
2]רען [

Frg. 43

1]◦[
2 ב]דיל כדן [

Frg. 44

1]א [
2 של]יטין [
3]◦כוהי [

Frg. 45

1] אבׄתׄ [
2]ל[

Frg. 46

1] ומונק[
2]ן [

Frg. 47

1]שמהת ◦[
2]◦◦◦ל[

Frg. 48

1]אׄנון עמא [

Frg. 49

1]ל עׄל [

Frg. 50

1]חׄזה ואמ[ר

Frg. 51

1 י]הב כ◦ה[
2]ל[

Frg. 52

1]שׄ[
2]כו[

Frg. 53

1]ע הואׄ[
2] שלטן [

Frg. 54 Col. ii

1 [ ] באישׄין
2 [ ]הן די מ[
3 תמיניא לבחיר והא א◦[
4 לכן אשלח לאליה קשׁ[יטא
5 תוׄ[ס]ף {◦} ברקא וזי[קיא
6 [ ]◦◦[ ]אׄ ואמ[
7 [ ]עוד אלׄ[
8 [ ]ללאׄ [

Frg. 39

2.] within the loin (?) [
3.] to change [

Frg. 42

1.] and in the camp of [

Frg. 41

2.] *vacat* They fell with me/my people[

Frg. 44

2. ru]lers [

Frg. 43

2. be]cause of this [

Frg. 46

1.]and suckling (?)[

Frg. 48

1.]they/them, the people [

Frg. 47

1.]the names of [

Frg. 50

1.]he saw and he sai[d

Frg. 49

1.]l upon/he entered [

Frg. 51

1. he] gave [

Frg. 53

1.]` they were[
2.] dominion [

Frg. 54 Col. ii

1. [ ] bad
2. [ ] which [
3. the eighth to the chosen and behold [
4. to you I will send Elijah [the] righ[teous
5. you/she/it will add lightning and me[teors
6. [ ] and [
7. [ ]again [

Frg. 55

1] ודי [

Frg. 56

1 מ]ערתא ◦[
2] ימין תל[

Frg. 57

1]שׁ֯ן֯[
2]סמו[

Frg. 58

1]מ֯◦ה֯ וארך עלי[
2 א]ח֯ד֯ במאנה֯[
3 ל]מלקטה [
4]רב ידוהי ל◦[
5]◦א מתא֯בד [

Frg. 59

1] הו֯ח[
2]די הוא ◦[
3]◦ למ◦[
4]ל֯ תזף[
5] תקף [

Frg. 60

1]ין וקו[
2]א להן ◦מ[

Frg. 61

1]◦◦[
2 ש]ליטא י[

Frg. 62

1]◦◦◦◦◦[
2]◦ם למפ֯נא וד◦[

Frg. 63

1]◦ שסהתהן ◦[
2]◦ט֯ן ובחדשא ◦[

Frg. 64

1] {◦} יבש[
2]ל חי֯בי֯הון פ[
3]יד די[
4]לל[

Frg. 65

1]◦◦◦ ◦◦[
2] אדם די י◦[ ] א◦◦[
3 לש]לחותה לארע מצ֯ר֯י֯ן֯ [
4]ל[

Frg. 66

1]◦◦[
2]שנו מן [ע]שׂב[א
3] בחדוה *vacat*[
4]◦◦◦◦[

Frg. 55

1.] and which [

Frg. 56

1. the c]ave [
2.] right [

Frg. 58

1.] and the length of [the] upper room (?) [
2. he se]ized his vessel[
3. to] gather it [
4.] his hands to [
5.] destroyed [

Frg. 60

2. [ ] except [

Frg. 59

2.]which he .[

4.] lend[
5.] strong [

Frg. 62

2.] to turn and [

Frg. 61

2. r]uler [

Frg. 64

1.] dry[
2.] their sinners [
3.] which[

Frg. 63

1.] their names [
2.] and in the month [

Frg. 66

2.]changed (?) from the grass[
3.] in joy. *vacat* [

Frg. 65

2.] Adam who [
3. to]send him to the land of Egypt [

Frg. 67

1] מת∘∘ [
2]לה לה למנטר[
3] ושבק לה למ֯[
4]∘ ל∘ט֯[

Frg. 68

1] חזית כען[
2]∘∘∘[

Frg. 69

1]∘ער֯א ערעין ודא[
2]ד תחוה לנא מה [די

Frg. 70

1] למל[
2] ערעין [
3 ∙]∙∙∙ די [
4]ך שמש֯[
5]אל אשתנ֯[י
6]אמכון ויאמ֯[ר

Frg. 68

1.] I/you saw now [

Frg. 67

2.] to him/her to guard[
3.] and he left/forgave her/him [

Frg. 70

2.] meeting [
3.]the **LORD** who [
4.] sun/ministered[
5.] was changed[
6.]your mother (?) and he will sa[y

Frg. 69

1.] meeting and this (?)[
2.] you/she will tell to us what [

C. Eschatological Texts

4Q**238** (4QWords of Judgement) ed. P. Flint, *DJD* XXVIII

top margin

1 [מתלש נתכת מא◦[
2 ר[מיה להגלות ועו֯]לה
3]ח֯לבים חלה הם[
4 א[ר֯ד ואראה [
5]◦עך ואיׄ[
6]ם֯ ב֯[

4Q**249p** (4Qpap cryptA Prophecy?) ed. S. J. Pfann, *DJD* XXXVI

1]◦[
2]◦כ◦[
3]◦[ ]◦[ ]ב֯ב֯[
4]א֯תׄ המ֯[
5] *vac* [
6 ל[ך֯ לך מיׄ[
7 כו[ל חברי֯]ך
8]ור שבע֯[
9 ב[ק֯ץ הקצׄ]ים
10 עד [הגמר[
11]◦◦◦[

4Q**457b** (4QEschatological Hymn) ed. E. Chazon, *DJD* XXIX

Col. I (Frg. 1)

1]◦ׄ?[
2 ה֯גויםׄ[
3 ומי יעמ֯[
4 יולד בה ◦[
5 עדת אל גׄ[
6 ו֯יׄ◦◦ב ◦◦[
7 חרים בצעם [
8 ◦[ ]ר֯םׄ כלל ◦ל[
9 ◦[

C. Eschatological Texts

4Q238 (4QWords of Judgement) trans. P. Flint

1.] uprooting, a cu[rse?] is about to be poured out[
2. de]ceit to be uncovered, and false[hood
3.]fat portions, cake they[
4. I will] come down and I will see [

4Q249p (4Qpap cryptA Prophecy?) trans. S. J. Pfann

4.]the [
5.] *vacat* [
6. G]et yourself up and go from[
7. a]ll of [your] associates[
8.] seven[
9. at the] end of tim[es
10. until]the consummation[

4Q457b (4QEschatological Hymn) trans. E. Chazon

Col. I (Frg. 1)

2. the nations[
3. and who will [
4. he/it will be born in it [
5. congregation of God [

7. banning their ill-gotten gain [
8.] all/total [

Col. II (Frg. 2)

top margin

1 נלחם אל בהם וא֯◦[
2 שמח ד֯ויד להשיב [
3 יעשה עליון בשמים [
4 מלכיה לעשות ב֯יד֯י֯[
5 אלוהינו כול קדושים[
6 וכבודו עליהמה ירא]ה
7 *vacat* ויאומרו לעליו֯[ן
8 אש֯[ ] כול מעש֯י֯ה֯◦◦[

4Q**472** (4QEschatological Work B) ed. T. Elgvin, *DJD* XXXVI (corrected, 2004)

Frg. 1

1 [ ]ב֯יום ◦[
2 [י]שמחו ו֯[ירננו יהפוך(?)]
3 [חב]ליהם לברכה [ ] ושלום ג֯◦[
4 את֯ כול ר֯עו מש֯[מ]ר֯י פני מלך [ויביאו(?)]
5 זהב ופז מנבלי֯[ ]כ֯ול כתם֯ [אופירים]
6 ולוא ש֯חרו פניו[

bottom margin

Frg. 2 (formerly frg. 3)

1 [ ]◦◦[ ]
2 [ ]◦[ ]◦ לכל֯[ ]כ֯ליום[הבאים]
3 [ב]ל֯ישנה דכי ליחד נזיר֯י[ ]
4 נדיבים לכבוד וד◦[ ]
5 לפנות [ ]ל֯[ ]◦ם ב֯[ ]
6 כ֯אופרים[ ]
7 לכליל ת֯[פארת]
8 למלואה֯[ ]
9 מ֯לך[ ]

4Q**475** (4QRenewed Earth) ed. T. Elgvin, *DJD* XXXVI (corrected, 2004)

1 [ציו]ן֯(?) י]ב֯חר ו֯בחי֯י֯ צד֯ק֯[
2 [חוקותיו(?)]ש֯כחום ולוא ידורשום וא֯רץ֯[
3 [והוא שלח(?) י]דים בתוכם והגיד להמה את כול֯ ה֯[משפטים(?)]
4 [כ]ו֯ל תבל ולוא יהיה עוד אשמות בארץ ולוא יה֯[יה עוד(?)]

Col. II (Frg. 2)

1. God fought against them and [
2. David rejoiced to bring back [
3. The Most High will do in heaven [
4. her kings, to do by the hands of[
5. our God. All holy ones[
6. and upon them His glory will appea[r
7. *vacat* And they shall say to the Most Hi[gh
8. [ ] all (their?) deeds [

4Q472 (4QEschatological Work B) trans. T. Elgvin

Frg. 1

1. [ ]in the day of [
2. [ ] they [will] rejoice and [be glad He will turn(?)]
3. their [labour pa]ins to blessing [ ] and peace [
4. all His friends, the gu[ar]ds in <the> King's presence [and they will bring (?)]
5. gold and pure gold from jars of[ ]all [Ophir]-gold [
6. and they did not eagerly seek His presence[

Frg. 2

2. [ ] to all[ ]every day [those who come]
3. pure [of] tongue into the *Yaḥad*, who are consecrated[
4. noble ones to glory, and [
5. to turn [
6. like Ophir-gold[
7. for a g[lorious] crown[
8. to its fullness[
9. King[

4Q475 (4QRenewed Earth) trans. T. Elgvin

1. [Zio]n (?) [did] He choose, and by a righteous life[
2. [His laws (?)]they forgot and did not seek them, and a land[
3. [He stretched out (?) (His) h]ands in their midst, and told them all the[precepts(?)
4. [a]ll the earth, and there will no longer be any guilt in the land, and there will not b[e any more (?)

5 [והיו(?) מש]חית וכול משטם והיתה כול תבל כעדן וכול יש]בי בה
6 [ו]שקטה הארץ לעולמים וידרשו(?)[ ]יושב]יה
7 [וישראל יהיה לו(?)]לבן אהוב וידרישו את כולה וצ]דקה(?)
8 [ ]◦ה כיא ה◦[
9 [ ]◦ל[

4Q**521** (4QMessianic Apocalypse) ed. É. Puech, *DJD* XXV

Frg. 1

	Col. i	Col. ii
1		]◦◦[
2	]ם	ו]שמעת[ם(?)
3	]ים	ופעלת[
4	]ים	ימה עברת[ם(?)
5		וליראה א[
6		רבו צדיקי[ם
7		וקימים[
8		ואהב[
9		ואת[

Frgs. 2 Col. i + 3

7]◦[ ]ו\ייטב לנו
8]משפט *vacat*
9]קויך לתשועה
10] *vacat*
11]ט יעלה

Frgs. 2 Col. ii + 4

top margin

1 [כי הש]מים והארץ ישמעו למשיחו
2 [וכל א]שר בם לוא יסוג ממצות קדושים
3 התאמצו מבקשי אדני בעבדתו *vacat*
4 הלוא בזאת תמצאו את אדני כל המיחלים בלבם
5 כי אדני חסידים יבקר וצדיקים בשם יקרא
6 ועל ענוים רוחו תרחף ואמונים יחליף בכחו
7 כי יכבד את חסידים על כסא מלכות עד
8 מתיר אסורים פוקח עורים זוקף כפ[ופים]
9 ול[ע]לם אדבק [במ]יחלים ובחסדו י[ ]
10 ופר[י מעש]ה טוב לאיש לוא יתאחר

5. [There will be (?) destruc]tion and great envy, and then all the earth will be like Eden, and all who li[ve there
6. [ ]the land will be quiet for ever, and those who live[there] will seek (?)[
7. [Israel will be unto Him (?)]a beloved son, and they will seek it all, and ri[ghteousness (?)
8. [ ] for [

4Q521 (4QMessianic Apocalypse) trans. M. Wise, M. Abegg, and E. Cook with N. Gordon

Frg. 1

Col. ii

2. [and] you have heard[
3. and the function of[
4. westward. You have transgressed[
5. and to fear [
6. and the righteou[s] multiplied[
7. and those standing[
8. and [ ]loved[
9. and [

Frgs. 2 Col. i + 3

7.]and it shall be well with us
8.]justice. *vacat*
9.]your [ ] for salvation
10] *vacat*
11.] shall go up

Frgs. 2 Col. ii + 4

1. [For the hea]vens and the earth shall listen to His Messiah
2. [and all w]hich is in them shall not turn away from the commandments of the holy ones.
3. Strengthen yourselves, O you who seek the Lord, in His service. *vacat*
4. Will you not find the Lord in this, all those who hope in their heart?
5. For the Lord seeks the pious and calls the righteous by name.
6. Over the humble His spirit hovers, and He renews the faithful in His strength.
7. For He will honour the pious upon the th[ro]ne of His eternal kingdom,
8. '*setting prisoners free, opening the eyes of the blind, raising up those who are bo[wed down*' (Ps 146:7-8).]
9. And for [ev]er (?) I (?) shall hold fast [to] the [ho]peful and pious [ ]
10. A man's rewa[rd for]good [wor]k[s] shall not be delayed

11 ונכבדות שלוא היו יעשה אדני כאשר ד[בר
12 כי ירפא חללים ומתים יחיה ענוים יבשר
13 ו[דלי]ם ישב[יע]נתושים ינהל ורעבים יעשר
14 ונב[ונים (?)]◦ וכלם כקד[ושים ?]
15 וא[ ]

Frg. 2 Col. iii

top margin

1 ואת חק חסד{יך}ך ואתר אותם ב[כי( )]
2 נכון באים אבות על בנים א[שרי(?)]
3 אשר ברכת ˙אדני ברצונו[ ]
4 גלה הארץ בכל מקו[ם]
5 כי כל ישראל בגיל[ ]
6 ואת שבט[ו ו]ירממו[כי(?)]
7 מצא[ו]

Frgs. 5 Col. i + 6

1 [ ]ם
2–3 [ ]
4 (?) יעשה אד]ני לו [א]שר ל<ו>א יעב<ו>ד עם אלה
5 [ו(י)יט(י)ב עם ר]עהו ועם שכנ[ו]
6 [ואז(?) יהיה]טוב לך ואמץ כוח
7 [ובעבור רוב]מזון אמונ[י]ם יגדלו

Frgs. 7 1–8 + 5 Col. ii 7–16

1 [ ]ראו [א]ת כל א[שר עשה
2 [אדני האר]ץ וכל אשר בה ימים[וכל]
3 [אשר בם] וכל מקוה מים ונחלים *vacat*
4 [כ]ל[כם]העושים את הטוב לפני אדנ[י]
5 [מברכים ולו]א כאלה מקלל[ים] ולמות יהי[ו כאשר]
6 [יקי]ם המחיה את מתי עמו *vacat*
7 ונ[ו]דה ונגידה לכם צדקות אדני אשר[ ]
8 בנ[י תמ]ותה ופתח[קברות-]
9 ופ[תח(?)]
10 ו[ ]
11 וגי מות ב[ ]
12 וגשר תה[ומ-(\ות)]
13 קפאו ארור[ים]
14 וקדמו שמים[ ]
15 וכ]ל מלאכים[
16]ל[

11. and the Lord shall do glorious things which have not been done, just as He s[aid.]
12. For He shall heal the critically wounded, He shall revive the dead, '*He shall send good news to the afflicted,*' (Isa 61:1)
13. He shall sati[sfy] the [poo]r, He shall lead the uprooted, and the hungry He shall enrich (?).
14. The wi[se (?)] and all of them like hol[y ones (?)]
15. and [

Frg. 2 Col. iii

1. and the law of Your lovingkindness. I shall set them free with[ ]
2. fathers are coming upon (or going for) their sons. B[lessed]
3. for whom the blessing of the Lord is his delight [ ]
4. the earth rejoices in all the pl[aces]
5. 'all Israel in rejoicing [ ]
6. and [his] staff [and] they will exalt[for]
7. [they] found [ ]

Frgs. 5 Col. i + 6

4. [the Lo]rd [shall do] to him [wh]ich he shall not do with these
5. [He shall do well with]his [fri]end and with [his] neighbour
6. [Then it shall be]beneficial for you and he shall increase strength
7. [Because of he multitude of] food, the faithf[u]l shall increase.

Frgs. 7 1–8 + 5 Col. ii 7–16

1. [ ] see all t[hat the Lord has made,]
2. [the eart]h and all that is on it, the seas [and all]
3. [that is in them] and every reservoir of water and the streams. *vacat*
4. [a]l[l of you] who do good before the Lor[d]
5. [shall bless and no]t as these who curse. They shall b[e] destined to die, [when]
6. the One who revives [rai]ses the dead of His people. *vacat*
7. Then we shall [giv]e thanks and relate to you the righ[teous acts] of the Lord that [ ]
8. thos[e destined to d]ie. And He shall open [graves]
9. and he shall o[pen (?)]
10. and [ ]
11. and the Valley of Death in[ ]
12. and the Bridge of the De[ep]
13. the accursed shall be little esteemed (?) [ ]
14. and the heavens shall meet [ ]
15. and a]ll the angels[

Frg. 8

]כ֯ותל ב[י]ן 1
[2–4
]הׄ יפיעו 5
]את אדם 6
ב]ר֯כׄות יעקוב 7
היכ]ל וכל כלי קדשו 8
כהנ]ה וכל משיחיה 9
]<ידב[רו]> 10a
]ל֯[התקד]ש ודבר אדני ו[10
{ידברו} 11a
בר]ך את אדני 11
] עיני 12

Frg. 9

]לוא תה[יה 1
]◦ים ובׄ[ע]בד אׄ[דני 2
]בׄה תעזוב ב[י]ד משיׄח֯[3
]הל[ ]ר֯ץׄ[4

Frg. 10

]◦ש֯[ר 1
]י֯שמרו ברי֯[ת 2
עו]ד֯ רשע ביניהם 3
]ה בתוכם 4
bottom margin?

Frg. 11

]◦[1
]*vacat*[2
]ים ינחלוה[3
]קׄה ממנו ◦[4
]כׄהׄנה ת[5

Frg. 12

ויתן כ◦[1
[ומ]לׄכ֯וׄתׄ[2

Frg. 13

]הם ◦◦[1
]◦◦[ ]◦[2

Frg. 8

1.]a wall be[twe]en

5.] they shall shine out
6.] Adam
7. bl]essings of Jacob
8. Temp]le and all His holy vessels
9.]its[priest] and all its anointed ones

10a. they] shall spea[k

10.] and [t]he[y] spo[ke] the word of the Lord, and [ ]

11a. {they shall speak}

11. Ble]ss the Lord
12.] the eyes of

Frg. 9

1.]you sh[all] not [
2.] s and by [the se]rvant of the L[ord
3.]you have left, by the [ha]nd of[ ]messiah[

Frg. 10

1.]whi[ch
2.]they shall keep [my] covena[nt
3. furthe]r wickedness among them
4.] in their midst.

Frg. 11

2.] *vacat* [
3.]s they shall inherit it[
4.] from us [
5.]priesthood [

Frg. 12

1. and he gave [
2. [and the ki]ngdom[

Frg. 14

]ם̊[
בין צדי]ק̊ לרש̊[ע
]ל̇[

Frg. 15

]ץ̊ מ◦[ ]ם̊[
]*vacat*[
י]שראל̇[
]את א[

Frg. 16

]◦◦ כ̊ל̇[
]צת א̇[
]ג̊[

Frg. 14

2. between the righteo]us and the wic[ked

Frg. 15

2.] *vacat* [
3. I]srael[

Frg. 16

1.] all[

D. Magic and Divination

1. Curses

4Q**280** (4QCurses) ed. B. Nitzan, *DJD* XXIX

Frg. 1

1] את [
2]ה֯ ולהדב֯יק [
3]ו֯י◦ה֯ ל֯[

Frg. 2
Parallel: 1QS II

1]ויבדילהו אל]ל֯רעה מתוך בני הא֯[ור בהסוגו מאחריו *vacat* והוסיפו[
2]ואמרו *vac* אר[ור אתה מלכי רשע בכול מח]שבות יצר אשמתכה יתנכה[
3 א֯ל לזעוה ביד נוקמי נקם לוא יחונכה אל]ב[ק֯וראכה֯]ישא פני אפו[
4 לכה לזעמה ולוא יהיה לכה שלו]ם[בפי כול אוחזי אבו֯]ת ארור אתה[
5 לאין שרית וזעום אתה לאין פליטה וארורים עוש֯]י מחשבות רשעתמה[
6]ומ[ק֯ימי מ֯ז֯מתכה בלבב֯מה לזום על ברית א֯ל֯] ול◦◦◦◦ על התורה ועל[
7]דבר[י֯ כול ח֯ו֯ז֯י֯ א֯מ֯]תו וכ[ו֯ל המואס֯ ל֯ב֯ו֯א֯]בברית אל ללכת בשרירות[

Frg. 3 (also published as 4Q**271** 1 [part 1])

1]◦◦◦[
ס
2]מ֯{ש֯}יגי הגב]ו[ל֯[

5Q**14** (5QCurses) ed. J. T. Milik, *DJD* III

1]ים ועל ימים גם ע֯ל ◦[
2]◦י֯ניך מעליך יפלו [
3]ת֯י֯כם תפלו בכול תפ֯ל֯[
4]ישמידוך מכ֯ול הח֯ול֯[
5]מ֯עט לו֯ ואין דיו֯ כי ◦[

D. Magic and Divination

1. Curses

4Q**280** (4QCurses) trans. B. Nitzan

Frg. 1

1.] the [
2.]*h* and to cleave [
3.]*wy.h l*[

Frg. 2

1. [And God will set him apart]for calamity from the midst of the sons of li[ght for he has turned away from following Him. *vacat* And they shall continue]
2. [saying: *vacat* Cur]sed be you, Melki-rešaᶜ, in all the sch[emes of your guilty inclination. May] God [give you up]
3. to terror at the hand of those who exact vengeance. May God not be merciful unto you [when] you call (on Him). [May He lift up His angry face]
4. upon you for a curse. And there will be no pea[ce] for you at the mouth of any intercesso[rs. Cursed be you]
5. with no remnant and damned be you with no escape. And cursed be those who execu[te their wicked schemes]
6. [and those who] confirm your purpose in their heart, by plotting evil against the covenant of God[and against the Law and]
7. [the word]s of all the seers of [His] tru[th. And who]ever refuses to enter [the covenant of God, walking in the stubbornness]

Frg. 3

2.]the ones removing the bou[nd]ary[

5Q**14** (5QCurses) trans. M. Wise, M. Abegg, and E. Cook

1.] and upon the seas also upon [
2.] your [ ] shall fall from you [
3.] your [ ] shall fall on every [
4.]they shall destroy you from among all the [
5.]a little for him, and he does not have enough because [

2. EXORCISMS

4Q**444** (4QIncantation) ed. E. Chazon, *DJD* XXIX

Frgs. 1–4 Col. i + 5 (Col. I)

top margin

1 ואני מיראי אל בדעת אמתו פתח פי ומרוח קודשו ◦[

2 אמת לכ[ו]ל[אל]ה ויהיו לרוחי ריב במבניתי חוק[י אל

3 [ב]תכמי בשר ורוח דעת ובינה אמת וצדק שם אל בל[בבי

4 [ ]וה ותתחזק בחוקי אל ולהלחם ברוחי רשעה ולוא ◦◦[

5 [ ]ל[ ]ת דיניה *vac* ארור

6 [ ]רון האמת והמשפט

7 [ ]ה עד תום

ממשלתה

8 [מ]מזרים ורוח הטמאה

9 [ ]◦◦קל והגנב[ים

10 [צ]דיקים ארו[

11 [ ]◦דת תועב[ה

Frg. 6 (Col. I 5–8)

1]◦[

2]ם המו[

3]◦תו ארורה ו◦[

4]◦יד רוחי אמת[

Frg. 4 Col. ii 1–3 (Col. II 6–8)

1 ד◦◦ה[

2 להט◦[

3 בלו◦[

4Q**510** (4QShir[a]) ed. M. Baillet, *DJD* VII

Frg. 1
Parallel: 4Q**511** 10 1–8

top margin

1 ([ ] תשבוחות בר[כות למ]לך הכבוד דברי הודות בתהלי

2 [ ] לאלוהי דעות תפארת ג[בור]ות אל אלים אדון לכול קדושים

וממש[לתו]

3 על כול גבורי כוח ומכוח גבור[ת]ו יבהלו ויתפזרו כול ויחפזו מהדר מע[ון]

2. Exorcisms

4Q444 (4QIncantation) trans. E. Chazon

Frgs. 1–4 Col. i + 5 (Col. I)

1. And as for me, because of my fearing God, he opened my mouth with his true knowledge; and from his holy spirit [
2. truth to a[l]l[the]se. They became spirits of controversy in my (bodily) structure; law[s of God
3. [in]blood vessels of flesh. And a spirit of knowledge and understanding, truth and righteousness, God put in [my] he[art
4. [ ] And strengthen yourself by the laws of God, and in order to fight against the spirits of wickedness, and not [
5.] its judgements. *vacat* Cursed be
6.] of the truth and of the judgement.
7.] until the completion of its dominion
8. ba]stards and the spirit of impurity
9.] and the thieve[s?
10. ri]ghteous ones [
11.] abominati[on

Frg. 6 (Col. I 5–8)

3.] cursed [
4.] the spirits of truth[

Frg. 4 Col. ii 1–3 (Col. II 6–8)

2. flame [
3. with[out

4Q510 (4QShir[a]) trans. M. Wise, M. Abegg, and E. Cook

Frg. 1

1. [ ] praises. Ble[ssings to the K]ing of Glory. Words of thanksgiving in psalms of
2. [ ] to the God of knowledge, splendour of s[treng]th, the God of gods, Lord of all the holy ones. [His] domini[on]
3. is over all the mighty strong ones, and by the power of His streng[th] all will be dismayed and scattered, running hurriedly from the majesty of the dwe[lling]

4 כבוד מלכותו *vacat* ואני משכיל משמיע הוד תפארתו לפחד ולבׄ[הל]

5 כול [1]רוחי מלאכי חבל ורוחות ממזרים שד אים) לילי(ת [2]אחים ו[ציים]

6 והפוגעים פתע פתאום ל)תעות רוח [3](בינה ולהשם לבבם ונׄ◦◦תם ב)קץ ממשל[ת]

7 רשעה [4](ותעודות תעניות בני או[ר] באשמ)ת קצי [5](עוונות ^נגוע[י]^ ולוא לכלת עול)ם

8 [כי א]ם לקץ [6](תעניות פשע] *vacat*] [7]רננו צדיקים) באלוהי פלא

9 ולישרים תהלי *vac* (וׄל] [8] י)]רוממו[ה]וׄ כ[ו]ל תמימיׄ דרך

bottom margin

Frg. 2

top margin

1]דׄם בגורל רשע *vac* וכול[

2 א]לוהי ישע וקדושי[

3]חׄ עולמים וכול רוחי [

4 א]שׁׄ עולמים בוערׄת בסוׄ[

5]◦◦[ ]ל◦◦ בגוׄ[

Frg. 3

top margin

1]ים ◦[

Frg. 4

top margin

1]◦ו בוׄ◦[

Frg. 5

top margin?

1]ו[

Frg. 6

1]אור[

Frg. 7

1]תׄוש מ◦[

2]תׄאומרו ל◦[

3]תׄשבכה[

4]◦רה א[

5]◦שׁׄ[

Frg. 8

1]וש ב[

2]וׄמר לׄ[

3]◦◦◦[

Frg. 9

1] הׄואהׄ[

2]ם ◦[

Frg. 10

1]עשׄ[

2]תת◦[

Frg. 11

1] חצׄ◦םׄ[

2]בלתׄ[

Frg. 12

1]מודה[

4. of His royal glory. *vacat* And I, the Instructor, proclaim His glorious splendour so as to frighten and to te[rrify]
5. all [1]the spirits of the destroying angels, spirits of the bastards, demons, Lilith, [2]howlers and [desert dwellers]
6. and those which fall upon men without warning to lead them astray from a spirit of [3]understanding and to make their heart and their [ ] desolate during the present dominion of
7. wickedness [4]and predetermined time of humiliations for the sons of lig[ht], by the guilt of the ages of [those] [5]smitten by iniquity—not for eternal destruction,
8. [bu]t for an era of [6]humiliation for transgression. [*vacat*] [7]Sing for joy, O righteous ones, for the God of Wonder.
9. My psalms are for the upright. *vacat* And [[8]let] all those who are blameless exalt Him!

Frg. 2

1.] with the lot of the wicked *vac* and every[
2. G]od of salvation and holy ones[
3.] eternal and every spirit of [
4.]eternal fire burning in [
5.] [ ] in [

Frg. 6

1.]light

Frg. 7

2.]you will say [

Frg. 9

1.] he[

Frg. 12

1.]give thanks

4Q**511** (4QShir[b]) ed. M. Baillet, *DJD* VII

Frg. 1

1 [מ]מׄשלותם
2 [ ]◦◦◦ וׄכׄוׄ[ל בא]רׄץ ובכול
3 רׄוחות ממשלתה תמׄיד יב[רכו]הו בקציהם
4 הימים וכול חיתם ישמיעוׄ[ ]יׄ תפארת
5 כולם יגילו לאלוהי צדק ברׄנׄ[ות]ישועות
6 כיא א[ין] משחית בגבוליהם ורוחי רשע
7 לו יתהלכו בם כיא הופיע כבוד אלוהי
8 דעות באמׄרׄיׄו וכול בני עולה לוא יתׄכלכלו

bottom margin

Frg. 2 Col. i

1 לׄמשכיל שירׄ[ ]יׄ[הללו את שם]
2 קודשו ורוממוהו כול יודעי [צדק]
3 וׄרוש ממשלוׄתׄ הׄשׄבית לאין [שמחת]
4 [ע]ולמים וחיי נצח לאיר אוׄר [ ]
5 [ג]וׄרלו רשית ביעקוב ונחׄלת אל[והי]םׄ [ ]◦לׄ◦◦[ ]יׄשׄראׄ[ל]◦[ ]
6 [שומ]רׄי דרך אלוהים ומסל[ת ק]ודשו לקדושי עמו בדׄעׄ[ת]
7 [אלוה]יׄםׄ הנבונה שם [י]שראל [בש]נׄים עשר מחנות קׄדׄוׄשׄ[ ]ה לוׄ
8 [ ]גורל אלוהים עם מלׄאׄ[כי]מאורות כבׄוׄדו בשמוׄ תׄ[ש]בׄוׄחׄת

9 [ ]הׄם תכן למועדי שנה [ומ]משלת יחד להתׄהׄלׄךׄ[ב]גורל
10 [אלוהים]לׄפׄיׄ כבודׄ[ו ו]לשרתו בגורלׄ עׄם כׄסׄאו כיא אלוׄהׄיׄ

bottom margin

Frg. 2 Col. ii

1 [ ]◦[ ]◦[ ]◦◦[
2 וׄדרושו למו כׄ[
3 ועדת ממזׄרׄים כׄ[ו]לׄ ◦◦[
4 ובוׄשת פנים למׄסׄפר אב[
5 [א]ל[ו]הים הׄא◦[ ]ד בכוחׄ◦[
6 [רז]יׄ אלוהיׄם מׄיא ידׄעׄ[
7 אלוהׄיׄ גבורׄות יעדׄם לׄ[
8 כמוהם וׄטׄמׄאים כנדתם [
9 יודע יושׄר יׄשרים ביש[ראל
10 ובׄישראל מׄ[ ]רים בׄ◦ל[

bottom margin

4Q511 (4QShir^b) trans. M. Wise, M. Abegg, and E. Cook

Frg. 1

1. [their d]ominions
2. [ ] [3]and al[l on the e]arth and with all
3. the spirits of its domain, [let them] continually b[less] Him in their times,
4. the seas and every creature. Let them proclaim[ ] the splendour of
5. it all. Let them rejoice before the righteous God, with sho[uts of joy for] salvation
6. for the[re is no] destroyer within their borders
7. nor do wicked spirits walk among them. For the glory of the God of knowledge has shone forth
8. through His words, and none of the sons of injustice shall be sustained.

Frg. 2 Col. i

1. For the Instructor: [ ] song [Praise the name of]
2. His holiness. Let all who know [righteousness] exalt Him.
3. And He put a stop to the head of the dominions without [ ]
4. eternal [joy] and life everlasting, making the light shine [ ]
5. His [l]ot is the first fruits in Jacob, the inheritance of God [ ] Israe[l]
6. [those who kee]p the way of God and His [h]oly highw[ay] for the saints of His people. By the discerning knowledge of
7. [Go]d, he placed Israel [in t]welve camps [ ] for Himself
8. [ ]the lot of God with the ange[ls of] His glorious lights. In His name the praises of
9. their [ ] He established as the festivals of the year, [and the d]ominion of the Yahad, to walk [in] the lot
10. [of God] according to [His] glory [and] to serve Him in the lot of the people of His throne. For the God of

Frg. 2 Col. ii

2. let them [not (?)] seek Him, [
3. and the congregation of bastards, all [
4. and open shame, as the number of [
5. [G]od with might [
6. [the mysterie]s of God, who knows[
7. the God of strengths has appointed them for[
8. like them, and the unclean according to their impurity [Who]
9. knows the uprightness of the upright in Is[rael (?)
10. and in Israel [ ] in [

Frg. 3

1]ב֯ע֯ו֯ל֯מ֯[י]ם כ֯י֯אׄ[
2 תוע]ב֯ותיכם *vacat* ו֯א֯ח֯[ר
3 ק]צׄיׄ רשעתה ופ◦[
4]◦ הגבורות וכחכום[
5]◦◦ם֯ וא֯ין֯ לכ֯ם֯[ש]ל֯ום [
6]מלו֯נו ו֯פחדו כול ◦[
7 שמי]ם וארץ ירועו מ֯[
8]◦ב֯ו֯ ו֯כ֯ו֯ל[

Frg. 4

1]◦◦[ ]◦[
2]◦ אלוהי [
bottom margin

Frg. 5

1]◦בד֯ ו֯◦[
2]ר֯עתו ◦[
3]ל[

Frg. 6

1]וׄא◦ א◦[
2]ג֯◦לם[

Frg. 7

1]◦י֯הׄם
2]כול
3] לכול בשר
4]י֯

Frg. 8

1]ם ב◦◦[
2]יגילו באלוהים[
3] *vacat* [
4 למשכיל ש]יר שני לפחד מיראיו֯[
5]ת֯ע֯ותו בתענ֯ייות ולוא לכל֯[ת עולם
6]◦◦י֯ א֯ל֯ בסתר שׁדי ◦[
7]לשׁ֯יו יחביאני [ ]ל֯[
8]◦נ֯י֯ בקדושיו֯[
9 יח]ד֯ עם קדוש֯[יו
10 מ]ו֯ד֯ים [ל]אל *vac* כיא [
11 ב]ב֯תי כבודם יחברו֯[
12]אתה א֯ל֯[וה]י֯ ה[א]ל[והים
13]ל[

Frg. 9

1]צדקׄ[
2]*vac*[
3]םׄ[

Frg. 3

1.]forever. For[
2.] your [abomin]ations *vacat* And the[n
3. the ti]mes of its wickedness and [
4.] the strengths. And as the wise[
5.] and you have no [p]eace [
6.]His habitation. And all [ ] shall fear [
7. heave]ns and earth shall shatter (*or*: shout) [
8.] and all[

Frg. 5

2.]his evil [

Frg. 4

2.] God of [

Frg. 7

1.] their
2.]all
3.] to all flesh

Frg. 8

2.]they shall rejoice in God[
3.] *vacat* [
4. For the Instructor:] the second [so]ng so as to frighten those who terrify[
5.]his straying through humiliations but not for [eternal] destructi[on
6.] God in the secret of the Almighty (Shaddai) [
7.] His [ ] He shall hide me [
8.] with his holy ones[
9. togeth]er with [His] saint[s
10. giving th]anks [to] God. *vacat* For [
11. in] the houses of their glory they shall be united[
12.]You are the Go[d] of the [g]o[ds

Frg. 9

1.]righteousness[
2.] *vacat* [

Frg. 10
Parallel: 4Q**510** 1

◦◦◦]רוחי מלאכי חבל ורוחות ממזרים שד אים] לילי[ת]
]אחים ו(ציים *vac?*) [6]והפוגעים פתע פתאום ל]תעות רוֺחֺ
]בינה *vacat?* ולהשם לבבם ונ◦◦תם ב]קֺץ מֹמשל(ת) [7]רשעֹהֹ
]ותעודות תעניות בני או(ר) *vacat?* באשמ]ת קצי נגוע(י)
]עוונות ולוא לכלת עול]םֺ (◦חֺוֺקֹ[ ]◦◦ [8]כי א)ם לקֺץֺ
]תענייות פשע [*vacat*
]רננו צדיקים [*vac?* באלוהי פלא [9]ולישרים תֹהלי (כבודו
[י)]רוממו(ה)ו כ(ו)ל תמימי דרך *vac* (בכנור ישועות
]יפת]חו פהֹ לרחמי אל ידרושו למנו *vacat* הושיֺעֹה אלוהֺ[ים]
]שומר חס]דֺ בֹאמת לכול מעשיו ושופט בצדֺ[ק מ]הֺויי עד
]ע]דֺ נֺהיי עולמים בסוד אילים ואנשים ישפוט
ברום שמים תוכחתו ובכול מוסדי ארץ משפטי יוד
bottom margin

Frg. 11

]◦[ ]◦ וֺבֺ[
מו]עֺדֺי צֺרֺוֺתֺ [
]ה וֺ[מ]קֹלל לכול ◦[
]יֺפגעו לענות בֹ[
]עֹרו מיראיו [
]ם מתוך מֺ◦[
]לוא תרֹאוֺ[
]הֺפגועים הֹ◦◦[
עו]למים כיא אחרֺוֺןֺ[
]*vac* ואחרוןֺ מֺוֺ[
] בחר לכל[
א]לוֺהֺיםֺ הֺ◦[

Frg. 12

]◦די רשעֺ[ה
י]תֺפֺחדו כול [
]באלוהים לֺ[
]לֺ[

Frg. 10

1. [spirits of the destroying angels, spirits of the bastards, demons,] Lili[th,]
2. [howlers and desert dwellers *vac*? [6]and those which fall upon men without warning to] lead them astray from a spirit of
3. [understanding *vacat*? and to make their heart and their desolate during] the present dominion of [7]wickedness
4. [and predetermined time of humiliations for the sons of light, *vacat*? by the guil]t of the ages of those smitten by
5. [iniquity—not for etern]al [destruction] [8]but for an era of
6. [humiliation for transgression.] *vacat*
7. Sing for joy, O righteous ones,] *vacat*? for the God of Wonder. [9]The psalms of his glory are for the upright.
8. [And let] all those who are blameless exalt Him! *vacat* With the lyre of salvation
9. they [shall ope]n their mouths for God's compassion. They shall seek His manna. *vacat* Save me, O Go[d,]
10. [He who preserves lovingkindne]ss in truth for all His works and judges in righteous[ness] those who exist forever
11. [unt]il eternity. He judges in the council of gods and men.
12. In the height of heaven is His rebuke, and in all the foundations of the earth, the judgements of the Lord

Frg. 11

2. sea]sons of distress [
3.] and cursing to all [
4.]they fall upon [ ] to afflict [
5.] those who make him fear [
6.] from the midst of [
7.]you shall not see[
8.]the demon possessed [
9. ever]lasting for the latter[
10.] *vacat* And the latter [
11.] he chose for[
12. G]od [

Frg. 12

1.] wickedne[ss
2.] all [ ] shall tremble [
3.]in God [

Frg. 13

1] ופ י֯[
2]◦◦[

Frg. 14

1]מוד֯◦[
2]י֯ עול֯[ם
3]◦◦◦◦[

Frg. 15

1]ם מ[
2]עולמים[
3 בכול מ]א֯ודם כ֯י֯א֯ ◦[
4 ל]פ֯ני גבורתו[ ]◦◦[
5]◦◦ה֯ רוחי הבלים ל֯[
6]יר ומעשיו הקדוש֯[ם
7 רו]ח֯ רעה ה[ ] ב֯ו֯[
8]ל֯[

Frg. 16

1]◦◦◦◦[
2]כול משלוחותי֯ו֯ ◦מ֯ע֯◦◦[
3 אש]א֯וכלת במוסדי עפרו֯[
4 בר]וך אתה אלוהי אל֯[ים
5]תיהם ופוקח או֯[זנים
6]א֯◦◦[

Frg. 17

1]א֯מונת֯[ ] כ֯ו֯ל֯ [
2]◦ד֯ל אב֯יונ֯י֯[
3]גבו֯ר֯ה אין משא[
4] רוב֯ א֯ונ֯י֯ם֯ לוא י֯[
5]◦◦מ֯◦[

Frg. 18 Col. i

8]]י֯
9]]אה
10]]ת֯

bottom margin

Frg. 18 Col. ii

1]]◦י
2]]◦רו

Frg. 13

1.] and [

Frg. 14

2.] everl[asting

Frg. 15

2.]everlasting[
3. in all] their [str]ength for [
4. be]fore His might[
5.] vain spirits [
6.] His holy deeds [
7.] evil [spiri]t [

Frg. 16

2.]all its companies [
3. a fire which] devours the foundations of its dust[
4. Ble]ssed are You, O God of go[ds
5.] their [ ] and opening [their] e[ars

Frg. 17

1.]faithfulness[ ] all [
2.] poor [
3.]might, their is no burden[
4.] abundance of strength [ ] not [

Frg. 18 Col. ii

3 [ ]בׄ[ג]בׄורתו

4 [ ]יׄ *vacat*

5 [אם נבלות]בדברי ואין וׄ[ב]מׄוצא שפׄתי ולוא בליעל

6 [ ]ורוח בינתי וׄ◦◦הׄ עבודת רשעה כיא

7 אׄ[לו]הׄיםׄ ע ני *vac* וכולׄ מעשי נדה שנתי כיא

8 הׄאׄיר אלוהים דעתׄ בינה בלבבי ומוכיחי

9 צׄדׄק עם נעוותי ושופטׄי אמונה בכול פשעי

10 אשמתי כיא אלוהים שופטי וביד זר לוא

bottom margin

Frg. 18 Col. iii

2 בׄמׄ[ ]◦[ ]

3 [ו]אׄלוהיׄ[ ]◦◦[ ]וׄ◦[ ]

4 [ו]משפׄ[ט]◦◦[ ]

5 וׄעׄם התׄנׄגׄפׄיׄ[ ]

6 כנפי אליׄכׄהׄ ◦[ ]

bottom margin

Frg. 19

1]◦בׄ◦[

2]◦ עׄמׄוׄ [

3] כדׄעתי [

4]◦ אלוהים [

5]גׄבורות פלאוׄ[

6]◦[ ]◦[

Frg. 20

	Col. i	Col. ii
1	בצד]קׄתׄו יטׄהׄ[רני]	
2	]ומלאך כבוׄדׄוׄ	יׄרׄוׄאׄ ◦[
3	]◦ ביד אשמה	ירועו ◦[
4	]◦ ורפואות	יתמוגגׄ[ו
5		תתעׄ[

Frg. 21

1 י]בׄיׄאום[

2]פט ש◦[

3. [ ]in His [s]trength
4. [ ] *vacat*
5. [Is there any foolishness] in my words? There is none. Or [in] the utterance of my lips? There is no worthlessness
6. [ ]and the spirit of my understanding and work of wickedness, for
7. G[o]d is concerned with me. *vac* And I have hated all the works of impurity, for
8. God has shined the knowledge of understanding in my heart. Righteous instructors
9. correct my sins, and faithful judges correct all my guilty transgressions.
10. For God is my judge and in the hand of a stranger [He shall] not

Frg. 18 Col. iii

3. [and]God[ ]
4. [and]judgeme[nt] [ ]
5. and when I stumble[ ]
6. my wings are to You [ ]

Frg. 19

2.] His people [
3.] according to my knowledge [
4.] God [
5.]His wondrous might deeds[

Frg. 20 Col. i

1. in] His [righte]ousness He shall clean[se me]
2.]and His glorious messenger
3.] by guilt
4.] and healing

Frg. 20 Col. ii

2. fearing [
3. they shall break [
4. they shall come apart[

Frg. 21

1.]they [shall] bring them[

Frg. 22

1] שו]פטי̊
2]] כיא עם כול
3] מענה כול לש]ון ישמע ומזל
4 [כול שפתים ומח]שבת כול לבב הואה
5 [ידע]ו̊ל◦] [◦ת
6] ה̇]

Frg. 23

1]דו וע̇צת̊[
2]ורות מצ̊[
3]עולמים [
4 כו]ל מחשב[
5]ת̊ה̊ל[

Frg. 24

1]ו̊ש̊[
2]ר̇וחות ◦[
3]ג̇דופיה̊[ם
4]ו בם [
5]פחז ו̊[

Frg. 25

1]◦ר̊ו מחני[
2]ל◦◦ למלא̊[

Frg. 26

1]ה̊ מ̊◦[ ]◦◦[ ]◦[
2]ח̊סדיו וכול מח̇ש̊[בותיו
3]מבני אדם ומסוד̊[בשר
4]ג̇בורותיו̇ ו[מ]ו̊פת̊[יו
5]לספר ◦[

Frg. 27

1]כ̊ו̊◦ ◦ה̊ש̇[
2 ע]ליה יגיל[ו
3]ם ירוממו̊[
4]ר̇ לרשעה̊[
5]ל◦[

Frg. 22

1. [jud]ges of
2. [ ] for with all
3. [ ] He shall hear the [appropriate respo]nse and the utterance of
4. [the lips and the thou]ght of every heart He
5. [knows] [ ]

Frg. 23

1.] and the council of[

3.]everlasting [
4. ever]y though[t

Frg. 24

2.]spirits [
3.]th[eir] slanders[
4.] with them [
5.]lewdness [

Frg. 25

1.] camps[
2.] to [

Frg. 26

2.]His mercies and all [His] thou[ghts
3.]from humanity and [fleshly] counsel[
4.]His mighty deeds and [His wo]nder[s
5.]to tell [

Frg. 27

2. bec]ause of it/her [they] shall rejoice[
3.] they exalt[
4.] for wickedness[

Frgs. 28–29

[ ]כׄהׄ ב∘∘[ ]∘ מׄגׄוׄיׄים
[י]גילו באלוהים רנׄה וׄא[ני אודכ]ה כׄיא למען כבודכה
[ש]מתה דעת בסוד עפרי לה[ללכה] ואני מצי֯רוק יצר
[חמר]קׄוׄרצתי ומחושך מגבׄ[לי]הׄ ^[∘∘וׄהׄ^ וׄעׄולה בתכמי בׄשׄרי
[ ] *vacat* [ ] *vacat*
[ ]∘∘[ ]ל[ ]∘∘[ ]∘∘ ואתה[ ]ל[

Frg. 30

חׄתמתׄהׄ[א]רׄץ גׄ∘∘[ ]
ויעמקוׄ[השמים ושמי ה]שׄמׄיׄם ותהומות ומחׄ[שכי ארץ]
אתה אלׄיׄ חׄתׄמׄתה בעד כולם ואין פותח ולאשרׄ[אענה]
הימדו בשועל אנשים מי רבה וׄאׄם בזרת[יתכנו שמים ומי בשליש]
יכול עפר הארׄץ וישקׄ[ו]ל בפלסׄ[ ]הרים וגׄבׄעׄוׄתׄ בׄמׄוזנׄ[ים]
את אלה לוא יׄעשה[ ]אׄדׄםׄ[ואיכה]יׄוׄכל איש לתכן את ריחׄ[אלוהים]
bottom margin

Frg. 34

[ ]כׄוׄ[
[ ]וׄ[

Frg. 35

top margin

א[לו]הׄיׄםׄ בכול בשר ומשפט נקמות לכלתׄ רשעה ולזׄעׄ[ף]
אפי אלוהׄים במזוקקי שבעתׄים ובקדׄושים יקדׄיׄ[ש]
אלוהים לו למקדש עולמים וטהרה בנברים והיׄוׄ
כוהנים עׄם צדקו צבאו ומשרתים מלאכי כבודו
יהללוהו בהׄפלא נוראות *vacat*
ואני מירא אל בקצי דורותי לרומם שם דברׄ[תי לפחד]
בגבורתו כוׄ[ל]רוחי ממזרים להכניעם מירא[תו ולוא לכול]
[מ]וׄעדי[עולמים כי אם ל]קׄץ ממשלתם[
ר]שׄעׄ[ה

Frgs. 28–29

1. [ ] from the nations
2. [ ] they [shall] rejoice in God with joy. And a[s for me, I shall thank Yo]u that, for the sake of Your glory,
3. You [pl]aced knowledge in my frame of dust in order to that I might p[raise You.] And I was formed of spittle (?).
4. I was molded [of clay] and [my] format[ion] was in darkness [ ] and injustice is in the filth of my flesh
5. [ ] *vacat* [ ] *vacat*
6. [ ] and you[ ]

Frg. 30

1. You sealed[l]and [ ]
2. and they are deep [the] heavens and the deeps and the dar[k places of the earth]
3. You, my God, have sealed all of them forever, and there is none to open. And to who[m]
4. Shall the abundant waters be measured by the hollow of a man's hand? [Shall the heavens be measured] by a span? [Who with a measure]
5. can calculate the dust of the earth or weigh the mountains in a balance or the hills with scale[s?] (cf. Isa 40:12)
6. Man did not make these things. [How then] can a man measure the spirit [of God?]

Frg. 34

2.] and[

Frg. 35

1. G[o]d with all flesh, and a judgement of vengeance to wipe out wickedness and by the fierce
2. anger of God among those who have been refined sevenfold. But God will consecrate some of the holy ones
3. for Himself as an eternal sanctuary; a refining among those who are purified. And they shall be
4. priests, His righteous people, His army, and ministers, His glorious angels.
5. They shall praise Him for His awe-inspiring wonders *vacat*
6. And I am pouring out the fear of God to the ends of my generations, to exalt the Name [to frighten]
7. by His strength al[l] the spirits of the bastards, to subdue them by [His] fear [
8. [eternal fe]stivals [ ] the end of their dominion[

Frg. 36

1]וׄתם [
2]חסד֯[י]ו וטהרם וה֯◦[
3]לפדויים כ֯י֯א֯ אלוהי֯]ם
4]◦י֯ ו֯א֯[נ]י֯ ל[

Frg. 37

1]ם֯[
2]◦י֯ ◦[ ]◦ ב֯מקׄום ◦[
3 יזדעזעו יס]ו֯ד֯ותם ות֯ח֯ול ה֯א֯ר֯ץ֯[
4 י]ר֯ו֯עו כול מ֯ח֯שביה וכו֯[ל אשר עליה
5]י֯ב֯ה֯לו ויחפ[זו
6]הׄ תהום [

bottom margin

Frg. 38

1]ת֯ו ו֯נ֯ח֯ל֯ת֯ו֯[
2]◦ בט֯חתי[
3 י]ש֯ועתו יענה֯[
4]◦[ ]◦◦◦[

Frg. 39

1]◦ר֯ון א֯◦◦[
2]◦◦ו֯תם [
3]◦◦◦◦[

Frg. 40

1]◦ הׄג֯בל֯]תה
2]ו֯ת והגבהׄ]תה
3]ה֯ וכ֯גב]ורתכה
4]◦ונו ◦[

Frg. 41

1]בׄמרומי ר֯ום מ֯ע֯ו֯ן ש◦[
2]ת לכרובי קודש[

bottom margin

Frg. 42

1]◦[
2 לוא י]עשה כולׄ [
3]◦י תעודתי֯ פלגתה ליׄא[
4]◦ *vacat* ובשמיני אפצהׄ] פי
5 ד]ו֯רות אשמתי ואצפה אל [
6]◦בותם ואל מוסדי הארץ[

Frg. 36

2.]His merci[es] and He shall cleanse them and [
3.]for the redeemed, for Go[d
4.] and I [

Frg. 37

2.] in the place [
3.] their [founda]tions [will tremble] and the earth will shake[
4.] all its designs are bad/shattered and al[l which is upon it
5.]they shall be terrified and pani[c
6.] deep [

Frg. 38

1.] and His inheritance[
2.] I trusted[
3.]His [sa]lvation, He shall answer[

Frg. 39

2.] their [

Frg. 40

1. You]established boundaries [
2.] and [You] made high[
3.] and according to [Your] might[y deeds

Frg. 41

1.]highest heaven a dwelling [
2.] for the holy cherubim[

Frg. 42

2.] he [shall not] do anything [
3.] my testimony You assigned to me (?)[
4.]*vacat* And on the eighth I will open [my mouth
5.] my guilty [g]enerations. And I will watch for [
6.] their [ ] and to the foundations of the earth[

7]עפרה ואדעה מחשבתכה[
8]◦ כיא בידכה לפתוׄ[ח
9]לעין־ לוא ינחׄ[
10]◦◦ין ואם[

Frg. 43

1 ◦◦אׄ◦◦[
2 בדעתׄ כׄ[
3 נחלה ומׄ◦[
4 ומשפטי צדׄ[ק
5 תעב קדוש א◦[
6 רוחי חבל למׄלׄ[
7 לבבם כנדת תועׄ[בותיהם
8 כׄזדון לבבם בׄתׄ◦◦[
9]םׄ וב◦[

Frgs. 44–47 Col. i

top margin

1 כיא לצדׄיקים [   ]יו במקור
2 ◦[ ] נצי◦[ ]ם ואׄ[כ]וׄל סודי
3 ◦יׄת טׄ◦◦[   ]םׄ ואש
4 גבור◦[   ]א למכותם
5 וׄיׄסׄוד [   ]אדםׄ על
6 צׄדׄיק ב[   ]רׄזׄיׄ פׄלׄאו
7 [ ]◦א מׄלׄ[   ]◦ם
8 [   ]◦◦

Frgs. 48–49 + 51 Col. ii

top margin

1 בעצת אל כיא[   ]תׄ בינתו נתן [ב]לב[בי]
2 הודות צדקו וׄ◦[   ]עׄה ובפיׄ יׄפחד [כול רוחות]
3 ממזרים להכׄניׄע[   ]טׄי טׄמׄאה כיא בׄתׄכׄמי
4 בׄשרי יסוׄדׄ דׄ◦[וב]גויתי מׄלחמׄוׄתׄ חוקי
5 אל בלבבי ואועיׄ[ל   ]עׄל כׄוׄל מופתי גבר מעשי
6 אשמה ארשיׄע[   ]אל ◦◦◦◦וׄתׄ *vacat* הואה
7 ידע וברזיוׄ ◦◦[   ]◦◦◦◦ ריבי כׄוׄל
8 רוחי ◦◦[   ]◦[ ]◦[ ]מ[ ]מׄימ◦[ ]ל

Frgs. 52, 54 + 55, 57 + 59 Col. iii

top margin

1]דׄתם ואתה אליׄ[אל חנון ורחום]וׄארוך אפים רׄב החסד יסוד הא[מת
2]◦ לאדם ולבנׄ[יו   מ]קור הטׄוהר מקוי הכבוד גדול הצדׄ[ק

7.]its dust. And I know Your purpose[
8.] for it is in Your hand to ope[n
9.]for the eye, [ ] shall not [
10.] and if[ ]

Frg. 43

2. in the knowledge of [
3. inheritance and [
4. right[eous] judgements [
5. he abhorred [the] holy [one
6. the spirits of destruction [
7. their heart as the impurity of [their] abomi[nations
8. as the arrogance of their heart [

Frgs. 44–47 Col. i

1. for to the righteous [ ] his [ ] by source
2. [ ] and [al]l the foundations of
3. [ ] and might fire
4. [ ] for their wounds
5. and [the] foundation [of] man
6. upon a righteous one [ ] His wondrous mysteries

Frgs. 48–49 + 51 Col. ii

1. in the council of God, for [ ] His knowledge he put [in my] hear[t]
2. the praises of His righteousness, and [ ] and by His mouth he frightens [all the spirits]
3. of the bastards to subdue [ ] uncleanness. For in the filth of
4. my flesh is the foundation of [and in] my body are conflicts. The statutes of
5. God are in my heart, and I prof[it] from all the wonders of man. The works of
6. guilt I condemn [ ] God. *vacat* He
7. knows and in His mysteries [ ] the disputes of all
8. the spirits of [ ].

Frgs. 52, 54 + 55, 57 + 59 Col. iii

1.] their [ ] And You, my God, [are a merciful and gracious God,] slow to anger, abounding in steadfast love, the foundation of tr[uth
2.] for Adam and for [his] son[s] the [s]ource of purity, the reservoirs of glory, great in righteousn[ess

3]עשה ל◦[ ] משפטים למעשי כול ומשיב ברכות [
4 ברוך את]ה אלי מלך הכב[ו]ד כיא מאתכה משפט[
5 ארו]רים ומאתכה סוד לכול יראיכה ב[
6 בר]וכים ל [ ]◦ המה [
7]מגערתכה י [ ] ברוב [
8]ל[ ]ל[

Frg. 56

1]◦◦◦◦◦[
2]רתי כיא[
3]◦ עוונותי[
4]הל[

Frgs. 60–62 Col. iv

top margin?

1]ם ולישרים]ודו[
2]ו כולכם רוח[י]ל[
3]חי כלא[
4]◦את[
1]תה [

Frg. 63 Col. i

4 כ]ול קצוו[ת]
5 [*vacat*
6]◦י ברזי
7]נו

Frgs. 63–64 Col. ii

top margin

1 [מ]עשי אלוהי פדותי ◦◦◦דיו◦[ ]◦הב בסודי
2 [ ]◦ ◦◦◦◦◦ובכול מה רצו◦◦[ ]◦חם אברכה שמכה ובמועדי תעודותי אספרה
3 נפלאותיכה ואחורתם חוקי הודות כבודכה ברישית כול מחשבת לבב
4 דעת ותרומת מזל שפתי צדק ובהנכון לכול עבודת אמת ועם כול
5 [אנ]שי ברית ד◦◦[ ]◦[ ]◦[ ]ו[ש]לומי בתודה אד◦[ ]מעשה ובכול

Col. iii

top margin

1 ואני תרנן לשוני צדקכה כיא פתחתה ובשפתי שמתה מקור
2 תהלה ובלבי סוד רישית כול מעשי איש ומולות פעולות

3.] judgements for the works of all and giving blessings in return [
4. Blessed are Yo]u, my God, the glorious King. For from You judgement [
5.] and from You is the foundation for all who fear You [
6. bles]sed [ ] they [
7.] because of Your rebuke [ ] in the abundance of [

Frg. 56

2.] for[
3.] my transgressions[

Frg. 60 Col. iv

1.] and for the upright[
2.] all of you [are] spirit[s
3.] prison[

Frg. 63 Col. i

4. [al]l [the] end[s of]
5. [ ] *vacat*
6. [ ] in the mysteries of

Frgs. 63–64 Col. ii

1. [w]orks of the God of my redemption [ ] in the foundations of
2. [ ] and in everything. [ ] I will bless Your name. And in my appointed times I shall relate
3. Your wonders. I shall engrave them, the statutes of thanksgiving for Your glory. The beginning of every purpose of the heart
4. is knowledge and the beginning of every blessed utterance is righteous lips and in being prepared for every true service. And with all
5. [the m]en of the covenant [ ] my [p]eace is in thanksgiving [ ] work and in all.

Col. iii

1. And as for me, my tongue shall sing out Your righteousness, for You set it free. You placed on my lips a fountain
2. of praise and on my heart the secret of the origin of all the works of man, and the fulfillment of the deeds

3 תמימי דרך֯ ו֯משפטים לכו֯ל עבודת מעשיהם להצדיק
4 צדיק באמתכה ולהרשיע רשע *vac* באשמתו להשמיע שלום
5 לכול אנשי ברית ולה֯[ר]ים בקול פחד הוי֯ לכול מפר֯י֯ה֯
6 [ ]ש֯◦◦[ ]ו֯[ ]ל כו֯ל[ ]ל[ ]◦[ ]א [ ]ות ח֯◦[ ]

Col. iv

top margin

1 י֯ברכו כול מעשיכה
2 ת֯מיד וברוך שמכה
3 לעולמי עד אמן אמן

bottom margin

Frg. 65

top margin

1] צומחי [
2]נ֯יתו ל֯[

Frg. 66

top margin

1]◦ים כש֯[
2]◦ן֯ צדק◦[

Frg. 67

top margin

1] אמונים [
2 מ]ש֯פ֯ט֯י֯כה [

Frg. 68

1]ג֯ב[
2]ח֯ ◦◦ה֯[
3]שר נע◦[
4]ה֯זיד ב◦[
5]◦ו֯ר֯ו֯[

Frg. 69

1]◦רי֯[
2]אותם [

Frg. 70

1]א֯ לו[
2]אוזן ומענ֯[ה
3]ע֯ם ל[

Frg. 71

1]ם ◦[
2]ו֯משפטיהם[
3]◦שי רוש בב֯[
4]דעת ◦◦[
5]ל֯[

Frg. 72

1]אה [
2]ל[

Frg. 73

1]י֯ ה֯כו֯ו֯ה גדול
2]ים פני אלוהים
3]י֯ם֯ מיסודו֯
4]ח֯

Frg. 74

1]ו֯לוא
2]חדון֯
3]◦◦[

3. of the blameless, the judgements for all the toil of their works, in order to justify
4. the righteous one in Your truth and to condemn the wicked one *vacat* in his guilt, to proclaim peace
5. to all the men of the covenant and to e[xal]t with a terrifying voice, "Woe to all who break it!"

Col. iv

1. Let them bless all Your works
2. continually, and blessed be Your name
3. for ever and ever. Amen, amen.

Frg. 65

1.] sprouts of [
2.] his [

Frg. 67

1.] faithful [
2.] your [ju]dgements [

Frg. 70

2.]ear, and [the] respon[se

Frg. 69

2.]them [

Frg. 71

2.]and their judgements[
3.] head on [
4.]knowledge [

Frg. 74

1.]and not

Frg. 73

1.] the great burning
2.] face of God
3.] His foundation

Frg. 75

1]◦הׄ◦ וׄ◦◦[
2 בלוא פתח]תׄה פי מׄה [אדבר
3]◦◦ם לוא[
4]◦ ◦[

Frg. 76

1]שׄפט◦[
2 י]שראל ◦[
3]ל[ ]ל[

Frg. 77

1]בׄהׄ◦◦ ◦[
2]◦רׄ דׄבׄ◦[

Frg. 78

1]וׄם

Frg. 79

1]◦וׄרׄ◦[

Frg. 80

1]בׄרורי[
2]מׄ ◦◦[

Frg. 81

1 יר]וׄממוׄ[
2] ובכוח גב[ורתו
3 ר]וׄחׄ רעׄהׄ[
4]לכם לׄ[
5]בׄכׄבׄוׄדׄוׄ [

Frg. 82

1]◦◦ערו[
2]בכם [
3]ל◦[

Frg. 83

1]◦◦[
2]◦ת גבור[
3] כול גׄ[
4]*vacat*[
5]◦◦[

Frg. 84

1]ראׄ[
2]הׄ◦[

Frg. 85

1]◦וׄ[
2]◦ אליו וא[
3]◦[ ]ל[

Frg. 86

1]מׄתׄוׄךׄ[
2]◦נׄי כׄ◦[
3]לבׄכׄ◦[

Frg. 87

1]לׄי לׄ◦[
2]◦תׄי[

Frg. 88

1]יׄ◦[
2]כׄול מׄ◦[

Frg. 89

1]לו[

Frg. 75

2. unless] You [have opened] my mouth. What [shall I say
3.] not[

Frg. 76

2. I]srael [

Frg. 81

1.]they [shall] exalt[
2.] and in the power of [His] str[ength
3.]evil [spi]rit [
4.]to you [
5.]in His glory [

Frg. 80

1.]purified[

Frg. 83

2.] streng[th
3.] all [
4.] *vacat* [

Frg. 82

2.]with you [

Frg. 85

2.] to Him and [

Frg. 86

1.]from the midst[

3.]heart [

Frg. 88

2.]all [

Frg. 90

1]◦ הכבו̊[ד
2]ונה רם [

Frg. 91

1]◦ת[

Frg. 92

1]איו̊[
2]י כ◦[

Frg. 93

1]◦ ב̇ד̊ע[ת
2]◦◦◦◦◦ת̊◦[

Frg. 94

1]◦תו [
2]◦ם ◦[
3] ע[

Frg. 95

top margin?
1]◦ב̊ו ש̇ם̊[
2]ים בכבוד [
3]א̊שר יתהל[

Frg. 96

1]◦◦◦[
2]◦◦ ה̊נבונ◦[
3] אדם לבד[ו
4 ב]ד̊עתו הנבונה[
5]◦◦[

Frg. 97

top margin
1]צפור כנף י[
2]לב̊[ ]ל[

Frg. 98

top margin
1]ברנה̊[ ]ל̊[ ]ל̊[

Frg. 99

1 כאשמ̊[ת
2 מלך ◦[
3 על ב◦◦[
4 כול[

Frg. 100

top margin?
1]גדול ◦[
2 מח]שבות◦[

Frg. 101

top margin?
1]ר̇ומ̊ ע̊ולמ̊[ים

Frg. 102

1]◦י̇ ◦[
2]ב̇לוא̊[
3]◦◦[

Frg. 103

1]◦◦◦◦
2]ו̊רות ע̇ד̇
3]◦ גבורתו
4]ב̇ליעל
5]◦נ̊ע̇ו מ◦

Frg. 104

top margin
1 אל̊[

Frg. 105

1]◦ ומ̇ו̊[ ]◦[
bottom margin

Frg. 90

1.] the glo[ry
2.] exalted [

Frg. 93

1. with [the] knowle[dge of

Frg. 95

1.] name[
2.] in glory [
3.]that [ ] shall [

Frg. 97

1.] winged bird [

Frg. 96

2.] the understanding [
3.] man alon[e
4. in] His understanding knowledge[

Frg. 99

1. according to [ ] guil[t
2. king [
3. upon [
4. all[

Frg. 98

1.]with a shout of joy[

Frg. 101

1.]everlas[ting]praise [

Frg. 100

1.]large [
2. tho]ughts [

Frg. 103

2.] until
3.] His might
4.]Belial

Frg. 102

2.]without[

Frg. 105

1.] and [

Frg. 106

top margin

1]תֺם [

Frg. 107

top margin?

1]אֺ [

2]◦◦[

Frg. 108

1 אור]ךֺ אפים רובׄ

2]◦כול בדבריכה

3 *vac*[

4 ◦[

Frg. 109

1]◦אֺ

2 עֺלץ ל[

3 עם ◦ל[

Frg. 110

1]ין ב[

2]י הד[

3]ל[

Frg. 111

1]◦ אדם

2]◦ הוא[ה]

3 *vacat* [

4]בקצו

5]י כבוד

6 מי]ראיו

7 מ]יראיו

8]מבנית[ ]

9] אמן א[מן]

Frg. 112

top margin?

1]◦ר

2]◦

Frg. 113

1]שֺ◦

2]◦ו

Frg. 114

1]םֺ

2]ם

3]◦

Frg. 115

1 וֺבשֺ[

2 השורץֺ[

3]]חֺל◦[

Frg. 116

1]◦יֺו

2]◦◦ וֺלברֺכֺו

3]שדי

bottom margin?

Frg. 117

1]◦ם עֺם

2]ל[

Frg. 118

1]◦◦יֺ

Frg. 119

1] קומ[

bottom margin?

Frg. 106

1.] their[

Frg. 109

2. he exulted [

Frg. 108

1. slo]w to anger, abounding
2.] all in your words
3.] *vacat*

Frg. 111

1.] man
2.] he
3.] *vacat*
4.]in His time
5.] glory
6. those who cause] him to [f]ear
7. those who cause] him to fear
8.]structure[ ]
9.] Amen, a[men.]

Frg. 115

1. and [
2. the creeping thing[

Frg. 116

2.] and to bless Him
3.]Shaddai.

Frg. 120

1]◦[ ]◦ל̇

2 ע]ולמים

bottom margin

Frg. 121

1]◦[

2] תעני̇ות ו̇עד תום[

3]מ̇יראיו כול ◦[

4]ל[

Frg. 122

1]◦ י̇◦◦◦ ◦[

2]◦ות בכול ב̇◦[

3]◦ ◦שמ̇ים ו◦[

4]◦ל̇[

Frg. 123

1]◦ם̇[

2]◦עו ממ◦[

3]◦ יענו למ[

4]ל̇[ ]ו̇[

Frg. 124

1]ירוממוה̇[ו

2]כ̇בודו וח◦[

3]ל דעת [

Frg. 125

1]◦[

2] כול[

3]עזר ע̇◦◦[

4]ב̇קש̇ו̇ א̇◦[

Frg. 126

1]ים ת̇[

2 ואני עפר וא]פר מה אד̇[בר

3]י̇כ̇ה לו̇א̇[

Frg. 127

1]אבינ̇ו̇[

2 ל]ו̇א תכיר ◦◦[

3]כ̇ו̇ל נ̇עדר◦[

4]ל̇[

Frg. 128

1]◦[

2]י כול י̇[

3]◦ו̇◦[ ]◦◦◦[

Frg. 129

1]◦מ̇ו̇ ◦◦◦[

2]ב̇רוך א̇נ̇ו̇ ב◦[

3]◦[

Frg. 130

1]◦◦◦ [

2]כ̇ה אלי וא̇[

3]◦◦◦◦[

Frg. 131

1]ל̇ם [

2] דעת ◦◦[

3]◦ו̇ש̇ אל̇◦◦[

Frg. 132

1]ישמ̇[

2]◦ שרו [

3]ה̇מש̇[

Frg. 133

1]כיא אל̇[

2]◦ א̇לו̇ה̇י̇[

Frg. 134

1]שר̇[

2]לכול [

3]ל̇[

Frg. 121

2.] humiliations and until the end[
3.]those who cause him to fear, all [

Frg. 120

2. ev]erlasting.

Frg. 123

3.] they shall answer [

Frg. 122

2.] with all [
3.] heavens [

Frg. 125

2.] all[
3.]help [
4.]seek [

Frg. 124

1.]they shall exalt H[im
2.]His glory and [
3.] knowledge [

Frg. 126

2. and I am but dust and a]shes, what shall I [say
3.] your [ ] not[

Frg. 127

1.]our father[
2.] you shall [no]t recognize [
3.]all were missing [

Frg. 130

2.]your[ ] to me and [

Frg. 129

2.]blessed, we [

Frg. 132

2.] they loosed [

Frg. 131

2.] knowledge [

Frg. 134

2.]to all [

Frg. 133

1.]for God[
2.] God[

Frg. 135

1]◦י֯ים [

2]שמים[

Frg. 136

top margin?

1]ו֯עשו ו֯◦[

2]לבׄ[

Frg. 137

1]◦מׄ[

2]ים ב[

3]◦י עולמי֯]ם

4 מ]שׄפׄטיׄו ול֯[

Frg. 138

1]ו֯קות [

2]◦ בׄגׄ[

3]מתו ◦[

4]◦◦◦[

Frg. 139

1]ל֯ אׄל◦[

2]◦ תוע◦◦[

3] *vacat* [

4]מאת ◦[

bottom margin?

Frg. 140

1]◦ם [

2]ת ◦◦לאׄ [

3]י֯גילו֯ [

4]◦ל[

Frg. 141

1]◦◦[

2]◦ים[

3]משׄ[*vac*]

4]◦◦[ ]ם [

Frg. 142

1]תׄבׄ[

2]◦◦[ ]מאו[

3]◦ל *vacat* [

4]◦תכׄרׄ◦[

Frg. 143

1]ימים[

2]ד֯עות [

3]למ◦[

4]◦ [

Frg. 144

1]הים ינואׄ[

2]י֯תן ושר[

3]אׄלהים[

Frg. 145

1]שׄ [

2]אשר [

3 [להכנ]יע

Frg. 146

1]◦ו֯◦[

2]ויז◦[

3]טומׄ[

Frg. 147

1]◦ל֯ מׄ◦[

2]◦שו ו◦[

3]יע ל[

Frg. 148

1]◦[

2 א]מׄתו אׄ[

3]חסׄדו [

Frg. 136

1.]and they did and [

Frg. 138

3.] His [

Frg. 140

3.]they shall rejoice [

Frg. 144

1.] shall forbid[
2.]He shall give and [
3.]God[

Frg. 148

2.] His [tr]uth [
3.]His mercy [

Frg. 135

2.]heaven[

Frg. 137

3.] everlast[ing
4.] His commandments and [

Frg. 139

3.] *vacat* [

Frg. 141

3.] *vacat* [

Frg. 143

1.]days[
2.]knowledge [

Frg. 145

2.]that [
3.] to sub[due

Frg. 147

2.] and [

Frg. 149

1]◦◦[
2]ו֯יאי◦[
3]ל[

Frg. 150

1 א]מן [
2]◦ ה[
3]◦◦[

Frg. 151

1]◦ מ◦[]ו֯ת֯[
2]◦ ב֯צ֯ד֯]ק

Frg. 152

1]שב◦[
2]רפת[
3]ש֯טמ֯[

Frg. 153

1]◦[
2]ו֯ד֯י ◦[
3]ד֯ו֯◦[

Frg. 154

1]מ֯אז ב֯[
2]היו ◦◦[
3]◦[

Frg. 155

1]◦ו֯◦[
2]◦ ◦◦[
3]◦[

Frg. 156

1]ב֯כ◦[
2]פ֯תח פ֯[
3]ל֯[

Frg. 157

1]ו֯צדק֯[
2]ת֯יר [
3]◦[

Frg. 158

1]ש֯ו֯ ת֯[
2]פ֯ר כמב[

Frg. 159

1]לו֯יר֯[
2]ם [

Frg. 160

1]צ֯ו֯ [
2]מ֯ר֯י֯◦[

Frg. 161

1]י֯מס◦[
2]בוד֯[

Frg. 162

1]◦מ֯◦[
2]◦דם[

Frg. 163

1]ר֯ם ל֯[
2]ע ו֯◦[

Frg. 164

1]ו֯ב ו◦[
2]◦ לא֯[

Frg. 165

1]◦◦ז֯ר֯עמ֯[
2]ב֯ם ל◦[

Frg. 166

1 [א◦[
2]פ֯לא ◦[
3]◦[

Frg. 150

1. A]men [

Frg. 154

1.]from then [

Frg. 156

2.]open [

Frg. 157

1.]and righteousness[

Frg. 166

2.]wonder [

Frg. 165

1.] their seed[

Frg. 167

1]ה֯[
2]הגבו֯[

Frg. 168

1]מו ול֯◦[
2]◦[

Frg. 169

1 ב]רוך[
2]בע◦[

Frg. 170

1]אכו֯[
2]◦א֯[

Frg. 171

1]צכם[
2]ש֯ר֯[

Frg. 172

1]◦◦◦[
2]מים ש◦[

Frg. 173

1]◦ון ול֯◦◦[
2]◦מׄה [

Frg. 174

1]מ֯ו֯[
2]שפט֯[

Frg. 175

1]את◦[
2]ה ◦[

Frg. 176

1 א]ל֯והי֯[
2]י֯◦◦[

Frg. 177

1]◦ונו◦[
2]ראי֯[

Frg. 178

1]◦◦כת [
2]◦◦◦א֯ות֯[

Frg. 179

1 ג]ב֯ו֯ר֯ת֯[
2]◦ כו֯[

Frg. 180

1]ו֯◦[
2]הגע[

Frg. 181

1]◦[
2 ח]ט֯אות ◦[

Frg. 182

1 רוח]י ממזרי֯[ם
2]ל[ ]ם֯[

Frg. 183

1]◦ ימׄ◦◦ [
2]◦[ ]ל[

Frg. 184

1]ב֯ענ֯◦◦[
2]◦ ◦ל◦[

Frg. 185

1]◦◦◦◦א֯[
2]◦◦[

Frg. 186

1]ב֯י֯נת[
2]◦ ◦◦[

Frg. 187

1]◦◦◦או֯[
2 א]ל֯[ו]ה֯י[

Frg. 169

1. B]lessed[

Frg. 171

1.] your [

Frg. 176

1. G]od[

Frg. 179

1. s]trength of[

Frg. 182

1. spirit]s of the bastards[

Frg. 181

2. s]ins [

Frg. 186

1.]understanding of[

Frg. 187

2. G]o[d

Frg. 188

1]◦[
2] יהל֯[
3]◦◦[

Frg. 189

1]◦גע◦[
2] ב◦[

Frg. 190

1]◦י֯ ◦◦[
2]◦ם [

Frg. 191

1]ל֯◦[ ]ל֯ו֯א֯[
2]מ֯י֯רא֯[

Frg. 192

1] ה֯נ֯ורא[
2]ל◦[

Frg. 193

1]◦ים ו[
2]◦לל◦[

Frg. 194

1]◦אוד֯ [
2]ל◦◦◦מ֯[

Frg. 195

1]עינים֯[
2]◦[

Frg. 196

1]◦[
2]שפ◦[

Frg. 197

1]◦ עמׄ[
2]ל[

Frg. 198

1]בו
2]◦

Frg. 199

1]שמי[
2]◦◦[

Frg. 200

1]תׄ מ֯[
2]◦ם [

Frg. 201

1]◦מׄותׄ[
2]ת֯◦ ◦[

Frg. 202

1]קׄכה֯[
2]◦ה֯[

Frg. 203

1]כ֯ול כ[
2]◦מ֯◦[

Frg. 204

1] אש[

Frg. 205

1]◦[
2]◦◦◦סה֯[

Frg. 206

1] ה[

Frg. 207

1]איר[

Frg. 208

1]כבוד֯[

Frg. 209

1]ע֯ב[

Frg. 191

1.]not[
2.]cause to fear[

Frg. 192

1.] awesome[

Frg. 195

1.]eyes[

Frg. 203

1.]all [

Frg. 202

1.] your [

Frg. 208

1.]glory[

Frg. 210

1]עׄלי [

Frg. 211

1]לב◦[

Frg. 212

1]בׄוׄ משׁ[

Frg. 213

1]◦עׄל◦[

Frg. 214

1 [א◦]

Frg. 215

1]◦צׄ◦[

6Q**18** (6QpapHymn) ed. M. Baillet, *DJD* III

Frg. 1

1 מׄ[
2 וא[
3 אב[
4 ידׄ◦[
5 תרוע]ה
6 להכני]ע
7 הוי[

Frg. 2

1]◦[
2]חׄיׄיׄ נצח וכבׄ]וד
3]וׄל חושך ואפ]לה
4 אל ח]ושך תשוקתנׄ]ו
5]לׄחי עולמים ויהי[
6]◦[ ] עד שמח[
7]מר בן ישחק [
8]בתשבחׄות ע]ולמים
9]ל[

Frg. 3

1]◦[
2]ת עולמים[
3]בבליעל ו[

Frg. 4

1 [אילים א[
2]וׄלי לוא [
3]לׄ[ ]יׄפלוׄ ל[

6Q**18** (6QpapHymn) trans. N. Gordon

Frg. 1

2. and [

4. hand [
5. shou[t
6. to subd[ue
7. Woe[

Frg. 2

2.]eternal life and glo[ry
3.] darkness and glo[om
4. to the d]arkness of ou[r] desire[
5.]for eternal life and it shall come to pass[
6.] [ ] until joy[
7.] son of Isaac [
8.]with e[ternal] praises[

Frg. 3

2.] eternal[
3.]with Belial [

Frg. 4

1.] rams [
2.] no [
3.]they shall fall [

Frg. 5

1]◦[ ]ל ומׄ◦[
2 מל]אכי צדק במע[
3 י]חׄזקו ברוח דעתׄ[
4 לעו]למים לוא יׄכׄלוׄ[

bottom margin

Frg. 6

1]◦[ ]עליוׄ[
2 ל]פני הד[
3]מׄושלים[
4]אמתו ל[
5]הלל 𐤀𐤋[

Frg. 7

1]◦[
2]את[
3]ם ל[
4]כׄל [
5]ל[

Frg. 8

1]ב𐤀𐤋 ישר]אל
2]◦ם ביום[
3]◦ל עלינו[
4 כ]ול מו[
5]◦ ◦[

Frg. 9

top margin

1]משטמה ב◦[

Frg. 10

1]םׄ מצ◦[
2]עד וא[
3 𐤀𐤋] להׄ[

Frg. 11

1]הזה [
2]בחרב[

Frg. 12

1]עׄ כבו]ד
2]◦שכה[
3]ל֯[

Frg. 13

1]וׄ א[
2]תׄ לע[
3] ורני א]ל

Frg. 14

1]◦◦◦ם [
2]קׄהלנו ב[
3]עליכה[

Frg. 15

1]וׄבׄ[
2]◦יח[
3]ה ◦[

Frg. 16

1]דׄ ◦[
2]◦ כיא[

Frg. 17

1]◦ עׄ[
2]לכׄוׄ[

Frg. 18

1]טח [
2]ל[

Frg. 19

1]חׄבל֯וׄ[

Frg. 5

1.] [ ] and [
2. an]gels of righteousness in [
3.]they [shall] hold fast to the spirit of knowledge[
4. for eter]nity, they shall not destroy[

Frg. 6

1.]upon him[
2. be]fore [
3.]rulers[
4.]his truth [
5.]praise **God**[

Frg. 7

4.]all [

Frg. 8

1.]by the **God** of Isra[el
2.] on the day[
3.] upon us[
4. a]ll [

Frg. 9

1.]Malevolence [

Frg. 10

3. **G]od** [

Frg. 11

1.]this [
2.]by sword[

Frg. 12

1.] glor[y

Frg. 13

3.] and shout t[o

Frg. 14

2.]our assembly [
3.]upon you[

Frg. 16

2.] for[

Frg. 19

1.]his destruction[

Frg. 20

1]ה ותפארת [

2]כיא לכה המ[

3]◦ת◦[ ]הׄןׄ ל◦[

Frg. 21

1]◦◦◦◦◦[

2]◦ׄי וׄרוחׄ[

Frg. 22

1]לׄגׄ◦[

Frg. 23

1]לוא [

Frg. 24

1]נׄוׄת [

Frg. 25

1]◦[

2]כׄה◦[

Frg. 26

1]◦ח[

Frg. 27

1]דׄ[

8Q**5** (8QHymn) ed. M. Baillet, *DJD* III

Frg. 1

top margin

1 [בשמכה] ג]בור אני מירא ומעׄ[

2]◦ני האיש הזה אשר הוא מבני ה◦[

3]הזׄה ומה תשביׄתׄו אורוׄ להׄ[ ]◦◦ל[

4]למׄ[ז]לות השמׄ[ים

Frg. 2

1]וׄבׄ[

2]◦ר וׄתׄשביׄ[

3]◦לׄתׄ יהוה ◦[

4]כׄה רבה למעלה מכולׄ[

5]◦מרדפׄוׄתׄ והמשפטים[

6]וׄכול הרוחות לפניכה ע]ומדות

bottom margin?

11Q**11** (11QapocrPs) ed. F. García Martínez, E. J. C. Tigchelaar, and A. S. van der Woude, *DJD* XXIII

Frg. 1

1]וה[

2]כב[

3] האׄ[

4]ם ע[

5]דם ◦[

Frg. 21

2.] and spirit[

Frg. 20

1.] and splendour [
2.]because for you [
3.] their [

Frg. 23

1.]not [

8Q**5** (8QHymn) trans. M. Wise, M. Abegg, and E. Cook

Frg. 1

1.] in Your name, [O M]ighty One, I intimidate and [
2.] this man, who is from the sons of [
3.] this [ ] and why do you cause his light to cease to [ ] [
4.]to the co[nste]llations of the heave[ns

Frg. 2

2.] and you cause [ ] to cease [
3.] LORD [
4.] exceedingly great above all[
5.] persecutors (?). And the judgements[
6.]and all the spirits are s[tanding] before You [

11Q**11** (11QapocrPs) trans. F. García Martínez, E. J. C. Tigchelaar, and A. S. van der Woude

6]סׄוכות ◦[
7]לם וׄ[

Frg. 2 Col. i

1]
2]ה
3]ת
4]◦יׄך

Frg. 2 Col. ii

5 ב[
6 את [
7 שבעים[
8 [ ]ל[

Frg. 3

1]◦[
2] למיׄם [
3]אחתׄ[

Frg. 4

1]תׄ[
2] וׄריק [

Col. I

2]וׄבוכהוׄ [
3]שבועהׄ[
4]בׄיהוה[
5]תׄנין [
6 א]תׄ הארׄ[ץ
7] משבׄ[יע
8]את ב[
9]הזואתׄ[
10]אׄת השד[
11]יׄשבׄ[

Col. II

1 [ ]שׄם[
2 [ ]הׄ שלומה[ ]ויקרׄ[א
3 [הרו]חותׄ[ ]והשדים [
4 [ ] אלהׄ [הש]דים וׄשׄ[ר המשט]מה
5 [א]שר[ ]לׄ תהוׄ[ם]ך
6 [ ]לש◦[ ]הׄגד]ול]וׄהי
7 [ ]◦◦[ ]עמוׄ תׄ◦וׄ רפואה
8 [על]שמך נשען וקרׄ[א
9 [יש]ראל החזק
10 [ביהוה אלוהי אלים אשר עשה] את השמים
11 [ואת הארץ ואת כול אשר בם א]שׄר הבדיל[בין]
12 [האור ובין החושך]◦ עדׄ[

Frg. 2 Col. ii

7. seventy[

Frg. 4

2.] and empty [

Frg. 3

2.] to the water [
3.]one[

Col. I

2.]and the one who weeps for him [
3.]oath[
4.]by YHWH[
5.]dragon [
6.] the ea[rth
7.] exor[cis]ing[

9.]this[
10.]the demon[
11.]he will dwell[

Col. II

2. [ ] Solomon,[ ] and he shall invo[ke
3. [the spi]rits, [ ]and the demons, [
4. [ ] These are [the de]mons. And the p[rince of enmi]ty
5. [w]ho [ ] the a[byss]
6. [ ] [ ]the gre[at]
7. [ ] [ ]his nation [ ] cure
8. [ ]relied [upon] your name. And invo[ke]
9. [Is]rael. Lean
10. [on YHWH, the God of gods, who made] the heavens
11. [and the earth, and all that is in them, w]ho separated[ ]
12. [light from darkness] [

Col. III

] [תה] [התהומ]ות
הארץ וׄ◦]   ה[ארץ מי ע]שה את האותות[
וׄאת המופ]תים האלה ב[ארץ יהוה הואׄ]ה אשר[
עשה את הׄ]אלה בגבור[תׄו משביע לכול מׄ]לאכיו[
]וא[תׄ כול זרׄ]ע הקודש [אשר הׄתׄ]י[צׄבו לפני]ו ויעיד א[ת
]כול הש[מׄים וׄ]את כול[הארץׄ] בהם [אשר יעׄשׄ]ו [על
]כול אי[שׄ חטא ועל כול אׄ]דם רשע ו[הׄם יודעים
]רזי פל[או אשר אינם]   [ה אם לוא
]ייראו [מלפני יהוה ל]   ו[להרוג נפש
]   [יהוה ויירא]ו את המכה ה[גדולה הזואׄ]ת
]וירדף א[חד מכם א]לף   [◦עבדיׄ יהו]ה[
]   ג[דׄוׄלה וׄ]   [רׄת]

Col. IV

]ו[גדול]   [משביע]
והגדול בׄ]   [תקיף ורׄ]
כול הארץ]   [השמים וׄ]
יככה יהוה מ]כה גדול[ה אשר לאבדך]
ובחרון אפו] ישלח [עליך מלאך תקיףׄ] לעשות[
]כול דב[רו אשר] בלוא[רחמ]ים[עליך אש]ר
]   [עׄל כול אלה אשרׄ] יורידו[ךׄ לתהום רבה
]ולשאול[התחתיה ומיׄ]   [◦כב וחשך
]בתהום ר[בׄה מואדה]לוא   ע[וׄד בארץ
]   [עד עולם ואׄ]   [בׄקללת האב]דון[
]   [חׄרון אף יׄ]הוה   ב[חושך בכׄ]ול[
]תעודות [תׄעניות]   [מתנתך
]   [לׄ] [◦]   [ה הׄ◦]

Col. V

] [◦]   [דׄ◦]   [◦]
אשרׄ]   [הׄפגוע]ים   [
נדבי א]   ר[פׄאל שלמ]ם אמן אמן סלה[*vacat*
לדויד עׄ]ל   ל[חׄש בשם יהו]ה קרא בכו[לׄ עת
אל הׄשמׄ]ים כי [יׄבוא אליך בליׄ]לה וא[מרתה אליו
מי אתה]הילוד מ[אדם ומזרע הקדׄ]ושי[םׄ פניך פני
]שו[וׄ וקרניׄךׄ קרני חל]ו[םׄ חושך אתה ולוא אור
]עו[ל ולוא צדקה]   [שׄר הצׄבׄה יהוה]יוריד[ך
]לשאו[ל תחתית]ויסגור דל[תי נחושת בׄ]אלה לו[א
]יעבור[אור ולוא] יאיר לך ה[שמש אש]ר יזרח[
על ה[צׄדיק לה]   ו[אמרתה ה]
] הצ[דיק לבואׄ]   [הׄרע לו ש]ד

Col. III

1. [ ] [ ]the depth[s
2. the earth and [the] earth. Who ma[de these portents]
3. and won[ders on the] earth? It is he, YHWH[who]
4. made [these through] his [strength,] who summons all [his] an[gels]
5. [and] all the [holy] see[d] to st[a]nd before [him, and calls as witness]
6. [all the hea]vens and[all] the earth[against them]who committe[d]against
7. [all me]n sin, and against all p[eople evil. But] they know
8. his [wonder]ful [secrets] which they do not [ ] If they do not
9. [refrain out of fear]of YHWH from[and] from killing,
10. [ ]YHWH and [t]he[y] will fear tha[t] great [blow.]
11. [O]ne among you [will chase after]a th[ousand] servants of YHW[H]
12. [g]reat and[ ] [

Col. IV

1. [and] great[ ]adjuring[
2. and the great [ ]powerful and [
3. all the earth[ ] the heavens and[
4. YHWH will strike you with a [grea]t b[low] to destroy you[
5. And in his fury[he will send]against you a powerful angel[to carry out]
6. his [entire comm]and, who[will not show] you mercy, wh[o
7. [ ]over all these, who[will bring] you [down] to the great abyss
8. [and to] the deepest [Sheol.] And [,] and it will be very dark
9. [in the gr]eat [abyss. No any]more on the earth
10. [ ]forever and [ ]by the curse of Ab[addon]
11. [ ]the fury of Y[HWH in] darkness for a[ll]
12. [periods of] humiliation [ ] your gift

Col. V

2. which[ ]the possessed[
3. the volunteers of [Ra]phael has healed [them. Amen, amen. Selah.] *vacat*
4. Of David. A[gainst An incanta]tion in the name of YHW[H. Invoke at an]y time
5. the heav[ens. When]he comes to you in the nig[ht,] you will [s]ay to him:
6. 'Who are you, [oh offspring of] man and of the seed of the ho[ly one]s? Your face is a face of
7. [delu]sion and your horns are horns of ill[us]ion, you are darkness and not light,
8. [injust]ice and not justice.[ ]the chief of the army, YHWH [will bring] you [down]
9. [to the] deepest [Sheo]l, [and he will shut the] two bronze [ga]tes th[rough which n]o
10. light [penetrates,] and [the] sun [will] not [shine for you] tha[t rises]
11. [upon the] just man to [And] you will say: [
12. [the j]ust man, to go[ ] a de[mon] mistreats him, [

13 [א]מת מח◦[אשר הצ]דקה לו[

14 [ ] ולֿ[ ]ל[ ]ה[

Col. VI

1 [ ]ג[ ]ד[ ]◦ ל[ ]◦ין

2 [ ]תו[ ]יה[ ]יה◦[ל]עֿולם

3 Ps 91 [את כול]בני בלֿ[יעל אמן אמן] סלה [1לדויד יושב]בסתר[עליון בצל] שדי

4 [יתלונן]2האומר [ליהוה מחסי] ומצודתֿ[י אלוהי] מבטח [אבטח] בו

5 [3כי ה]ואה יצילך מֿ[פח יקו]ש מדבר הֿוֿ[ות 4ב]אברתו יסך[לך]ותחת

6 [כנפ]יו תשכון חסדֿ[ו ע]לֿיך צנה וסוחרהֿ אמתו סלה *vac* 5לואֿ תירא

7 מפחד לילה מחץ יעוף יומם 6מקטב ישוד[צ]הרים מדבר[בא]פל

8 יהלך 7יפ[ו]ל מצדך אלף ור[בבה מי]מינך אל[יך לו]א יגע 8רק[תבי]ט

9 בעיניך[ותרא]הֿ שלום רשע[ים 9קר]את מח[סך]ת מחמדו[10לוא]

10 תרא[ה רעה ו]לוא יגע [נגע באה]ליך 11כ[י מלאכיו]יצוה לך

11 לשומ[רך בדרכי]ך 12על כפיםֿ[ישאונ]ך פן[תגוף בא]בן רגל[ך 13על]

12 פתן [ואפעה תד]רוך תרמו[ס כפיר] ותנין [14ביהוה ח]שקתה ו[יפלטך]

13 ו[ישגבך 16bויר]אך בישוע[תו סלה *vac*]*at* *v*]*aca*[*t*]

14 ויע[נו אמן אמן] סֿלה *vaca*]*t* *v*]*aca*[*t*]

15 [*v*]*aca*[*t* *v*]*aca*[*t*]

3. OMEN LISTS

4Q186 (4QHoroscope) ed. J. M. Allegro, *DJD* V (written in square, paleo-Hebrew, Greek, and cryptic characters in reverse order; see *DJD*)

Frg. 1 Col. i

1 ◦◦[

2 ה[

3 *vacat*[

4 ואיש אשר יהיה קֿ[

5 רחבים וֿגֿלגֿלים[

6 מעורבים ולוא שאר הֿיֿש[

13. [of tr]uth from [because] he has [jus]tice [
14. [ ] and [ ] [ ]

Col. VI

2. [ ] [ ] [ ] [for]ever
3. [all]the sons of Bel[ial. Amen, amen.] Selah. [[Ps 91:1]Of David. He that lives]in the shelter[of the Most High, in the shadow of] the Almighty
4. [he stays.][2]He who says [to YHWH: ‘My refuge] and [my] fortress,[my God] is the safety in which [I trust.]
5. [[3]For h]e will save you from [the net of the fow]ler, from the calam[itous] pestilence. [[4]With] his feathers he will cover[you]and under
6. his [wing]s you shall stay. [His] kindness [up]on you will be a shield, and his truth a breastplate. Selah. *vac* [5]You shall not fear
7. the dread of night or the arrow that flies by day, [6]the plague that rages at [no]on or the pestilence that [in dark]ness
8. proceeds. [7]A thousand will f[a]ll at your side, and t[en thousand at] your [ri]ght; [y]ou it shall [no]t strike. [8]Only,[look]
9. with your eyes,[and you will see] the retribution of the wicked [ones.] [9]You have [invok]ed [your] shel[ter,] his happiness.
10. [10]You will [not] see[evil, and a plague] will not strike [in] your [ten]ts. [11]F[or] he has commanded [his angels] concerning you
11. to gua[rd you on] your [paths.] [[12]They shall lift] you upon their palms, lest[you strike your] foot [against a st]one. [13] [Upon]
12. cobra [and viper shall you s]tep, you shall tramp[le lion] and dragon. [14]You have [lo]ved [YHWH] and [he will rescue you]
13. and [protect you [16b]and sh]ow you [his] salvation. [Selah] *va*[*cat v*]*aca*[*t*]
14. And [t]he[y] shall an[swer: Amen, amen.] Selah *va*[*cat* *v*]*aca*[*t*]
15. *v*]*aca*[*t* *v*]*aca*[*t*]

3. Omen Lists

4Q**186** (4QHoroscope) ed. J. M. Allegro with N. Gordon (see note in transcription)

Frg. 1 Col. i

3. *vacat*[
4. and a man who will become [
5. broad and rounded[
6. pleasing and not the flesh of [

Frg. 1 Col. ii

1]ג טמא
2]אבן צונם
3]איש עי[
4]◦◦ות וה[נ]ה֯ נ֯צ֯י֯[ו]ת
5 ושוקיו ארוכות ודקות ואצבעות רגליו
6 דקות וארוכות והואה מן העמוד השני
7 רוח לו בבית האור שש ושלוש בבור
8 החושך וזה הואה המולד אשר הואה ילוד עליו
9 ברגל השור עני יהיה וזה בהמתו שור

Frg. 1 Col. iii

1 וא◦ה[
2 וראושו[
3 מיראות[ ]ושניו רומות לאבר ואצבעות
4 ידיו ע֯בות ושוקיו עבות ומלאות [ש]ער לאחת
5 ואצבעות רגליו עבות וקצרות ורוח לו בבית
6 [החושך ש]מ֯ונה ואחת מבית האור וא֯י֯ש

Frg. 1 Col. iv

1]שמה אלה
2]יהיה תוך
3]ל[

Frg. 2 Col. i

1 סרכ◦[ע]י֯נ֯י֯ו בין שחורות וב[ין] ה֯ג֯מ֯ריות וזקנו
2 ממ◦[ ]והיאה תרגל ובת קולו עניה ושניו
3 דקות ויושבות על סרכמה והואה לוא ארוך
4 ולוא קצר והואה֯ ממי֯ל◦[ו]אצבעות ידיו דקות
5 וא֯ר֯ו֯[כ]ות ושוקיו חלקות וכפות רגליו *vac*
6 [ ]ל֯[ ]יושבות על סרכמה ורוח ל֯[ו
7 [ ]ע֯מוד השני שמונ֯ה וא[חת
8 [ ]מולדו ילוד הו[א]ה עליו
9 [ה]ואה בהבת֯ו ◦◦◦[
10 [ ]◦ני זות[
11 [ ]◦◦◦[ ]ל֯[

Frg. 2 Col. ii

1]הוא
2 מ]ע֯ורב
3]שלוג/גולש

Frg. 3

1 מבי [
2 בכת[
3]◦[ ]ו֯פי֯[

Frg. 1 Col. ii

1.] unclean
2.]granite
3.]a man of

5. and his thighs are long and thin, and his toes
6. are thin and long, and he is of the Second Vault.
7. He has six (parts) spirit in the House of Light, and three in the Pit of
8. Darkness. And this is the time of birth on which he is brought forth—
9. on the festival of Taurus. He will be poor; and this is his beast— Taurus.

Frg. 1 Col. iii

2. And his head[
3. terrifying [ ]and his teeth are elevated, and the fingers of
4. his hands are thick, and his thighs are thick and each covered with [h]air;
5. and his toes are thick and short. He has [ei]ght (parts) spirit in the House of
6. [Darkness] and one (part) from the House of Light. And a man

Frg. 1 Col. iv

1.]there. These
2.]he will be in the middle

Frg. 2 Col. i

1. order. His [ey]es are both black and glowing coals, and his beard
2. [ ] and it is curly. And the pitch of his speech (?) is subdued, and his teeth
3. are fine and well ordered. He is neither tall
4. nor short, and he is [and] the fingers of his hands are fine.
5. and tapering. His thighs are smooth and the soles of his feet *vac*
6. [ ]arranged in good order. [He] has of spirit [
7. [ ]Second Vault eight (parts) and o[ne]
8. [ ]his time of birth [at which] he is born [
9. [th]at is his beast [

Frg. 2 Col. ii

1.]he
2.]pleasing
3.]white as snow (*or*: flowing)

4Q**318** (4QZodiology and Brontology ar) ed. J. C. Greenfield and M. Sokoloff, *DJD* XXXVI

Col. IV

5] ב]־///
וב־/[///]

6] ב־//]/ ///
/// ובב ובב[/]

7]]ב֯ב///
//// ובב//// ////

8]בתולתא בב/// /// /// ובב־ מוזניא va[*cat*

9]תשרי ב/ וב// עקרבא ב/// וב//// קשתא וב///// וב/// /// וב/// ////] גדיא
ב//// ////

Col. VII

1 וב־/// וב־[/]/// ס֯רטנא ב־///// וב־/// /// אר֯י֯א֯ ב־/// //// //// וב־[//]//
////

2 בת֯ו֯לתא ב־/[/]֯ /// /// ובב ובב/ מוזניא בב// ו֯ב֯ב[/]// עקרבא בב////

3 ובב///// קש]תא[בב/// //[/] ובב//// /// ובב//// /[/// גדי]א֯ בב/[// /]//
///

4 ובב־ דול]א v[*acat* שבט ב/ וב//[נוני]א ב[///
ו]ב֯////

5 [דכר]א֯ ב///// וב[/// /// וב/]///// תורא ב///[/ //// וב/// /// /// תאומיא]
ב־֯

6 [וב־/] סרטנא ב־//[/ וב]־/// וב־//// אריא [ב־///// וב־/// /// בתולתא]

7 ב־/// //// וב־//// //// מוזניא ב־/// /// /// ב[ב ובב/ ע]ק֯רבא בב//

8 ו֯בב/// ק֯שתא בב//// ובב///// גדיא ב֯ב֯[/// /// וב]ב֯/// //// /// ובב////
////

9 דולא בב/// ///[/]֯// ובב־ נוניא *vacat*

Col. VIII

1 אדר ב / וב// דכרא ב/// וב//// תורא ב///֯[// וב/// /// וב/// //// תאומיא]

2 ב//// //// ב/// /// /// ס֯ר֯ט֯נ֯א֯ [ב־ וב־/ א]ריא ב־// ו[ב־/// וב־////]

3 בתול[ת]א ב־/// // וב[־/// /// מוזניא ב־]/[/]/ //// ב־////[//// עקרבא]

4 ב֯[־//]/ /// /// ובב <ובב/> קשת֯[א בב// ובב/// ג]דיא [בב////
ובב/////]

5 דולא֯ בב/// /// ובב[/// //// ובב//// ///]/ נו[ניא בב/// /// /// ובב־]

6 דכרא *vacat* [אם בתורא] ירעם מסבת על[

7 [ו]ע֯מל למדינתא וחרב֯ [בד]רת מלכא ובמדינתא ב[

8 להוא ולערביא [ ]א כפן ולהוון בזזין אלן בא[לן vac[*at*

9 אם בתאומיא י֯רעם דחלה ומרע֯ מנכריא ומ[

4Q**318** (4QZodiology and Brontology ar) trans. J. C. Greenfield and M. Sokoloff

Col. IV

5. [in]13 and in 14
6. [in 1]9 and in 20 and in 2[1
7. [ ]in 27 and in 28
8. [Virgo, in 29 and in 30 Libra *vac*]*at*
9. [Tishri, in 1 and in 2 Scorpio, in 3 and in 4 Sagittarius, and in 5 and in 6 and in 7] Capricorn, in 8

Col. VII

1. and in 13 and in 14 Cancer, in 15 and in 16 Leo, in 17 and in 18
2. Virgo, in 19 and in 20 and in 21 Libra, in 22 and in 23 Scorpio, in 24
3. and in 25 Sagitt[arius,] in 26 and in 27 and in 2[8 Capricor]n, in 29
4. and in 30 Aquari[us. *v*]*acat* Shevaṭ, in 1 and in 2 [Pisc]es, in [3 and] in 4
5. [Ari]es, in 5 and in [6 and in] 7 Taurus, in 8 [and in 9 Gemini,] in 10
6. [and in 11] Cancer, in 12[and in] 13 and in 14 Leo, [in 15 and in 16 Virgo,]
7. in 17 and in 18 Libra, in 19 in [20 and in 21 S]corpio, in 22
8. and in 23 Sagittarius, in 24 and in 25 Capricorn, in 2[6, in] 27 and in 28
9. Aquarius, in 29 and in 30 Pisces. *vacat*

Col. VIII

1. Adar: In 1 and in 2 Aries, in 3 and in 4 Taurus, in 5 [and in 6 and in 7 Gemini,]
2. in 8 in 9 Cancer, [in 10 and in 11 L]eo, in 12 and[in 13 and in 14]
3. Virg[o], in 15 and in [16 Libra, in 1]7 in 18 [Scorpio,]
4. in [1]9 and in 20, and <in 21> Sagitt[arius, in 22 and in 23 Cap]ricorn, [in 24 and in 25]
5. Aquarius, in 26 and in 2[7 and in 28] Pi[sces, in 29 and in 30]
6. Aries. *vacat* [If in Taurus] it thunders (there will be) *msbt* against[=
7. [and] affliction for the province, and a sword [in the cou]rt of the king, and in the province, [
8. will be. And to the Arabs [ ], hunger, and they will plunder each oth[er *vac*]*at*
9. If in Gemini it thunders, (there will be) fear and sickness from the foreigners and *m*[

Unidentified Fragments

Frg. 1

1 ב//]/ /// /// וב[ד

Frg. 2

1 /]/ וב//[/
2]ל[

Frg. 3

1 [/// ///\]

Frg. 4

1]בב̱[
2]בב̱///[

Frg. 5

1 /]/ ובב̱[//
2 [ ]

4. MAGIC BOOK

4Q**560** (4QExorcism ar) ed. D. Penney and M. Wise

Frg. 1 Col. i

1] ולׄבב וׄכׄ◦[[
2] מׄילדתה מרדות ילדן פקר באיש ש]יד [
3 [אנה מומה לך כל] עלל בבשרא לחלח<ל>יא דכרא וחלחלית<א> נקבתא
4 [אנא מומה לכן בשם יהוה הנ]שא עואן ופשע אשא ועריה ואשת לבב
5]ואסיר לבהלה בליליא בחלמין או בימממ]ה בשנא פרכ<יא> דכר<א> ופ<ר>כית<א> נקבתא מחתוׄרי
6] ר]שׄיעין◦◦◦[ ]◦◦[ ]ל[ ]◦◦◦
7]]◦◦◦[

Frg. 1 Col. ii

1]
2 קודמוׄ]הי
3 ו◦◦◦]
4 קודמוהי וממׄ]
5 ואנה רוח מומה [לך די
6 אומיתכ רוחה [די
7 עׄלׄ ארעא בעננין [
8] ל[*vacat* ◦]

Frg. 2

1]כן [
2]נין שנין תדׄול ות]

4. Magic Book

4Q**560** (4QExorcism ar) trans. M. Wise

Frg. 1 Col. i

1.]heart [
2.] the midwife, the punishment of childbearers, an evil madness, a de[mon
3. [I adjure all you who en]ter into the body, the male Wasting-demon and the female Wasting-demon
4. [I adjure you by the name of the YHWH, "*He Who re*]*moves iniquity and transgression*" (Exod 34:7), O Fever-demon and Chills-demon and Chest Pain-demon
5. [You are forbidden to disturb by night in dreams or by da]y during sleep, O male Shrine-spirit and female Shrine-spirit, O you demons who breach
6. [walls w]icked [

Frg. 1 Col. ii

2. before h[im
3. and [
4. before him and [
5. And I, O spirit, adjure [you that you
6. I adjure you, O spirit, [that you
7. On the earth, in clouds [

Frg. 2

2.] changed, you will diminish (?) and [

4Q561 (4QPhysiognomy/Horoscope ar) ed. M. Wise

Frgs. 10 + 6 (Col. I)

5 [◦◦]
6 [לׄשמקמיק] [◦]
7 כ]דרי וסגלגל להוׄ[ה
8 להוו]ןׄ לה שער רשה]
9 [כתפה]
10 [להוון על]
11 [ולא רב]

Frgs. 5 + 1 (Col. II)

5 בׄ] [
6 די אפׄהׄ בׄין [אריך לק]צׄר יׄ[ד]ין
7 פתין שקוהי [המו בין] מתקן
8 לעבׄין כׄף רגלוׄ[הי תהוה ע]בה ולא
9 שג[יא] לה רגלה [ ] מׄן דׄיׄ
10 [ ]לׄתׄ ופקׄ[ ] לא [ ]
11 [ל]מסף ◦[ ] דפ[נה]
12 [ ]◦◦◦[ ]◦[ ]

Frgs. 4 i + 7 + 8 (Col. III)

1 [ו]הי מערבין ולא שגיא עינוה[י]
2 בין אׄורין לאכומן אפה נגיד
3 שׄפיר שנוהי שוין ודקנה
4 דקׄ להוהׄ [ו]לא שׄ[ג]יא אברוהי
5 [מ]מחקי[ן וה]מׄ[ו בין] דקין לעבׄי[ן]
6 [ור]וח לה
7 [ ] עקא
8 [ומן די יהוין לה] שׄערן עׄבׄות
9 ושגיאן [ ]
10 [ ]◦◦ת עב [ ]

Frg. 4 ii (Col. IV)

1 להוה קל[ה]
2 קׄלׄ תׄמלי ותׄ[קף אפה לא קצר]
3 [ול]אׄ אריך [והו]אׄ [ ]
4 [ו]שער דקנה שגׄ[יא ואברוהי]
5 להוון בין עבין ל[דקין]
6 ואנון קטינׄי[ן אצבעת ידוהי]
7 כעבין טפרוהׄ[י]
8 לקומתה ו[ ]

4Q561 (4QPhysiognomy/Horoscope ar) trans. M. Wise

Frgs. 10 + 6 (Col. I)

6. [Anyone whose is between] and reddish-yellow [
7. [whose forehead (?)] will b[e] gl]obular and round [
8. his [will b]e [ ]. The hair of his head [
9.] his shoulder [
10.] they will be; concerning [his spirit (?)
11.] but not a great man [

Frgs. 5 + 1 (Col. II)

6. whose nose is between [long and sh]ort, whose ha[n]ds
7. are bro[a]d, whose thighs [are between] well-formed
8. and thick, the sole of whose fee[t will be th]ick but not
9. exce[edingly so,], whose foot [ ] because
10. [ ] not [ ]
11. [to] come to an end [ ]

Frgs. 4 i + 7 + 8 (Col. III)

1. [Anyone] whose [ ] is medium and not extreme, whose eyes are
2. neither light nor dark, whose nose is extended
3. (and) attractive, whose teeth are even, whose beard
4. will be sparse [but] not ex[tre]mely so, whose limbs
5. are [s]mooth [and a]r[e between] thin and thick
6. [ ] He will possess a [sp]irit [characterized by (?)]
7. [He will suffer (?)] oppression.
8. [Anyone whose body] hair [will be] thick
9. and extensive [

Frg. 4 ii (Col. IV)

1. [Anyone whose] will be [, whose] voice [ ]
2. a voice full (?) and st[rong, whose nose is neither short]
3. [no]r long, [and] is [ ]
4. [and] the hair of whose beard is extremely th[ick, whose limbs]
5. will be between thick and [thin]
6. and are delicat[e, the fingers of whose hands]
7. are rather thick, whose fingernails are [ ]
8. Regarding his height and [ ]

Frg. 3 (Col. V)

[ ]◦[ ]רׄה ◦[
[ומ]תקף [ר]בׄתׄה רבאׄ [
ומתׄקׄף לקדׄמין ל◦[
וירפון [ ] ויהכון [
ישתארון עמה וׄאׄ[
עלוהי למהך באתרׄ[
[מ]נהון ומתקף להוׄן [
[ח]לפה כרגי עׄמׄלׄ[הון
ותהך [ו]תׄטשא בלבׄ[ב
[ט]הרין [ו]שפנין טׄה[ר
[י]שכחׄה עדנא תמׄ[
◦◦לׄ[ ] דכרין ויחזא[
[ ]ם בערימן ור◦[
[ ]לה למאל[פה ו]ירשמׄ[
[ ]וׄלמאׄ[לפה

Unidentified Fragments

Frg. 8

]◦ תתחמדון [
]◦תו◦[

Frg. 2

]◦לה ל[
]עׄד קמׄ[
] די

Frg. 11

ו]הׄמו
דקנה] תרגל
] וׄלאׄ

Frg. 3 (Col. V)

2. [and st]rengthening the [an]ointing, the great [
3. and strengthening first of all [
4. but they will forsake [ ] and they will go[
5. [a remnant] will be left with him and [
6. upon him to go after [
7. [fr]om them and strengthening them [
8. [pa]ssing, the taxes of [their] labor [
9. and you will go [and] hide in the heart of [
10. [p]ure [and] a pur[e] turtledove [
11. he [will] find the time [
12. [ ]rams, and he will see [
13. [ ] in heaps and [
14. [ ] ito lear[n it and] he will inscribe [
15. [ ]and to le[arn it

Unidentified Fragments

Frg. 8

1.] you will rejoice [

Frg. 2

2.] until [
3. Any]one [whose

Frg. 11

1. and th]ey are
2. whose beard] is curly
3.] but not [

E. Documentary Texts

1. Documentary Texts Concerned with Religious Law

4Q**340** (4QList of Netinim) ed. M. Broshi and A. Yardeni, *DJD* XIX

Frg. 1

1 אלה הנתינ[ים]
2 אשר כונו בׄשׁׄ[מותיהם]
3 יתרא ועקו◦[ ]
4 הסׄסרו[ ]
5 הרתו[ ]
6 קוׄוך טו[ביה ?]

4Q**477** (4QRebukes Reported by the Overseer) ed. E. Eshel, *DJD* XXXVI

Frg. 1

1]◦◦◦ הג◦[
2 ל]הׄזׄכיר את ל נעוׄתׄםׄ ואׄ[ת
3]◦ [ ] [

Frg. 2 Col. i

top margin

1]ים אנשי ה[יחד
2] נפשמה ולהוכיח אׄ[ת
3 מ]חׄני הרבים על[
4]◦◦ע◦ל [ ] [

Frg. 2 Col. ii

1 רׄ[
2 אשר[הואה וגם אש]ר היה מרע[ ]
3 הׄרׄבים [ו]את יוחנן בן אׄרׄ[הוכיחו אשר]
4 הואה קצר אפיםׄ [ ] עמו ◦[ ] העון עמו וגם רוח פארה עמׄ[ו
5 [ ]ה הואה ◦◦◦ים אשר[ ] ־ *vac* ואת חנניה נותוס הוכיחו אשר הואה[
6 [להע]כיר את רוח היחׄ[ד ו]גם לערב א[ת]אל[
7 [ ]◦פ הׄוׄכׄ[י]חׄו אׄשר רוע ◦[ ]עׄמו וגם אשר איננו ח◦[
8 [ ]ורו וגם אוהב את שיר בשרו [ולא
הוכיחו[

E. Documentary Texts

1. Documentary Texts Concerned with Religious Law

4Q340 (4QList of Netinim) trans. M. Broshi and A. Yardeni

Frg. 1

1. These are the *netin*[*im*]
2. Who were designated by [their] n[ames]
3. Yitra and *ʿqw* [
4. *hmsmrw*[
5. *hrtw*[
6. *qwwk* To[biah ?]

4Q477 (4QRebukes Reported by the Overseer) trans. E. Eshel

Frg. 1

2.]to make their offences remembered, and th[e

Frg. 2 Col. i

1.] the people of the [*Yaḥad*
2.] their soul and to rebuke [
3. the c]amp of the *Rabbim*, on[

Frg. 2 Col. ii

2. which[he and also because] he was an evildoer[ ]
3. the *Rabbim* [and] Yoḥanan son of *ʾr*[was rebuked, because]
4. he is short-tempered [ ] with him [ ] the offence is with him and also haughty spirit (is) with [him
5. [ ] he that[ ] ר *vac* And Ḥananiah Notos was rebuked because he[
6. [to dis]turb the spirit of the *Yaḥ*[*ad* and] also to share [ ]with[
7. [ ] they repr[o]ached because bad [ ]with him and also because he is not [
8. [ ] and he also loves his close kin [and (therefore) did not rebuke him]

9] [*vac* ד ואת חנניה בן שמ[עון
הוכיחו]
10 [אשר הואה וג]ם אוהב את טוב̇[הצואר]

Frg. 3

1] הוכיחו[

2. ACCOUNTS

4Q**352** (4QpapAccount of Cereal B ar or heb) ed. A. Yardeni, *DJD* XXVII

Frg. a

1]ד̇//[
2]כ \//[
3]כ //[
4 \ כ]//
5 \ כ /[/
6 \ כ /[/
7 \ כ/[/
8 \ כ]//
9 \ כ]//

Frg. b

1]כ /[
2 \ כ /[
3 \ כ [

Frg. c

1]◦[
2]ד ◦[
3]ד [

4Q**352a** (4QpapAccount A ar or heb) ed. A. Yardeni, *DJD* XXVII

Frg. a

1 //\// ◦[

Frg. b

1 \\//◦[
2 ◦[

Frg. c

1]\\//◦[
2 ◦[

Frg. d

1]\//

Frg. e

1]◦[
2]//\// [

9. [ ] *vac* ר And Ḥananiah son of Šim[ʿon was rebuked]
10. [because he and al]so he chooses the fair[neck

Frg. 3
1.] they rebuked[

2. ACCOUNTS

4Q**353** (4QpapAccount of Cereal or Liquid ar or heb) ed. A. Yardeni, *DJD* XXVII

1]° ק \\//

4Q**354** (4QAccount B ar or heb) ed. A. Yardeni, *DJD* XXVII

1]אֿ \// \\//

4Q**355** (4QAccount C ar or heb) ed. A. Yardeni, *DJD* XXXVI

Frg. a

1]מלֿ֗ן [ ]כֿ
2]°רא[א]° \/ \//[(?)
3]°°°ספ ס ק כ[ ] \/ מ[(?)
4]°°°[

Frg. b

1]°[(?)]°[
2]ריֿ°[
3]°°[

4Q**356** (4QAccount D ar or heb) ed. A. Yardeni, *DJD* XXVII

1]שאֿר°° °[
2]מן עֿלימֿאֿ ר ר\/ [

4Q**357** (4QAccount E ar or heb) ed. A. Yardeni, *DJD* XXVII

1]°א \// °[
2]° בֿבֿר[

4Q**358** (4QpapAccount F? ar or heb) ed. A. Yardeni, *DJD* XXVII

1] °°[
2]° לק°[
3]\//בֿ°[
4]°°° [

4Q**351** (4QAccount of Cereal A ar) ed. A. Yardeni, *DJD* XXVII

Col. i

1 י]הוחנ◦[?
2]חנטין ק ///\

Col. ii

3 ◦[
4 ק // [

4Q**350** (4QAccount gr) ed. H. Cotton, *DJD* XXXVI

1 *traces*
2]ορ γ \
3] δ \
4]. γ \
5]. ι \
6]. δ \
7]ƨ δ
8].βω̣ ƨ ς
9].π̣ε̣π̣ κ̂λ \
10]*traces* .ο .
11]α..υ ƨ ζ *traces*
12]α.[

3. VARIOUS DOCUMENTARY TEXTS

Kh.Q. Ostracon **1** ed. F. M. Cross and E. Eshel, *DJD* XXXVI

1 בשנת שתים לׄ◦[[
2 בירחו נתן חני ב]ן [
3 לאלעזר בן נחמׄני[[
4 את חסדי מחולנ[[
5 מהׄיום הזׄה ל<ע>ולׄ]ם [
6 וא<ת> תחומׄי הבית ו[[
7 והתאנים הזׄי]תים [
8 וכמׄלותו ליׄחׄדׄ[[
9 וׄחׄנׄיׄ [[
10 לו את חׄסׄ]די [

3. Various Documentary Texts

Kh.Q. Ostracon **1** trans. F. M. Cross and E. Eshel

1. In year two of the [ ]
2. in Jericho, Ḥōnî so[n of] gave
3. to ᵓElᶜazar son of Naḥămanî[ ]
4. Ḥisday from Ḥōlôn[ ]
5. from this day to perpetui[ty]
6. the boundaries of the house and[ ]
7. and the figs, the ol[ives (?),]
8. when he fulfills (his oath) to the community[ ]
9. and Ḥōnî (?) [ ]
10. to him Ḥis[day (?)]

11 ואת ◦◦◦] [
12 וביד ◦◦◦◦ה] [
13 לגׄ◦נן [[
14 חסדיׄ עבד חׄ]ני מן]
15 חלון [[

bottom margin

4Q**346** (4QDeed of Sale ar) ed. A. Yardeni, *DJD* XXVII

Frg. a

1 ◦] מן ◦] למעבד]
2 בה כל]די יצבה ◦]
3] שמען מן כל [מן נכסי
4 ודי אקנה מ]ן יומא דנה ועד עלם
5 וש◦◦]
6 למנשה ו/כש◦]

Frg. b

1]ה ◦◦]
2]◦ב/כ◦]

Frg. c

Two illegible lines

Frg. d

1]◦ך וכל ◦]

Frg. e

1]◦תה מן ◦]

Frg. f

Two illegible lines

Frg. g

1] בׄתר צ]

4. DOCUMENTARY TEXTS TOO FRAGMENTARY FOR FURTHER CATEGORIZATION

6Q**26** (6QpapAccount or Contract) ed. M. Baillet, *DJD* III;*for these symbols/letters, see *DJD* III

Frg. 1

1 הן על]
2 ◦לׄנׄ◦]
3 הלוׄ קׄ]
4 ** נׄ]
5 שׄ◦]

Frg. 2

1 אנ]שׄיׄ בׄיׄתׄ]
2]‚ *///]
3]‚ *ר]
4]◦/◦]

11. and the [ ]
12. And into the hand of [ ]

14. Ḥisday servant of Ḥ[ōnî (?) from]
15. Ḥōlôn [

4Q**346** (4QDeed of Sale ar) trans. A. Yardeni

Frg. a

1. [ ] of/from [to do]
2. with it anything]that he desires [
3.] Shimᶜon from all [from my property
4. and (from anything) that I shall acquire fr[om today and forever
5. and [
6. to Menashe and [

Frg. e

1.] from/of [

Frg. d

1.] and all [

Frg. g

1.] after [

4. Documentary Texts Too Fragmentary for Further Categorization

6Q**26** (6QpapAccount or Contract) trans. M. Wise, M. Abegg, and E. Cook

Frg. 2

1. me]n of [the] household[
2.] 1 s(eah) 3[
3.]1 seah 10[
4.] 1 [

Frg. 1

1. if on[

3. behold [

Frg. 3

1]◦◦◦ תׄעׄ◦[

2]נׄפׄשׁך ◦[

3]◦◦◦◦[

4]◦◦[

Frg. 4

1]גׄם[

2]* לׄנׄפׄשׁ[

3]◦ד מ[

Frg. 5

1]◦ם̇[

2]◦◦[

Frg. 6

1]◦[

2]◦בר[

3]◦◦◦[

Frg. 7

1]נׄ◦[

2]◦◦[

Frg. 8

1]וׄבׄ◦[

2]ל[

Frg. 9

1]◦*[

2]◦עה[

Kh.Q. Ostracon **2** ed. F. M. Cross and E. Eshel, *DJD* XXXVI

1]ק שׁ[

2]עת הו[

3 יהוס[פ בנ נתן]

4 ב[ניו מעין]

4Q**345** (4QDeed A ar or heb) ed. A. Yardeni, *DJD* XXVII

Recto
Upper Version

1 ב◦◦◦ באלול שׁ[נת]

2 יׄצׄ˹ו˺אׄהׄואׄ ◦[ ]

3 [ ]

4 ◦◦◦◦◦[ ]

5 בכסף˹ד˺ בד [ ]

6 ישׁוע אׄמׄר אׄיך ◦◦נ[ ]

7 ◦◦◦◦◦◦◦◦◦◦[ ]

8 ◦◦נׄש◦◦◦◦[ ]

9 ◦◦ס̇◦אׄ◦[ ]

Frg. 4

2.] to soul of[
3.] 10 [

Frg. 3

2.]your soul [

Frg. 6

2.] son[

Kh.Q. Ostracon **2** trans. F. M. Cross and E. Eshel

1.]*q š*[
2.]ᶜ*t hw*[
3. Jose]ph son of Nathan[
4. his [s]ons from ᶜEin[Gedi (?)

4Q**345** (4QDeed A ar or heb) trans. A. Yardeni

Recto
Upper Version

1. On the of Elul, y[ear ,]

5. for 30 silver q(uarters)/*d*(*enarii*)[ ]
6. Yeshuaᶜ said, as [ ]

Lower Version

10 ב∘∘∘ [באלול]

11 ∘∘[ ]

12 מן ∘∘∘∘[ ]

13 ∘∘ ודיר ע ∘[ ]

14 שטר מ∘[ ]

15 [ ]ל[ ]

16 ∘[ ]∘[ ]

17 ∘∘∘∘[ ]

18 ∘ך ו[ ]

19 ∘∘[ ]ל[ ]

Verso

20 ה[ו]שעיה בר[ ]∘∘ על נפש[ה כתבה]

21 ישמעאל בר ש[מ]עון ממוהא

4Q**348** (4QDeed B heb?) ed. A. Yardeni, *DJD* XXVII

Recto
Upper Version

1]מנח[ם]∘ל∘∘ ∘∘מח∘∘ ∘∘ בר אל[עזר

2 דֻ ∘∘∘ ∘∘[ ]∘∘∘ ∘∘∘ ∘∘∘∘∘ ∘∘∘∘ [

3 ד ∘∘∘[ ]∘∘ א∘ה∘∘[

4]∘ל∘∘∘∘∘∘∘ [ ]ל[ ]∘∘ע ב[

5]∘∘∘∘∘ ושמעון ∘∘∘∘∘∘∘ל∘[

6]∘∘∘ ∘∘∘∘ ∘∘∘∘∘∘∘∘∘ ∘∘ ∘∘∘[

7]ן א∘∘∘∘ ∘∘אק∘∘ ∘∘∘∘∘∘∘∘ ∘∘[

8]∘∘∘∘∘∘∘∘[ ]ל[ ]ל∘∘ר∘∘∘[

9]∘∘ ∘∘∘∘יהוחנן בר יהוסף ∘[

10–12 (*signatures?*)

Lower Version

13]∘∘∘∘וס כוהן גדול ∘∘∘[

14 בר י]הוסף מתתיה בר שמעון אלעזר [בר

15 בר] חנן אלעזר בר שמעון בר חוני ∘[

16]∘ ב[ר י]הוחנן יהוסף בר ∘∘∘∘[

17]∘מלה פתחנו ∘∘∘ [ ]∘∘ מנש[ה

18]שמעון משוק הקורות ∘∘ח∘ ∘∘[

19]∘∘∘∘ה למ∘∘ה[ ]∘∘לה∘[ ]∘∘[

20]∘ במ∘צמ∘ה א∘∘[

21]∘∘∘∘∘[

Lower Version

10. On the [of Elul,]

12. of/from [ ]

14. deed (of?) [ ]

(remains of five more lines)
(continuation missing)

Verso

20. H[o]shaʿyah son of[ ] , for [him]self [he wrote it].
21. Yishmaʿʾel son of Shi[m]ʿon, at his word.

4Q**348** (4QDeed B heb?) trans. A. Yardeni

Recto

Upper Version

1. Menaḥe[m(?)] son of ʾEl[ʿazar(?)
2.]20 [ ] [
3.]10 [ ] [

5.] and Shimʿon [

8.] [ ] 10(?)[
9.] Yehoḥanan son of Yehosef (?) [

10–12. (signatures?)

Lower Version

13.] *os* High Priest [
14. son of Ye]hosef, Mattatyah son of Shimʿon, ʾElʿazar [son of
15. son of] Ḥanan, ʾElʿazar son of Shimʿon, son of Ḥoni [
16.] so[n of Ye]hoḥanan, Yehosef son of [
17.] we have opened (?) [ ] , Menash[eh(?)
18.]Shimʿon from the Beam Market/street, [

4Q**359** (4QpapDeed C? ar or heb) ed. A. Yardeni, *DJD* XXVII

Frg. a

1]מתת בר חזק[
2 ◦[ ]◦◦[ ]◦[

Frg. b

ז
ד
1]◦חת ר◦[
ו
י

4Q**347** (4QpapDeed F ar [= part of XḤev/Se **32**]) ed. A. Yardeni, *DJD* XXVII

Recto
XḤev/Se **32** = lines 1–4
4Q**347** = lines 4–7

1]ב לכס]לו שנת תמנה ב◦[
2]ד̇י/רו בר̇ת לוי מן נ̇ וד/יר[
3]מסמרא א/ש כפ̇ רב◦[
4]◦ חד̇ מ̇ן בי/רר תד/הו סה ד/ר[
5 פ]לגות ט̇ב̇א[
6]◦כ/דה שותפות י/ו◦◦[
7]◦◦◦ [

4Q**344** (4QDebt Acknowledgement ar) ed. A Yardeni, *DJD* XXVII

1 [ ]ס̇ף ל̇ש̇ הו̇מ/ס/זז ◦◦◦◦ ש/אל̇פ̇י̇ ◦[ ]
2 [ ]עמי אנה אלעזר בר ה̇סף[ ]
3 [ ]◦◦ן̇ ש̇ב̇עה כ̇ ו/מ/ס ◦◦◦[ ]
4 [ ]◦◦ ◦שטמ/קתה ב/מ̇ה̇ ◦◦ל ◦◦◦◦◦[ ]
5 [תשלמתא מן נ]כ̇סי ודי אקנה לקבל<ד>ך
6 אלעזר בר יהוסף על נפשה כ̇ת̇ב̇[ה]
7 [ ]י̇ה̇ו̇ס̇[ף]
8]◦[ ]◦◦◦◦[ ]

4Q**359** (4QpapDeed C? ar or heb) trans. A. Yardeni

Frg. a

1.]Mattat son of Ḥazaq[

4Q**347** (4QpapDeed F ar [= part of XḤev/Se **32**]) trans. A. Yardeni

Recto

1. [On the of Kis]lev, year eight, at [
2.] , daughter of Levi, from [
3.]the nail (?), saddler/saddler/shoemaker [
4.] one of [

5. h]alf (?) the good[
6.] my/our partnership [
7.] [

(continuation missing)

4Q**344** (4QDebt Acknowledgement ar) trans. A Yardeni

(beginning missing?)

2. [ ]with me, I, ʾElʿazar son of <Ye>hosef[ ]
3. [ ] seven [ ]

5. [the payment from] my [p]roperty and (from) whatever I shall acquire, according to that.
6. ʾElʿazar son of Yehosef, for himself he wrote [it].
7. [ ] Yehose[f]
8.] [

(continuation missing?)

Kh.Q. Ostracon **3** ed. E. Eshel, *DJD* XXXVI

top margin

1]   ש[ת ש ש
2 ל ם ן ס ע פ צ ק ר
3 א א ב ג ד ה ו ז ח ט
4 י כ   ש   ט

bottom margin

Kh.Q. Ostracon **3**

1. [*š*] *t š š*
2. *l m n s ʿ p ṣ q r*
3. *ʾ ʾ b g d h w z ḥ ṭ*
4. *y k š ṭ*

F. Miscellanea

1. Treasure List

3Q15 (3QCopper Scroll) ed. D. Wilmot and M. Wise

Col. 1

1 בחרובא֯ שבעמק עכור תחת
2 המעלות הב֯יאה למזרח אמות
3 *<ארוה> ארבעין שדת כסף וכליה
4 משקל ככרין שבעשרה KEN
5 בנפש בנדבׄך הש֯ל֯ש֯י עשתות
6 זהב 100 בבור הגדול שבחצר
7 הפרסטלין <בור> בקרקעו סתום בחליא
8 נגד הפתח העליון ככרין תשע מאת
9 בתל של כחלת כלי דמע בלגין ואפודת
10 הכל של הדמע והאצר השבעי מעסר
11 שני מפוגל פתחו בשולי האמא מן הצפון
12 אמות שש עד ניקרת הטבילהׄ XAΓ
13 בשׂיא המער֯א של מנס בירדא לסמל
14 גבה מן הקר֯קע אמות שלוש [כ]סף <ארבעין>
15 *vacat* [כ]כר 40 *vacat*

Col. 2

1 בבור המלח שתחת המעלות
2 ככר<ין> 41 *vacat* HN
3 במערת בית המדח הישן֯ ברובד
4 השׁ(ל״)שי עשתות זהב ששין וחמש ΘE
5 בצריח שבחצר מתיה עצין וכתבן
6 בור בׄ[ו] כׄלין וכסף ככרין שבעין
7 בבור שנגד השער המזרחי
8 רחוק אמות תשע <ע>סרא בו כלין
9 ובמזקא שבו ככרין עסר ΔI
10 בבור שׄתחת החומא מן המזרח
11 בשן הסלע כדין של כסף שש
12 ביאתו תחת הסף הגדול
13 בבׄרכׄא שבמזרח כחלת במקצע

*For 3Q**15**, < > indicates modern corrections, both additions and deletions.

F. Miscellanea

1. Treasure List

3Q15 (3QCopper Scroll) trans. M. Wise

Col. 1

1. In the ruin that is in the Valley of Achor, under
2. the steps, with the entrance at the east a distance of forty
3. cubits: a strongbox of silver and its vessels—
4. seventeen talents by weight. ΚΕΝ
5. In the sepulchre, in the third course of stones:
6. one hundred ingots of gold. In the big cistern that is in the courtyard
7. of the peristyle, <pit> at its bottom concealed by a sealing ring,
8. across from the upper opening: nine hundred talents of silver coins.
9. In the mound of Kohlit: votive vessels—all of them flasks—and high-priestly garmenture.
10. All the votive offerings, and what comes from the seventh treasury, are
11. impure second tithe. The cache's opening is at the edge of the acqueduct, six
12. cubits to the north of the immerision pool, ΧΑΓ
13. In the plastered Reservoir of Manos, at the descent to the left,
14. three cubits up from the bottom: silver coins <forty>
15. *vacat* totalling forty talents. *vacat*

Col. 2

1. In the salt pit that is under the steps:
2. forty-one talents of silver coins. *vacat* ΗΝ
3. In the cave of the old Washer's Chamber, on the
4. third terrace: sixty-five ingots of gold. ΘΕ
5. In the burial chamber that is in the Courtyard of Matthias: wooden vessels, along with their inventory-list.
6. In a recess in the burial chamber: vessels and seventy talents of silver coins.
7. In the cistern opposite the eastern gate (i.e. of the courtyard),
8. at a distance of nineteen cubits: in it are vessels.
9. And in the conduit of the cistern: ten talents of silver coins. ΔΙ
10. In the cistern that is under the wall on the east,
11. at the crag of the bedrock: six jars of silver coins.
12. The cistern's entrance is under the big threshold.
13. In the pool that is on the east of Kohlit, in the

14 הצפני חפור אמ<ו>ת <ב֯>ארבע
15 *vacat* ככרין 22 *vacat*

Col. 3

1 בחצ[ר]°°° תחת הפנא הדרו
2 מית <חפר> אמות תשע כלי כסף וזהב של
3 דמע מזרקות כוסות מנקיאות
4 קסאות כל שש מאות ותשעה
5 תחת הפנא האחרת המזרח
6 ית חפר אמות שש עסרה כסף
7 ככ 40 *vacat* TP
8 בשית שבמלחמ בצפונו
9 כלי דמע לב֯ושי<ן> ביאתא
10 תחת הפנא המערבית
11 בקבר שבמלחמ ממזרחו
12 בצפנו אמות תחת המ
13 ת <חפר> אמות שלוש ככ 13 *vacat*

Col. 4

1 בבור הגדול שב֯[כ]ח֯לת֯ בעמוד
2 בצפונו כ֯כ֯[ ]14 ΣΚ *vacat*
3 באמא הבא֯[ה]°° בביאתך
4 אמות ארבע[ין ואח]ת֯ כסף
5 *vacat* ככ 55 *vacat*
6 בין שני הכ֯יפין שבעמק עכור
7 באמצען ח֯פ֯ו֯ר אמות שלוש
8 שם שני דודין מלאי֯ן כסף
9 בשית האדמא שבשולי העצ
10 לא כסף ככ מאתין
11 בשית המזרחית שבצפון כח
12 לת *vac* כסף ככ שבעין *vacat*
13 ביגר של גי הסככא חפור
14 אמת כסף ככ 12 *vacat*

Col. 5

1 ברוש אמת המי֯ם֯ [של גי ה]
2 סככא מן הצפון תח֯[ת האבן]
3 הגדולא חפור אמ[ות שלו]
4 ש כסף *vac* ככ 7
5 בסרק שבסככא מזר֯ח֯
6 אשיח שלומו כאלין של
7 דמע וכתבן אצלם *vacat*

14. northern corner, dig down four <*b*>cubits:
15. *vacat* ? twenty-two talents of silver coins. *vacat*

Col. 3

1. In the courtyard of under the southern
2. corner, <dig down> nine cubits: votive vessels of silver and gold,
3. sprinkling basins, cups, bowls,
4. and pitchers, numbering six hundred and nine.
5. Under the other corner—the eastern one—
6. dig down sixteen cubits: forty
7. talents of silver coins. *vacat* TP
8. In the dry well that is in Milham, on its north:
9. votive vessels, priestly clothes. Its entrance
10. is under the western corner.
11. In the grave that is in Milham, on the
12. northeast, <dig down> three cubits under
13. the corpse: thirteen talents of silver coins. *vacat*

Col. 4

1. In the b[ig] cistern [that is Ko]hlit, at the pillar
2. on its north: fourteen (?) talents of silver coins. *vacat* ΣK *vacat*
3. In the aqueduct that com[es from], at a distance of
4. f[orty-on]e cubits as you enter, silver coins
5. *vacat* totalling fifty-five talents.
6. Between the two boulders in the Valley of Achor,
7. right at the midpoint between them, dig down three
8. cubits: two cauldrons full of silver coins.
9. In the red dry well on the edge of the Wadi Atsla:
10. silver coins totalling two hundred talents. *vacat*
11. In the eastern dry well on the north of Kohlit:
12. silver coins totalling seventy talents.
13. In the cairn of the Secacah Valley, dig down one
14. cubit: twelve talents of silver coins. *vacat*

Col. 5

1. At the head of the aqueduct [of the]
2. Secacah [Valley], on the north, under the
3. big [stone], dig down
4. [thr]ee cub[its]: *vacat* seven talents of silver coins.
5. In the fissure that is in Secacah, to the east of
6. the Pool of Solomon: vessels of
7. votive offerings, along with their inventory-list. *vacat*

מעל החריץ של שלום
ו עד הרגם הגדול
אמות ששין חפור אמות
שלוש כסף *vacat* ככ 23 *vacat*
בקבר שבנחל הכפא
בביאה מירחו לסככא
חׄפוׄר אמות שבע ככ 32

Col. 6

[ב]מערת העמוד של שני
[ה]פתחין <ה>צופא מזרח
[ב]פתח הצפוני חפור
[א]מות שלוש שם קלל
בו ספר אחד תחתו
vacat ככ 42 *vacat*
במערא של הפנׄא
של הרגם הצופא
למזרח חפר בפתח
אמות תשע ככ 21
במשכן המלכא בצד
המערבי חפר אמות
שתים עסרה ככ 27
ביגר שבמגזת הכוהן

Col. 7

הגדול חׄפוׄר [אמות]
תשע ככ[2]2
באמא של קׄי◦[ ]
האשיח הצפו[ני הגד]ול
בארבע רוח[ות]
משח אמות עׄסׄר[י]ן [ואר]בע
ככרין ארבע מאות *vacat*
במערא שאצל המקׄוׄ[א] של
בית הקץ חפר אמות שש
כדין של כסף שש *vacat*
בדוק תחת פנת המשמרה
המזרחית חפור אמות שבע
vacat ככ 22 *vacat*
על פי יציאת המים של הכוז
בא חפור אמות שלוש עד הטור
ככ 80 זהב ככרין שתים

8. Above Solomon's Canal,
9. sixty cubits toward the large cairn,
10. dig down
11. three cubits: *vacat* twenty-three talents of silver coins. *vacat* ?
12. In the grave that is in the Wadi Ha-Kepah
13. at the point of entry as you go from Jericho to Secacah,
14. dig down seven cubits: thirty-two talents of silver coins.

Col. 6

1. [In] the cave of the pillar that has two
2. [o]penings and faces east,
3. [at] the northern opening, dig down
4. three [cu]bits: there, an urn
5. in which is one scroll; under it,
6. *vacat* forty-two talents of silver coins. *vacat*
7. In the cave at the corner
8. of the large cairn, the one that faces
9. east, dig down at the opening
10. nine cubits: twenty-one talents of silver coins.
11. In the Queen's Mausoleum, on the
12. western side, dig down twelve
13. cubits: twenty-seven talents of silver coins.
14. At the cairn by the ford of the

Col. 7

1. High Priest, dig down
2. nine [cubits]: twenty-[two] (?) talents of silver coins.
3. In the aqueduct of
4. the lar[ge] northe[rn] reservoir
5. having four si[des],
6. measure out from its [ri]m twent[y-fo]ur cubits:
7. four hundred talents of silver coins. *vacat*
8. In the cave that is next to the cold-chamber belonging to
9. the family of Hakkoz, dig down six cubits:
10. six jars of silver coins. *vacat*
11. At Dok, under the eastern corner of
12. the guardhouse, dig down seven cubits:
13. *vacat* twenty-two talents of silver coins. *vacat*
14. At the mouth of the wellspring of Kozibah,
15. dig down three cubits to the row of stones:
16. eighty talents of silver coins; two talents of gold coins.

Col. 8

[בא]מא שבדרך מזרח בית֯
אוצר <שמזרח אחור>
כלי דמע וספרין אס֯ר 10
בגי החיצונא בתך ד֯ר°
על האבן חפור אמות שבע
עסרא תחתיה כספ *vacat*
vac וזהב ככ 17 *vacat*
ביגר של פי צוק קדרון
חפור אמות שלוש ככ 7
בשלף של השוא הצופא
מערב בדרום בצריח
הצופא צפון חפור אמות
עשרין וארבע ככ 66
ברין <בדור> של השוא בצויח <בצריח> שבא חפו֯ר
אמות אחת עס֯רה *vacat*
כסף ככ 70 *vacat*

Col. 9

בשובך שבשולי הנטף משח משולי<ו>
אמות שלו<ש ע>שרא <שתין> חפור<ר> אמ<ש>ות שבע
<כ>כרין אסתרין ארבע *vacat*
בחבלת השניא בצריח הצופא
מזרח חפו֯ר אמות שמונא
vac ומחצא ככ 23.5
בצריחי החורון ב<צ>ריח הצופא ים
בזרב חפור אמות שש עסרה
vac ככ 22 *vacat*
בקומעה כסף מנה חרם
בקול המים הקרובין לכפת ביב
מ<ז>רח כלפיהם חפור אמות
vac שבע ככ 9 *vacat*
בשית שיבצפון פי הצוק של בית
תמר ב<י>צ<ה>י֯את גי פלע
vacat כל שבה חרם *vacat*
בשובך שבמצד נאב בתח[ום ה]

Col. 10

דרום בעליאה השנית ירידתו
מלמעלא ככ 9 *vacat*
בבור גר מזקות שרוו מהנחל
הגדול בקרקעו ככ 11

Col. 8

1. [In the aq]ueduct that is on the road east of the
2. storehou[se]: <which is east behind>
3. votive vessels and ten (?) books.
4. In the outer gorge, at the stone in the
5. middle of a sheepfold: dig down seventeen
6. cubits beneath it: *vacat*
7. *vacat* seventeen talents of silver and gold coins. *vacat*
8. In the cairn at the mouth of the gorge of the Wadi Qidron,
9. dig down three cubits: seven talents of silver coins.
10. In the fallow field of the Valley of Shaveh that faces
11. southwest, in the burial chamber
12. facing north, dig down
13. twenty-four cubits: sixty-six talents of silver coins.
14. In the courtyard in the Valley of Shaveh, at the burial chamber that is in it, dig down
15. eleven cubits: *vacat*
16. *vacat* seventy talents of silver coins. *vacat*

Col. 9

1. At the dovecote that is at the edge of the Wadi Nataf, measure from the dovecote's edge
2. thirteen cubits and dig down seven cubits: seven
3. talents of silver coins and four stater coins. *vacat*
4. In the second estate, at the burial chamber that faces
5. east, dig down eight
6. *vacat* and one-half cubits: twenty-three and one-half talents of silver coins.
7. At the Vaults of Beth Horon, at the burial chamber facing
8. west, in the recess, dig down sixteen cubits:
9. *vacat* twenty-two talents of silver coins. *vacat*
10. At the Pass: silver coins totalling one mina, and consecrated temple offering.
11. At the wellspring near the edge of the aqueduct,
12. on the east over against the wellspring, dig down seven
13. *vacat* cubits: nine talents of silver coins. *vacat*
14. At the dry well north of the mouth of Beth
15. Tamar's gorge, at the outlet of the Pele Ravine:
16. *vacat* all that is in it is consecrated temple offering. *vacat*
17. At the dovecote that is in the Fortress of Nob, at the bor[der]

Col. 10

1. on the south, in the second roof-chamber—whose entrance descends
2. from above—: nine talents of silver coins. *vacat*
3. In the lime-plastered cistern that has conduits drawing water from the Great
4. Wadi, at the cistern's bottom: eleven talents of silver coins.

באשיח שיבית הכרם בבואך
לסמולו <חפור> אמות עסר כסף *vacat*
vacat כ֯כ֯רין ששין ושנין
בים של גי זרד בצדו המער֯בׄי
אבן שחור<ר>ה אמו<ו>ת שתין
הי הפתח ככרין שלש מאות
vac זהב *vac* וכלין כפורין עסרין
תחת יד אבשלום מן הצד
המערבי חפורׄ אמות שתין עסרה
vacat ככ 80 *vacat*
ב֯ל֯ׄ בית ח֯מים של רחיל תחת
השקות *vacat* ככ 17
[בברכא העליונ]ה בארבעת

Col. 11

מקצועות זׄהב כלי דמע כתבן אצלם
מתחת פנת האסטאן הדרומית
בקבר צדוק תחת עמוד האכסדרן
כלי דמע◦ <ע>סרה דמע <ע>סנה וכתבן אצלם
בהכסה ⌈אש הסלע הצופא מערב
נגד גנת צדוק תחת המסמא ה
גדולא שבשול<יה> זהב חרם {בקׄ}
בקבר שתחת הסכין ככ 41
בקבר בני העמ טהור הו
בו כלי דמע א<ר>רב<ע> עסרה
vacat כתבן אצלן
בבית <א>אשוחין באשוח
בביאתך לימינ<מ>ית
שלו כלי דמ<ע> <ל>אחד <מ> עס<ו>רא
כתבן אצלם *vacat*
במבא רו[בד]ב֯ית המשכב המערבי
טיף על מ֯[כלין הכל] תׄש֯ע מאות

Col. 12

זהב ככ 5 ככרין ששין ביאתו מן המ<ע>רב
תחת האבן השחורא כוזין תחת סף
vacat הבור ככרין 42
בהר גר֯יזין תחת המעל<ה>א של השיח העליונא
שדא אחת וכלכליה וכסף ככ 61
בפי המבוע של בית שם כל<י> כסף וכלי זהב
של דמע וכסף הכ֯ל ככרין שש מאות
בביבא הגדולא של הבור מלבית הבור

5. At the reservoir of Beth Hakerem, on the left
6. as you enter, dig down ten cubits: silver coins totalling *vacat*
7. *vacat* sixty-two talents. *vacat*
8. At the tank of the Zered Gorge, at the western (burial chamber)—the one with
9. a black<k> stone for an opening—dig down two cubits:
10. three hundred talents of silver coins,
11. *vacat* gold coins *vacat*, and twenty vessels containing temple penalty fees.
12. Under Absalom's Monument, on the western
13. side, dig down twelve cubits:
14. *vacat* eighty talents of silver coins. *vacat*
15. At the tank of the water reserve of Rachel, under
16. the trough: seventeen talents of silver coins.
17. In the [Upp]er [Pool], in its four

Col. 11

1. corners: votive vessels, and their inventory-list is next to them.
2. Under the southern corner of the Stoa,
3. at Zadok's grave, under the column of the small portico:
4. ten votive vessels, and their inventory-list is next to them.
5. At the Throne—the peak of the cliff facing west—
6. opposite Zadok's Garden, under the great
7. closing-stone that is at the edge: gold coins and consecrated offerings.
8. At the grave that is under the Knife: forty-one talents of silver coins.
9. At the grave of the common people—it is ritually pure—
10. in it: fourteen votive vessels,
11. *vacat* and their inventory-list is next to them.
12. In the reservoir precinct, in the reservoir
13. lying on the left as you enter:
14. eleven votive vessels,
15. and their inventory-list is next to them. *vacat*
16. At the entryway to the terr[ace] of the western mausoleum,
17. at the stand along the [vessels totalling] nine hundred;

Col. 12

1. five talents of gold coins; sixty talents of silver coins. Its entrance is on the west.
2. Under the black stone: oil vessels. Under the threshold
3. of the crypt: forty-two talents of silver coins. *vacat*
4. On Mount Gerizim, under the upper step of the ditch:
5. one chest and all its vessels, and silver coins *vacat* totalling sixty-one talents.
6. At the mouth of the fountain of Beth Shem: silver and gold
7. votive vessels, and silver coins. The sum total: *vacat* six hundred talents. *vacat*
8. In the big pipe of the cistern, at the point where it joins the cistern:

9 הכל משקל ככרין 71 מנין עסרין
10 בשית שב<צׄחב>צפון כחלת פתח אצפון
11 וקברין על פיה משנא הכתב הזא
12 ופרושיו ומשחותיהׄם ופרוט כלׄ
13 *vacat* אחד ואח[ד] *vacat*

2. LETTERS

4Q**342** (4QLetter? ar) ed. A. Yardeni, *DJD* XXVII

1]◦חוהׄ ו א◦◦◦[
2]◦בוׄ/כיׄ כל מה די עב[ד
3]◦[ ]◦ יהודה ואלעזר [
4]◦חׄ◦ׄ ו דע לאלישוׄע די◦[

4Q**343** (4QLetter nab) ed. A. Yardeni, *DJD* XXVII

Recto

1]]◦◦◦[
2 ◦◦◦ אׄנׄהׄ[ ]מנה י◦[
3 ◦◦◦[ ]◦נ◦◦ בהׄ[
4 ש/ע ל◦◦◦וׄךׄ ו[ ]איך ◦[
5 ותנתנון ◦[ ]מׄעׄ[?]ל ם/ה ◦◦◦[
6 אׄחי הוא מׄן שמרׄיׄ[
7 לא ויעבךׄ ד לידיך הוׄ[
8 ביׄתׄה ואתרה בא[
9 ואהוא מחשךׄ ד לכוׄן במׄ[

bottom margin

Verso

10 מׄ◦◦◦[
11 מן ◦◦◦וׄןׄ ש/ע ◦◦◦◦◦◦[ ]◦[(?)
12 ובאׄיש עׄביׄד[
13 והבו עם שמׄעׄ[ו]ן וׄ[
14 שעדלהי
(space of two lines)
15 עׄמׄהׄוׄן

bottom margin?

9. a sum total, by weight, *vacat* of seventy-one talents and twenty minas.
10. In the dry well that is at the north of Kohlit, with an opening on the north
11. and graves by its mouth: a copy of this inventory-list,
12. with explanations and measurements and full detail for each
13. *vacat* and every hidden item. *vacat*

2. Letters

4Q**342** (4QLetter? ar) trans. A. Yardeni

2.] all that di[d
3.] [ ] Yehudah and ʾElʿazar [
4.] to ʾElishuaʿ (?) [

4Q**343** (4QLetter nab) trans. A. Yardeni

Recto

2. I[ ]from him/her(?) [

5. and you will give [ ] [
6. my brother was of [
7. no, and he will deliver (?) into your hands [
8. his/the house and his/the place in [
9. and I will be suspecting (?) you/ to you in [

Verso

11. from [
12. and evil was done[
13. and give with Shimʿ[o]n and[
14. *Sʿdlhy*
(space of two lines)
15. with them (?)

Unidentified Fragments

Frgs. a + b

1]◦א◦יא̇[ ]◦ באדני◦[ ]
2]◦א ◦◦[ ]ת בית אפ̇ק̇
3]כי א̇[ ]ע̇יני א◦[
4]◦◦[

3. Scribal Exercises

4Q**234** (4QExercitium Calami A) ed. A. Yardeni, *DJD* XXXVI

Frg. 1

Upside-down

אלי [

Sideways

ישחק [

Horizontal

1]אל [
2 לפנ[י ויאמר]ישחק אל יעקב[
3 [גשה] נא

4Q**360** (4QExercitium Calami B) ed. A. Yardeni, *DJD* XXXVI

Right Side (Vertical)

1 ליה/ח [
2 מנח[ם
3 נ נ◦[
4 מנח[ם
5 מע/ש [

Left Side

1 ◦◦◦ מנחם [
2 ◦צ◦ ח◦◦[

Bottom

1 רבק ל סמ

Unidentified Fragments

Frgs. a + b

1.] [ ] in the ears of[?]
2.] [ ] Beit ʾAphek
3.] [ ]the eyes of/my eyes

3. Scribal Exercises

4Q**234** (4QExercitium Calami A) trans. A. Yardeni

Frg. 1

Upside-down

to me [

Sideways

Isaac [

Horizontal

1.] to[his son]
2. before m]e. And [Isaac] said [to Jacob]
3.] come near,[please

4Q**341** (4QExercitium Calami C) ed. J. Naveh, *DJD* XXXVI

1 לבעפסאצגדהו[ ]טׄיכל

2 סחרה א◦◦◦א◦ס◦◦ס◦◦ס◦

3 תירקוסׄ [ ]א בי[ ]ק

4 שרחסי מגנס מלכיה מניס

5 מחתוש מׄקליח מפיבשת

6 [ ]לגוס בניבןׄ בסרי גדי

7 דלוי הלכוס הרקנוס וני ז

8 זוחלזלפ

9 זכריאל י◦י

a יתראיתישילא

b יטריסיסי

c עקילא

d עלי עדפׄי

4Q**341** (4QExercitium Calami C) trans. J. Naveh

1. *lbʿpsʾṣgdhw*[ ]*ṭykl*
2. *sḥrh ʾ ʾs s s*
3. *tyrqws* [ ]ʾ *by*[ ]*q*
4. *šrḥsy*, Magnus, Malkiah, *mnys*
5. *mḥtwš*, *mqlyḥ*, Mephiboshet
6. [ ]*lgws*, *bnybn*, *bsry*, Gaddi
7. Dalluy, *hlkws*, Hycanus, Wani, *z*
8. *zwḥlzlp*
9. Zakariel

a. *ytrʾytyšylʾ*
b. *yṭrysysy*
c. *ʿqylʾ*
d. *ʿly, ʿdpy*

G. Unclassified Manuscripts

1. Unclassified Manuscripts with Specific Names

1Q**25** (1QApocryphal Prophecy) ed. J. T. Milik, *DJD* I

Frg. 1

◦[
המ[ה
וירא ו◦[
חקקתי להם המ̊[צות
להמה ויש̊מ̊[ו
ובשומרון יש̊םׄ [
בוז על נדיבים [
[   ]ל◦ר̊ בציׄו̊[ן
[   ]תׄרימו ◦[

Frg. 2

◦[לה]ג̊יע [
שמכה ◦[
תפלה [
ליהו̊[ה/דה

Frg. 3

] ת̊שחו [
י]הודה וׄ[

Frg. 4

]ך ה̊[
]ממצוקותיהם [
יפ]תח ואל יעונו̊ בׄ[
]וכופר̊ם [
]א̊שר לו אם[
ה]מׄ[ה ו]נ̊אצו ולוא̊ [
י]שחו והשפלה [
]◦[   ]◦[

G. Unclassified Manuscripts

1. Unclassified Manuscripts with Specific Names

1Q25 (1QApocryphal Prophecy) trans. M. Wise, M. Abegg, and E. Cook with N. Gordon

Frg. 1

2. they[
3. and he looked and [
4. I decreed the j[udgements] for them [
5. for them, and [they] placed [
6. and in Samaria he put [
7. contempt upon the noble [
8. [ ] in Zio[n
9. [ ]you raised [

Frg. 2

1. [to a]rrive [
2. Your name [
3. prayer [
4. to the LOR[D/to Ju[dah

Frg. 3

1.] you shall cower [
2. J]udah and[

Frg. 4

2.]because of their afflictions [
3. he shall o]pen, and let them not practice witchcraft (?) [
4.]and their ransom [
5.]which is his if[
6. th]o[se, and]they shall despise and not [
7. they shall]throw down, and the lowland [

Frg. 5

1] כפלא [
2] הארץ [
3] לשמיעׄ ◦[
4]ל לעבדים [
5 ויה]וׄה ביהו]דה
6] הׄמלוכה [

Frg. 6

1]דׄו [
2]בבהמות ו[
3] קומה ולחכו [
4] להביא מ[
5] לחׄ◦◦[

Frg. 7

1]בׄןׄ [
2] מידה נע[
3]◦ ◦[

Frg. 8

1]כי מכרםׄ[

Frg. 9

1] ציון [
2]י ◦[

Frg. 11

1]◦◦ ציוׄןׄ[
2]לׄ [

Frg. 12

1]◦[
2] היה יש]ראל
3] נלוו עלי]הם
4] סׄפר [ ]ל[

Frg. 13

1] בקרב [
2] היׄ[

Frg. 14

1]ים [

Frg. 15

1]נׄהׄ[
2] נׄכרתה ותשׄ[
3]ל◦◦[

1Q**30** (1QLiturgical Text A?) ed. J. T. Milik, *DJD* I

Frg. 1

1]הׄ[
2 מ]שׄיח הקודש [
3 ב]שלישית את כול[
4 ס]פרים חומשים ◦[
5]ויותר על ארבעת ◦[
6] ופשריהם לפיׄ[

Frg. 2

1]לׄפניכה לתת[
2]ל◦ל[ ]טת הדרך [

Frg. 5

1.] as a wonder [
2.] the land [
3.] to declare [
4.] as servants [
5. and the LO]RD in Ju[dah
6.] the kingship [

Frg. 6

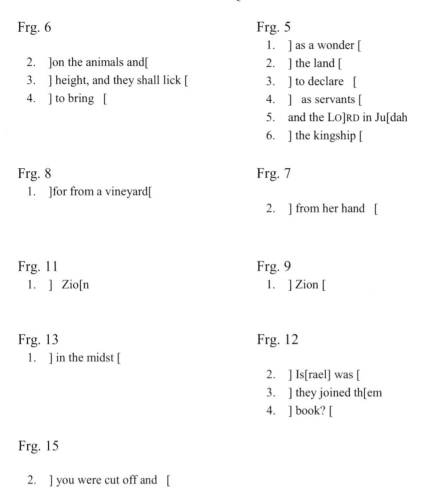

2.]on the animals and[
3.] height, and they shall lick [
4.] to bring [

Frg. 7

2.] from her hand [

Frg. 8

1.]for from a vineyard[

Frg. 9

1.] Zion [

Frg. 11

1.] Zio[n

Frg. 12

2.] Is[rael] was [
3.] they joined th[em
4.] book? [

Frg. 13

1.] in the midst [

Frg. 15

2.] you were cut off and [

1Q**30** (1QLiturgical Text A?) trans. M. Wise, M. Abegg, and E. Cook with N. Gordon

Frg. 1

2.] the holy [me]ssiah [
3. in the]third all[
4. b]ooks of the Pentateuch [
5.]and more than four [
6.] and their interpretations according to[

Frg. 2

1.]before you to give[
2.] [ ] the way [

Frg. 3

1 דב]ר̇תה ל̇[
2]מרננים לפני[כה
3]◦ השמים האמ̇[ר
4]פ̇ישים[

Frg. 4

top margin

1]לכה ולספר ר̇זי̇[
2]ב̇רית עליל̇◦[

Frg. 5

1]בבשול [
2]רישוני[ם

Frg. 6

1 traces of letters

Frg. 7

1]◦◦◦◦[
2] כי יוגד̇[
3]◦◦◦◦◦◦[

Frg. 8

1]א̇הו[
2]◦◦◦[

Frg. 9

1]כיא ◦[

Frg. 10

1]◦ רו ◦[

Frg. 11

1]◦ו ו◦[

Frg. 12

1]שרים[

1Q**31** (1QLiturgical Text B?) ed. J. T. Milik, *DJD* I

Frg. 1

1 [כ]ו̇ל אנשי היחד ה̇מ̇ת̇נ̇ד̇בי[ם
2 פיהם ישקו כול ◦◦[
3 [ ]◦ל◦ ◦ל◦ ◦[

Frg. 2

1 לאין כ◦[
2 ו̇בחירי̇[
3 במחנים̇[
4 למלח̇[מה

Frg. 3

1.]you [spok]e to[
2.]rejoicing before[You
3.] the heaven, who sa[ys

Frg. 4

1.] your[ ] and to tell of (the) mysteries[
2.]covenant [

Frg. 5

1.]in the ripening [
2.]firs[t

Frg. 7

2.] for it was told[

Frg. 9

1.]for [

Frg. 12

1.]officers[

1Q**31** (1QLiturgical Text B?) trans. M. Wise, M. Abegg, and E. Cook

Frg. 1

1. [a]ll the men of the Yahad who voluntee[r
2. their mouth/command all [ ] drank/were ruled [

Frg. 2

1. without [
2. and [the] chosen[of
3. in camps[
4. for wa[r

1Q**37** (1QHymnic Composition?) ed. J. T. Milik, *DJD* I

Frg. 1

1]עה֯ בו ישרא[ל]◦ ◦[ ]מיהו[
2]יהם אשר גמלו לנפשם רעה ו֯[
3]ב֯חירי ישראל למל[
4]לׄ[

Frg. 3

1]ם ה◦[
2]סוסי[

1Q**38** (1QHymnic Composition?) ed. J. T. Milik, *DJD* I

Frg. 1

1]כׄלׄבבם *vacat* בלבבי מׄרׄוקים לה֯ל[
2]ב֯אבן נגף *vacat* [ו]עם ל◦◦ים ◦◦◦◦[

Frgs. 2 + 12

1]◦יה לוא עזבו [ח]וקיכה [
2]לכבוד רב[

Frg. 4

1]◦◦ת◦[
2]כ֯ה ומוקדש֯[י
3]ה֯שפלתני ◦[
4 עש]יתה כל אל֯[ה
5]במוצׄל[י

Frg. 8

1]ן֯ בסוד עצתכׄה֯ [

Frg. 10

1 א]ל חרב[
2]אין כי לא ◦[

1Q**37** (1QHymnic Composition?) trans. M. Wise, M. Abegg, and E. Cook

Frg. 1

1.] in him Israe[l] [
2.] their [ ] that they did evil for themselves [
3.]the chosen of Israel for [

Frg. 3

2.]horses[

1Q**38** (1QHymnic Composition?) trans. M. Wise, M. Abegg, and E. Cook with N. Gordon

Frg. 1

1.]in their heart. *vacat* My heart (*or*: hearts of) beautification for [
2.]with a stone of stumbling. *vacat* [And] with [

Frgs. 2 + 12

1.] they have not abandoned Your [st]atutes [
2.]for great glory[

Frg. 4

2.] and sanctified[
3.]You have brought me low [
4.]You have [done] all the[se
5.]among [those] rescued[

Frg. 8

1.] in the confidential discussion of your council [

Frg. 10

1. t]o (the) sword[
2.]there is not, for not [

1Q**40** (1QHymnic Composition?) ed. J. T. Milik, *DJD* I

Frg. 1

1 [◦בי שמוע֯]
2 [ע רזיכה]
3 [כבינת]
4 [◦]

Frg. 2

1 [גבור]
2 [לא לכו֯]

Frg. 6

1 [◦ ◦]
2 [ם וכׄו֯]
3 [ועתה א]ל

Frg. 8

1 מ[שׄלחות או◦]
2 עו[למים֯]

Frg. 9

1 [במע֯ש]
2 [עולמים ותש]
3 [א] [◦] ב[ליעל וא◦]

2Q**23** (2QApocryphal Prophecy) ed. M. Baillet, *DJD* III

Frg. 1

1 [יׄוׄשב]   [
2 [והוי עליכה והוי] על
3 [וׄבׄשר הרבה אכלתמה
4 [◦ר תעשו כל
5 [בׄחרב וחנית
6 [תדוׄחוׄ[ן] מאבן פנת
7 תחת[יׄוׄת המלאה שעירים
8 לא [תתהללו בעצביכם
9 [ינו הנה ממזרח ומצפון
10 יכ[שׄלון ברכים ושׄ] [ןׄ
11 ונפלו [חׄללים רבים]   ]

bottom margin?

Frg. 2

1 [הׄ
2 [לע֯]   [ים
3 [דׄ שומ֯מים
4 [◦לוׄ

1Q**40** (1QHymnic Composition?) trans. M. Wise, M. Abegg, and E. Cook

Frg. 1
1.] report[
2.] Your mysteries [
3.] according to (the) understanding of [

Frg. 2
1.] mighty [
2.] to [

Frg. 6

2.] and [
3.] And now [my] G[od

Frg. 8
1. co]mmissions [
2. eve]rlasting [

Frg. 9
1.] in dee[d
2.]everlasting and [
3. Be]lial and [

2Q**23** (2QApocryphal Prophecy) trans. M. Wise, M. Abegg, and E. Cook

Frg. 1
1.]inhabitant[ ]
2.]and woe upon you and woe[upon]
3.]and you have eaten much flesh
4.] you shall do all
5.]with sword and spear
6.]you will push from (the) stone of the corner of
7. low]er [ ] full of goat-demons
8.]you will [not] be glorified by your idols
9.] behold, from the east and from the north
10.] knees [shall st]umble and [ ]
11. and] many slain [shall fall]

Frg. 2

3.] desolate

Frg. 4

1]ם̇[
2]ריד [
3 א]ויב כיס [
4]ו֯ שו֯[

Frg. 3

1]מ◦[
2]מ֯ים וירח֯[
3] חולה כ◦[

Frg. 6

1 מכ]מרם יתמ֯ל֯]א
2]כל מסלות[
3]משול בכל [
4]חם בדר֯[
5] לעשות[

Frg. 5

1]אש[
2]לת]פ[שמ֯[
3]ר עם שמ[
4]ת מל[

2Q**25** (2QJuridical Text) ed. M. Baillet, *DJD* III

Frg. 1

1 ימ]ל֯א פיהם[
2]◦י האסרים האלה[
3 כי]כן כתוב בספר מוש]ה

bottom margin?

Frg. 2

1]◦מע[
2]◦ לכ[
3]◦ בקע֯[
4]◦ ה֯ס֯פ֯ר֯י֯ם֯[
5]ל[

Frg. 3

1]לי מצ◦[
2 כ]ול֯[

3Q**8** (3QText Mentioning Angel of Peace) ed. M. Baillet, *DJD* III

Frg. 1

1]מכות [
2]מלאך שלו]ם

Frg. 2

1]ג֯שו ות[
2]הם ונמס ש֯[

bottom margin

Frg. 4

3. ene]my [ ] bag [

Frg. 3

2.] and the moon[
3.] sick [

Frg. 6

1.] their [n]et shall be fi[lled
2.]all the paths[
3. to]rule over all [
4.] in [
5.] to do[

Frg. 5

2.]to se[iz]e them[
3.] with/people [

2Q**25** (2QJuridical Text) trans. M. Wise, M. Abegg, and E. Cook

Frg. 1

1.]their mouth [is f]ull [
2.] these obligations[
3. for]thus it is written in the book of Mos[es

Frg. 2

4.] the books[

Frg. 3

2. a]ll[

3Q**8** (3QText Mentioning Angel of Peace) trans. M. Wise, M. Abegg, and E. Cook

Frg. 1

1.]wounds [
2.]angel of pea[ce

Frg. 2

1.] and [
2.] and shall melt [

3Q**9** (3QSectarian Text) ed. M. Baillet, *DJD* III

Frg. 1

1] ברו֯ח֯[
2]ה[י]ם לנ֯[
3]להשיב אשמׄ[
4] כיא[

Frg. 2

1]◦[
2]ע֯ושא אלה
3]נעוי֯תם

Frg. 3

1]◦ו֯תי֯[
2 אש]מת פשע[
3] אלה פת[
4]ו֯בעדתנו [

bottom margin

4Q**123** (4Qpaleo paraJosh) ed. P. Skehan et al, *DJD* IX

Frg. 1

1]מׄ◦◦◦◦[
2]ה֯ם·ומגרש֯[
3]דׄה·ומנ֯[
4]◦ס֯[ו]מגרשי[
5 קר]ית[ ]ארבע·א[
6]יהׄ[ ]◦[

Frg. 2

1]◦וה֯ ·ביׄד·מׄשה·עבׄד[
2]סׄ◦◦ו֯את·מגרשיהׄם· [
3]◦גׄים֯·הׄ◦◦טׄה· [
4]◦הׄ·[

Frg. 3

1]◦ת·מׄ[
2]ערים·אר[

Frg. 4

1 ומגר]שׄיה·את֯[
2]עׄ[ ]◦[ ] ו[

3Q**9** (3QSectarian Text) trans. M. Wise, M. Abegg, and E. Cook with N. Gordon

Frg. 1

1.] with [the] spirit/breath[
2. G]od to [
3.]to return (the) gui[lt
4.] for[

Frg. 2

2.]doing these things
3.]their offense

Frg. 3

2. si]n of rebellion[
3.] these foo[ls
4.]and in our congregation [

4Q**228** (4QText with a Citation of Jub) ed. J. VanderKam and J. T. Milik, *DJD* XIII

Frg. 1 Col. i

1 [ ]
2 [אות[ם]במחל[קׄ]ו[תׄ העתים
3 [ואגיד[הׄ לכׄמׄהׄ אשר תדעו
4 [ואספ[ר לפנו מחלקת עתו וכל
5 [[מע] [בׄה במשפט עתי עולה
6 [[אׄש בוערת אוכלת בסוד רשעה
7 [[ת במחלקת עתהׄ ימצאנׄה
8 [[מׄקשי שחת ומלאך שלומו
9 [חי[יׄ נצח כי כןׄ כׄתוב במחלקׄת
10 [[לׄמ ילכׄוׄ ואתמ]ה [את כל
11 [[יׄחזק ◦אׄתכמה בׄ] [◦◦◦
12 [[מׄתׄ וינחיל] [ת
13 [[לׄ◦וׄבׄיׄמׄ]ים [שׄרׄ
14 [[מצ◦] [יׄמׄ
15 [[הׄב◦]]

Frg. 1 Col. ii

1 ◦◦◦ היׄוׄמׄ] [בשר ולוא
2 משפחת הגויׄ]ם]
3 יעשו ואת ישר מׄ◦]]
4 ◦עת עם טעׄיכם]]
5–13 *vacat*] [

Frg. 2

1 [[◦ מׄ] [צׄ◦]]
2 [[אור בגׄוׄ]ים]
3 [[מדבר]]

Frg. 3

1 [[בׄכ]]

Frg. 4

1 [[◦הוא ל]]

Frg. 5

1 [[◦תא]]

4Q**228** (4QText with a Citation of Jub) trans. J. VanderKam and J. T. Milik

Frg. 1 Col. i

2. [the]m [in the divi]s[ion]s of the times
3. [and I tol]d you so that you may know
4. [and I recoun]ted before him the division of its/his time and all
5. [ ] *mʿ*[ ]*bh* in the judgement of (?) times of wickedness
6. [ ] a fire burning, devouring in a foundation of evil
7. [ ]*t* in the division of its/her time he will find it/her
8. [ ] snares of destruction, and the angel of his peace
9. [lif]e of eternity. For thus is it written in the divisions
10. [ ]*lm* they will walk. And you [ ] all the
11. [ ] he will strengthen you (?) in [ ]
12. [ ]*mt*, and he (?) will cause to posses [ ]*t*
13. [ ]*l* and in the day[s] *šr*
14. [ ]*mṣ* [ ] *ym*
15. [ ]*hb* [ ]

Frg. 1 Col. ii

1. the day (?) [ ] flesh (?) and not
2. the family of the nation[s]
3. they will do, and the upright one of *m*[ ]
4. time with your erring ones (?) [ ]

Frg. 2

1. [ ] *m* [ ] *ṣ* [ ]
2. [ ]light among the nati[ons (?)]
3. [ ]wilderness (?) [ ]

Frg. 4

1. [ ] it/he to[ ]

4Q**235** (4QUnid. Text nab) ed. E. Cook

Frgs. a–b

1 [◦א◦יא̇]   [◦ באדני◦]   [

2 [◦א ◦◦]   [ת בית אפ̇ק

3 [כי א̇]   [ע̇יני א◦]   [

4 [◦◦]   [

4Q**249j** (4Qpap cryptA Lev^{h}?) ed. S. J. Pfann, *DJD* XXXVI

Frgs. 1–2 Lev 26:14-16

1 [תעשו את כ]ל̊[המצות האלה [15]ואם בחקתי תמאסו ואם]

2 [את משפ]ט̊י̇[תגעל נפשכם לבלתי עש]ו̊[ת את כל]

3 [מצותי] להפ̇[רכם את בריתי [16]אף]אנ̇י [אעשה זאת]

4 [לכם וה]פ̇ק̇ד̇ת̇[י עליכם בהלה א]ת̇ הש̇[חפת ואת הקדחת]

5 [מכלות עינים ומדיבת נפש וזרעת]ם [לריק זרעכם ואכלהו]

6 [איביכם]

4Q**249k** (4Qpap cryptA Text Quoting Leviticus A) ed. S. J. Pfann, *DJD* XXXVI

0 [אף אני אעשה זאת לכם והפקדתי עליכם בהלה את השחפת]

1 [ואת הקד]חת מכל̊[ות עינים ומדיבת נפש וזרעתם זרעכם ואכלהו]

2 [איביכ]ם̇ לריק [17]ו̊[נתתי פני בכם ונגפתם לפני איביכם]

3 [ורדו בכם]שונאיכ̊[ם ונסתם ואין רדף אתכם   ]

4 [   ]◦◦[ ] הרש̇[   ]

5 [   ]◦ש ◦[   ]

4Q**249l** (4Qpap cryptA Text Quoting Leviticus B) ed. S. J. Pfann, *DJD* XXXVI

0 [ואתכם אזרה]

1 [בגוים והריקתי אחריכם חרב ו]ה̊י̇ת̇[ה ארצכם שממה ועריכם יהיו חרבה]

2 [34][אז תרצה הארץ את שבתתיה כ]ל̊ ימ̊י̊[השמה ואתם בארץ איביכם]

3 [אז תשבת ה]ארצ̊[והרצת את שבתתיה   ]

4 [   ]שב̇ת̇[   ]

5 [   ]ואת̇[   ]

6 [יש]ראל [   ]

7 [   ]שכ̊ ◦[   ]

4Q235 (4QUnid. Text nab) trans. N. Gordon

Frgs. a–b

1.] [ ] by Lord [
2.] [ ] Beth-Aphek
3.]because [ ]eyes of [

4Q249j (4Qpap cryptA Lev^{h}?) trans. S. J. Pfann

Frgs. 1–2 Lev 26:14-16

1. [and you will do a]ll[of these commands: [15]and if you shall despise my statutes, or if]
2. [your soul abhor]my [judge]ments,[so that you will not d]o[all]
3. [my commandments, but that you]bre[ak my covenant: [16]]I [also will do this]
4. [to you; I]will even appoint [over you terror,] con[sumption, and fever,]
5. [that shall consume the eyes, and cause sorrow of heart: and you shall sow you]r [seed in vain, for your enemies shall eat it.]

4Q249k (4Qpap cryptA Text Quoting Leviticus A) trans. S. J. Pfann

0. [I also will do this to you; I will even appoint over you terror, consumption,]
1. [and fe]ver, that shall consu[me the eyes, and cause sorrow of heart: and you shall sow your seed and shall eat it]
2. [your enemi]es for nought. And[I will set my face against you, and you shall be slain before your enemies.]
3. [And] they that hate yo[u shall reign over you; and you shall flee when none pursues you.]
4. [ ] [ ] the wick[ed]

4Q249l (4Qpap cryptA Text Quoting Leviticus B) trans. S. J. Pfann

0. [And I will scatter you]
1. [among the nations, and I will unsheathe the sword after you; and your land]shall b[e desolation, and your cities shall be a waste.]
2. [Then the land shall enjoy its sabbaths a]ll the days[of its desolation, while you are in your enemies' land;]
3. [then the]land[shall rest, and enjoy its sabbaths.]
4. [ ]sabbath[ ]
5. [ ]and the[ ]
6. [Is]rael [ ]

4Q**249m** (4Qpap cryptA Hodayot-like Text E) ed. S. J. Pfann, *DJD* XXXVI

1]◦[
2]היתׄה[
3]ׄמצא ב[
4]לׄי ישת[
5]יצא על ◦[
6]אפתח [
7 רׄ *vac* [
8]◦ שׄרׄ ◦[
9]נׄי[
10]אׄת[

4Q**249n** (4Qpap cryptA Liturgical Work E?) ed. S. J. Pfann, *DJD* XXXVI

Frg. 1

1 ל]שׄמוע[
2 גבו]רׄותיכ]ה
3]◦ל◦[ ]אתׄ[

Frg. 2

1]◦[
2]רׄ הׄ[
3]לׄה◦[
4]◦◦[

4Q**249o** (4Qpap cryptA Liturgical Work F?) ed. S. J. Pfann, *DJD* XXXVI

1]◦ ◦[
2]שׄ ◦[
3]יכהׄ[

4Q**249q** (4Qpap cryptA Fragment Mentioning the Planting) ed. S. J. Pfann, *DJD* XXXVI

1]נׄטׄעׄו[
2]שׄנ לאח[
3]ושקר לוׄ[
4]וׄכוׄלׄ קׄ[

4Q**249m** (4Qpap cryptA Hodayot-like Text E) trans. S. J. Pfann

2.]was[
3. will find in[
4. to me [
5. went out
6. I will open [
7. *vacat* [

4Q**249n** (4Qpap cryptA Liturgical Work E?) trans. S. J. Pfann

Frg. 1

1. to] listen[
2. yo]ur [mighty] works[

4Q**249q** (4Qpap cryptA Fragment Mentioning the Planting) trans. S. J. Pfann

1.]his/its planting[

3.]and he has lied to him[
4.]and every [

4Q**250** (4Qpap cryptA Text Concerning Cultic Service A) ed. S. J. Pfann, *DJD* XXXVI

1 [◦◦] [◦◦]
2 [ת יחׄל◦]
3 [לׄפני]
4 [ה֯משרתיםׄ]
5 ל]א יׄצאו]
6 [◦ורתו]
7 [וׄק בח] [◦◦◦]
8 [עמו לאׄ]
9 [וׄ ויתׄ◦]

4Q**250a** (4Qpap cryptA Text Concerning Cultic Service B?) ed. S. J. Pfann, *DJD* XXXVI

Frg. 1

1 [◦◦] [◦]
2 [מׄנחׄ]
3 [◦ול◦]

Frg. 2

1 [◦רׄ ש]
2 [◦הׄ◦]

Frg. 3

1 [◦הׄ◦]
2 [ומׄ]
3 [נׄ]

4Q**250b** (4Qpap cryptA Text Related to Isaiah 11) ed. S. J. Pfann, *DJD* XXXVI

1 [יחׄדיו ◦מ֯ץ
2 נ]ער קטנ]

4Q**294** (4QSapiential-Didactic Work C) ed. E. J. C. Tigchelaar, *DJD* XXXVI

1 [◦ש◦]
2 [אש◦]
3 [וב ב]
4 [יהגה יום]
5 [מ֯כול צׄו֯]רים

4Q**250** (4Qpap cryptA Text Concerning Cultic Service A) trans. S. J. Pfann

3.]before[
4.]ministers[
5.]they shall [n]ot go out[

4Q**250b** (4Qpap cryptA Text Related to Isaiah 11) trans. S. J. Pfann

1.]together
2. a s]mall boy[

4Q**294** (4QSapiential-Didactic Work C) trans. E. J. C. Tigchelaar

4.] he ponders day[
5.]from all enem[ies

4Q304 (4QMeditation on Creation B) ed. T. Lim, *DJD* XX

top margin(?)

1 ואת הארץ וכו[ל צבאם

2 החשך על כן נ◦[

3 עשה ◦◦◦[

4Q306 (4QMen of the People Who Err) ed. T. Lim, *DJD* XXXVI

Frg. 1

top margin

1 הׄזר◦◦◦ אשר ישׂגו ולא יעׄשו את] המצות

2 כי יעברוׄ [מיום] ליום וׄמחדש לחד[ש

3 אותׄו כל אשׁׄר ברית יׄ[שראל

4 ו◦◦רים את בשרו וׄירקוׄ[

5 וׄיקׄצף והכׄלבׄים אוכלים[מקצת עצמות המקדש

6 להוציאו מחצר הׄ[כל]בׄיׄם והי[

7 על י◦◦◦ אשר יע[ב]דו בם ◦[

8 הר◦[ ]שׄם ויצהר[

9 [ ]ל מׄ[

Frg. 2

1 [ ]◦◦[ ]

2 [ ]לבם[ ]

3 [וי]בׄקׄשו אׄת התורה ואׄ[ת] המׄ[צוה בכול לבבם]

4 ובכל נפשׄם היׄוׄ כמגששים ד[רך]

5 עינים התורה הׄולכת ומר◦[ ]

6 [ ]וד עד אשר יפקחו וראו[ ]

bottom margin

Frg. 3

1]◦◦[

2]הׄע◦[

3]יך הׄד◦[

4 [קצף גדו[ל

5]לשם ····[

6]◦[

4Q307 (4QText Mentioning Temple) ed. T. Lim, *DJD* XXXVI

Frg. 1

1]ע◦[

2]◦ר י[ ]יאוכלׄ[

4Q**304** (4QMeditation on Creation B) trans. T. Lim

1. and the earth and al[l their host
2. the darkness, therefore *n* [
3. He made [

4Q**306** (4QMen of People Who Err) trans. T. Lim

Frg. 1

1. the *zr* (descendants?) who will stray and not observe[the commandments
2. for they will transgress [from day] to day and from month to mon[th
3. it, all which is (in) the covenant of I[srael?
4. *w rym* its flesh and they will spit[
5. and he will be stirred to wrath (?) and the dogs eat[some of the bones of the sanctuary
6. by his sending out from the court the [do]gs and *hy*[
7. concerning *y* in which they will se[rv]e [
8.]*hr* [ ] *sm and* fresh oil[
9. [ ]*l m*[

Frg. 2

2. [ ]their heart [ ]
3. [and]they sought the Torah and the co[mmandment in all their heart]
4. and in all their soul, they were as gropers of (the) wa[y]
5. eyes the Torah going forth and *mr* [ ]
6. [ ]*wd* until (their eyes) shall be opened and they shall see[ ]

Frg. 3

2.]*hᶜ* [
3.]*yk hd* [
4.]grea[t] wrath[
5.]to the name **YHWH**[

4Q**307** (4QText Mentioning Temple) trans. T. Lim

Frg. 1

1.]ᶜ [
2.] *r y*[ ]he will eat[

3] מו◦תם]]לתע◦[
4]מׄו תמיד לכול[
5] *vacat* [
6 יׄהיה כול הגר הנש]אר
7 אתישראל בגו]ים[לׄ[
8 עד ת◦◦ר◦[

Frg. 2

1]ם]]מׄשי[
2] במקדש נפ[
3]ל ה◦שרתי[

Frg. 3

1]בני[
2]ם *vac* [
3]תמיד[
4]א◦◦◦[

Frg. 4

1]ואח[
2]שו[

Frg. 5

1]שמחה[
2 י]תיצבו[
3]לׄ[

Frg. 6

1]◦◦פו◦◦[
2]לוא ימ◦[
3]לב[

Frg. 7

1]בל[
2]מועדיׄ[ם
3] *vacat* [

Frg. 8

1]◦ר ומל◦[
2]לׄוא יחס]ר
3] *vacat* [

Frg. 9

1]לה[ ] ◦[
2]מושב[
3]◦ ◦◦[

4Q**331** (4QpapHistorical Text C) ed. J. Fitzmyer, *DJD* XXXVI

Frg. 1 Col. i

1]◦◦ןׄ
2]◦◦ןׄ
3]◦◦
4]◦◦◦ ◦[ ]◦ין
5]ם י◦[ ]◦
6 ה]כׄוׄהן אׄשר כׄול
7] יוחנן להבי אלׄ◦

bottom margin

3.]*mw. tm*[ ]*lt* ͑ [
4.]*mw* continually for all[
5. [ ] *vacat* [
6. *yhyh* any foreigner who remai[ns (?)
7. Israel among the nati[ons] for[
8. until *t r* [

Frg. 2
1.]*m*[ ]*msy*[
2.] in the Temple *np*[
3.]*l h srty*[

Frg. 3
1.]sons of[
2.]*m vacat* [
3.]continually[
4.] ͗ [

Frg. 4
1.]and brother[
2.]*sw*[

Frg. 5
1.]joy[
2.]they [will] take their stand[
3.]*l*[

Frg. 6
1.] *pw* [
2.]not *ym* [
3.]*lb*[

Frg. 7
1.]*bl*[
2.]appointed tim[es
3.] *vacat* [

Frg. 8
1.] *r wml* [
2.]he will not lac[k
3.] *vacat* [

Frg. 9
1.]*lh*[ ] [
2.]assembly[

4Q**331** (4QpapHistorical Text C) trans. J. Fitzmyer

Frg. 1 Col. i

6. the] priest who all
7.] Yoḥanan to bring to

Frg. 1 Col. ii

1 בׄןׄ]
2 מׄן]
3]
4]
5 אנושׄ]
6 תהזוׄיׄ◦]
7 שלמצׄו]ן

Frg. 2

1]◦[
2]◦ בן ◦[
3] ◦ד[
4]◦ק א[
5]ת כלׄ[
6]◦[

Frg. 3

1]◦[
2]אר ◦[
3]◦◦[

Frg. 4

1] בר[

Frg. 5

1]קו ◦[
2 יחז]קׄאל ◦[
3]◦◦ל ◦[

Frg. 6

1]לפפו[

Frg. 7

1]ן ק[
2]ל אלישׄ]יב

Frg. 8

1]חׄר ו[
2]*vacat*[
3]לׄ [
4]◦ [

Frg. 9

1]אׄ ◦[
2]כלׄ אש[
3]אׄ כמ[
4]ה זדׄ[

Frg. 10

1]ר ◦[
2]◦◦[

4Q**338** (4QGenealogical List?) ed. E. Tov, *DJD* XXXVI

] ◦◦◦ הוליד ◦◦◦[
הו]ליד

Frg. 1 Col. ii

1. son[
2. from[

5. a human being[

7. Salom[e

Frg. 5

2. Yehez]kel [

Frg. 7

2.] Eliash[ib

4Q**338** (4QGenealogical List?) trans. E. Tov

] he begat [
he be]gat [

4Q**418b** (4QText with Quotation from Psalm 107?) ed. J. Strugnell and D. Harrington, S.J., *DJD* XXXIV

Frg. 1 (formerly 4Q**418** 116)

1 תוׄ] [
2 מעוזכ[ ]◦לנׄ◦[[
3 יׄעלו הרים וירדו תהמוׄ]ת נפשם ברעה תתמוגג [
4]ינועו[ויחגו כשכור וכול חׄ]וכמתם תתבלע [
5]]שלך לבטחׄ[[

Frg. 2 (formerly 4Q**418** 112)

1]] צדׄקׄ[[
2]]אׄ יתע[[

bottom margin

4Q**419** (4QInstruction-like Composition A) ed. S. Tanzer, *DJD* XXXVI

Frg. 1

top margin

1 אשר תעשו על פי כול המשפׄ]טים
2 אליכם ביד משה ואשר יעׄשהׄ[
3 ביד כוהניו כיא המה נאמני בריׄ]ת אל
4 יודיע את אשר לׄ]ו[ואת הטׄ[
5]ויבחר בזרע אהרוןׄ להעׄ]מיד אותם
6 ד]רׄכיו ולגיש ניחוח אׄ]שה
7 ויתנם שׄ[ ]אשׄר לׄ]כו[ל עׄמׄו וׄ[
8 ויצוׄ ◦[ ]◦◦[
9 כסא אשר רם בהודׄ]י[עׄםׄ [
10 הוׄא חׄי עולם וכב]ו[דו לעׄ]ד
11 תשחרו ותועבת נדה ב◦[
12 אהבתםׄ ותגוללו בכול[דרכי[
13 ◦◦◦ ◦[

Frg. 2

1]בׄ פיהם[
2]לוׄאׄ רם בכׄוׄ]ל
3]היה ואת◦[
4]ם וח◦◦[
5]◦◦◦◦ [

4Q**418b** (4QText with Quotation from Psalm 107?) trans. J. Strugnell and D. Harrington, S.J.

Frg. 1

2. *thy refuge*[ ] [ ]
3. They go up on the mountains and descend into the depth[s; their courage melts away in their evil state]
4. [they stagger] *and reel* like a drunkard, and all [their] *s*[*eamanship* is confounded]
5. [ ]*cast* in security[ ]

4Q**419** (4QInstruction-like Composition A) trans. S. Tanzer

Frg. 1

1. which you will do in accordance with all the pre[cepts
2. unto you by the hand of Moses and which *he* will do[
3. by the hand of His priests, for they are the faithful ones of the coven[ant of God
4. He will make known that which is H[is] and the [
5.]and He chose the seed of Aaron to make [them] st[and
6. His [w]ays and to bring near a soothing [offering made by fire
7. and He appointed them [ ] for a[ll] his people and[
8. and He charged [them
9. a throne which is lofty. When *he* makes them know[
10. He lives forever and His gl[o]ry is forev[er
11. you will seek Him early. But an abomination of impurity (is) in [
12. their love and they defile themselves in all[the ways of

Frg. 2

1.] their mouth[
2.](is) not lofty in al[l

Frg. 3

1]◦[ ]◦◦◦[
2 [*vacat* ע]
3]םׄ אל א◦[
4]◦◦◦[

Frg. 4

1 ה]מׄשיל֯ בׄ[
2]םׄ מׄשפטם [
3]וׄחתרׄ וׄ[

Frg. 5

1]נׄוׄ נׄפרדהׄ ◦[
2 [◦◦]

Frg. 6

1] אׄזניםׄ ביׄד נכבדׄ◦[
2]תׄ הׄריב והמה לוׄ[
3]◦◦◦ [ ]ל֯[

Frg. 7

1]◦ בם [
2]אם לא י◦[
3]רשע לקׄ[
4]ל[

Frg. 8 Col. i

1] [
2]]צרור
3]החיים]אׄ *vac* אין
4]]◦ה הוא והוא
5]] כול
6]]רׄ לוא
7]]◦קׄ
8] [

Frg. 8 Col. ii

1 חפצוׄ ◦[
2 וׄבדברו ◦[
3 בשׄ[ ] וׄיספרםׄ [ ]◦[ ]◦[ ]◦[
4 מהמה דרכיהם עם פקוד[ת
5 לחושך ומאוצרו ישב[
6 תׄבואות לכול קׄצׄי עׄולׄם [ ]◦◦[
7 אם יקפוץ ידו ונאספה רוח כול [בשר
8 א]ל֯ אדמׄתם ישובון[

Frg. 9

1 [ו◦]
2]יׄם ◦[
3 [ ]
4]וׄביׄ[

Frg. 4

1. he do]minated [
2.] their judgement [
3.]and dug and[

Frg. 6

1.] ears through the honoured one [
2.] the strife and they will be to him[

Frg. 5

1.] it was divided [

Frg. 7

1.] in them [
2.]if not [
3.]wicked to [

Frg. 8 Col. i

2. [ ]bundle of
3. [the living] *vac* there is not
4. [ ] he and he
5. [ ] all
6. [ ] not

Frg. 8 Col. ii

1. His pleasure [
2. and in His word [
3. when [ ] and *he* will number/recount them [
4. confusing their ways with the punishme[nt of
5. to darkness. And from His treasure house He will restore[
6. (His) produce to all the times of eternity [
7. If He closes His hand, then the spirit of all [flesh] will be gathered in[
8. [t]o their earth/dust they will return[

Frg. 10

]לד֯
]◦

Frg. 11

]ו
] מימ֯י֯
הד֯ב֯]ר

4Q**440b** (4QFragment Mentioning a Court) ed. A. Lange, *DJD* XXXVI

]מ֯זר֯]ק]◦ש֯י֯]
]ק֯]]ו֯ילכו רבי֯ם֯]
]ב֯ט לוחצר צדי֯]קים
] *vacat?* ל֯כ֯ו֯ל ש֯י֯]

4Q**447** (4QPoetic Text B) ed. E. J. C. Tigchelaar, *DJD* XXIX

]◦◦ ולמאוס֯]
]תשכילנ֯ו]
]למ֯ע֯ן]

4Q**452** (4QPrayer D?) ed. E. Chazon, *DJD* XXIX

top margin?

]הי֯ מה גדל֯ת֯]
]את גבורות א]
]◦]]ל֯]

4Q**453** (4QLament B) ed. E. Chazon, *DJD* XXIX

top margin

איכ֯כה התאחרת֯]
]◦]

4Q**454** (4QPrayer E?) ed. E. Chazon, *DJD* XXIX

]ם֯
]◦ן֯ צדקכ֯ה֯
]ב֯ארץ חם ו֯נגועי
] *vacat* [
]כ֯יא מלוא◦◦] [

Frg. 11

1. and[
2. waters/from days [
3. the wor[d

4Q440b (4QFragment Mentioning a Court) trans. A. Lange

1.]sprinkling bo[wl] *šy*[
2.]*q*[ ]and many walked[(*or*: will walk[)
3.]*bṭ* for himself a court of righ[teous ones
4.] *vacat?* for all *šy*[

4Q447 (4QPoetic Text B) trans. E. J. C. Tigchelaar

1.] and to loathe[
2.]you teach him [
3.]in order that [

4Q452 (4QPrayer D?) trans. E. Chazon

1.]*hy* How you have (been) magnified[
2.] *ʾt* mighty deeds *ʾ*[
3.] [ ]*l*[

4Q453 (4QLament B) trans. E. Chazon

1. How were you late?[

4Q454 (4QPrayer E?) trans. E. Chazon

1.]*m*
2.] *n* your righteousness
3.]in the land of Ham and plagues of
4.]*vacat*[ ]
5.]for the (ful)filling of [ ]

6]שׁם במד[בר [

7]◦תם ל[[

8]◦◦[[

4Q**455** (4QDidactic Work C) ed. E. Chazon, *DJD* XXXVI

1]◦◦◦ הבר כ֯◦◦[ ]◦◦[ ]◦[

2] בכל אמ֯נה הגידו את ◦[

3]מ֯שקר ירחק֯ מ֯הזכירו[

4]ל֯[

4Q**457a** (4QCreation?) ed. E. Chazon, *DJD* XXIX

Col. I (Frgs. 1 + 2 Col. i)

Frg. 1

1]א֯ור

Frg. 2 Col. i

1]◦֯ [

2]מ֯◦◦◦כ֯[

3 ענג֯◦[ ]ו֯[

4 יט֯[

5 ומ֯◦ד◦ר א֯[

6 ובד[

7 ופל֯◦ חק֯[

8 ◦לו֯[

9 ב֯ימ֯י[

10 א ◦◦[

11 נב֯ר֯א֯[

12 ◦◦מ֯[

Col. II (Frg. 2 Col. ii)

top margin

1]ם֯

2]כ֯[ ]◦◦◦[

3]נ֯[ ]◦ו ◦◦[

4 ◦◦◦◦ון֯[

5 [

6 [

7]ב֯◦◦ורו[ ]◦ [ ]◦[

8 ◦֯יש֯כ֯◦[ ]◦[ ]◦

9]◦ו[

6.]there in the des[ert]
7.] *tm l*[ ]

4Q**455** (4QDidactic Work C) trans. E. Chazon

1.] the ble[ssing [ ] [ ] [
2.] in every sure covenant declare the [
3.]From falsehood let him be far from (?) mentioning it[
4.]*l*[

4Q**457a** (4QCreation?) trans. E. Chazon

Col. I (Frgs. 1 + 2 Col. i)

1.]light

7. and wonder/fulfill (the) law[

9. in the days of[

11. created[

4Q**459** (4QNarrative Work Mentioning Lebanon) ed. E. Larson, *DJD* XXXVI

Frg. 1

1 לבנון לב֯[ ] הגביהו רצון֯[
2 ידעו את אדני אלהי[הם
3 נתן למלאכים ואת◦[
4]ף לא ד֯א◦[

Frg. 2

1 א֯[
2 והיו[

4Q**461** (4QNarrative B) ed. E. Larson, *DJD* XXXVI

Frg. 1

1]◦◦ ל֯ה֯מׄית ◦◦[
2]ה֯י בהמה ויתנםׄ ב֯יד֯ ר֯[
3]◦◦בעבודה קשה ויתנו על֯ ◦◦◦[
4]ים עד קצה *vacat* ויתנם לש{ו}מה֯ ו֯[
5]◦ב֯◦[ובק]שוהו וימצאוה[ו
6]ל֯שמוע ומשכיל וה֯[
7 מ]ו֯סדות תבל עד נ֯[
8 ל]ע֯ש֯ות רצונו ול֯שמור חקיו ו֯◦[
9]◦ להשיב אל יהוה אלוהיהמה[
10] וראה יהוה את שיבתם א֯[

bottom margin

Frg. 2

1]ם סופרים[
2] ו֯מ֯כ֯◦[

Frg. 3

1]כ֯ו֯ל֯ ◦[
2]◦◦ ותה֯[
3]לע֯ליון֯[

Frg. 4

1]◦◦[
2]הרעים[
3]לא֯ורך אפך [
4]ם֯ עליו[
5]מ֯על֯י֯[ו

Frg. 5

	Col. i	Col. ii
1	]◦ם	
2	]◦ם	
3		◦[

4Q459 (4QNarrative Work Mentioning Lebanon) trans. E. Larson

Frg. 1

1. Lebanon [ ] they exalted the desire of[
2. they knew the Lord [their] God[
3. he gave to the messengers, and [
4.] not [

Frg. 2

2. and they were[

4Q461 (4QNarrative B) trans. E. Larson

Frg. 1

1.] to put to death [
2.] against them and he gave them into the hand of [
3.] with hard labour and they placed over [
4.] until its time. *vacat* And he made them a desolation and[
5.] [and]they[sou]ght him and they found hi[m
6.]to hear, and one who is wise and [
7. the foun]dations of the world as far as [
8. to]do his will and to keep his statutes [
9.] to bring back to the Lord their God[
10.] and the Lord will see their returning, (*or*: and see, Lord, their returning) [

Frg. 2

1.] scribes[

Frg. 3

1.]all [
2.] and [
3.]to the Most High[

Frg. 4

2.]the evil (ones)[
3.]to/by your patience [
4.] upon him/it[
5.]from upon h[im/i[t

4Q**464a** (4QNarrative E) ed. M. Stone and E. Eshel, *DJD* XIX

]ח֯[ ]ן֯[1
]ם ועמ֯ד ושפ֯[ט 2
]○○דת ברז להמה֯[3
]מילד֯ות לפרעוה֯[4
]עד קץ[5
]ל֯[6

4Q**465** (4QpapText Mentioning Samson?) ed. E. Larson, *DJD* XXXVI

]ב֯נ֯○[ ]○○[1
]○ ○○ג֯ ישׁלׄחׄ[2
פר[שגן האגר[ת 3
ש[מׄשו֯ן֯ אליו ○[4
] *vacat?* [5
] א○בׄ○[6
]י○[7

4Q**466** (4QText Mentioning the Congregation of the Lord) ed. D. Pike and A. Skinner, *DJD* XXXVI

]○ יניח֯[1
א[מר אל אלוהי]ישראל(?) 2
]○ עדת יהוהׄ[3
]כול הע֯[4
]כול[5

4Q**467** (4QText Mentioning 'Light to Jacob') ed. D. Pike and A. Skinner, *DJD* XXXVI

Frgs. 1–2
Parallel: 4Q**462** 1 3–4

]○[ ]○ב֯[1
]○○ ○○[ ]○[ ]○ז אור ליעקב ו[2
]הׄגוים לישראל כׄ○[ ]○ן יאמרו אי פה ה○[3

bottom margin

4Q**464a** (4QNarrative E) trans. M. Stone and E. Eshel

1.]*ḥ*[ ]*n*[
2.] and he stood and judg[ed
3.] *dt* in a mystery for them[
4.]midwives to Pharaoh[
5.]to the period[
6.]*l*[

4Q**465** (4QpapText Mentioning Samson?) trans. E. Larson

2.] he will send[
3. the co]py of the lett[er
4. Sa]mson to him [
5.] *vacat?* [

4Q**466** (4QText Mentioning the Congregation of the Lord) trans. D. Pike and A. Skinner

1.] he will give rest[
2. sa]id to the God of [Israel(?)
3.] the congregation of YHWH[
4.]all the ʿ[
5.]all[

4Q**467** (4QText Mentioning 'Light to Jacob') trans. D. Pike and A. Skinner

Frgs. 1–2

1.] [ ] *b*[
2.] *z* a light to Jacob, and[
3.]the nations to Israel *k* [ ] *n* they will say, 'Where is the [

4Q**468f** (4QHistorical Text G) ed. A. Lange, *DJD* XXXVI

]ב֯נ֯י֯ גלעד
] את הארץ
]◦ל֯ת֯ת בארץ
]ל֯א֯דם
] שבע
]אתה

bottom margin

4Q**468g** (4QEschatological Work A?) ed. A. Lange, *DJD* XXXVI

]ך֯[ ]ם֯[
גפם מגפא רבא [
ואדום ועזה ואש֯[קלון
בני קטורא פלטת֯[
לחם את הכרכים֯[
י֯שראל וש◦[

4Q**468i** (4QSectarian Text?) ed. A. Lange, *DJD* XXXVI

]ב֯לי ליץ֯[[
] כיא חזק עורפם
]צ֯ר לבני הרע ה֯שיבונו
]ל֯נו מעול֯ם כיא א֯בות֯ינו
נא]ר֯רו מכול שלת לבם
]◦ת איוב

4Q**468k** (4QHymnic Text B?) ed. D. Ernst and A. Lange, *DJD* XXXVI (also published as 4Q**418** 303)

]ה שמע֯ ◦[
]ל֯ תתע֯ו[
]ה אלה [
]פ֯גועים [
]מ֯ותם בג֯[
] ז֯רחי֯[ך

4Q**468l** (4QFragment Mentioning Qoh 1:8-9) ed. D. Ernst and A. Lange, *DJD* XXXVI

]וגע֯ *vac* ק֯[ ]◦[ ]ג֯[ ]ש֯[
אז]ן֯ מ֯שמוע מה ש]היה

4Q468f (4QHistorical Text G) trans. A. Lange

1.]the sons of Gilead
2.] the land
3.] to give in the land
4.]to Edom
5.] seven
6.]you

4Q468g (4QEschatological Work A?) trans. A. Lange

1.]*k*[ ]*m*[
2. their bodies (with) a great plague [
3. Edom, Gaza, and Ash[kelon
4. the sons of Keturah, the remnant of[
5. he will make war against the towns[
6. Israel and *š* [

4Q468i (4QSectarian Text?) trans. A. Lange

1.]without scorning[ ]
2.] because their neck is hard
3.]enemy? to the sons of evil, they returned us
4.]*l* us from eternity, because our fathers
5.]they [were cu]rsed because of all the insolence of their hearts
6.] *t* enemy

4Q468k (4QHymnic Text B?) trans. D. Ernst and A. Lange

1.]*h* listen [
2.]*l* you err/lead astray[
3.]*h* these [
4.]stricken ones [
5.]their death *bg*[
6.] [your]shining[

4Q468l (4QFragment Mentioning Qoh 1:8-9) trans D. Ernst and A. Lange

1.]*wgʿ vac q*[ ][ ]g[ ]*š/ś*[
2. *ʿea*]*r from hearing. Whatever*[*has happened*

4Q471a (4QPolemical Text) ed. E. Eshel and M. Kister, *DJD* XXXVI

1]ל֯עת צוית֯ם֯ לבלתי
2]◦ם ותשקרו בבריתו
3 ות]א֯מרו נלחמה מלחמותיו כיא גאלנו
4]◦יכם ישפלו ולוא ידעו כיא מאס
5]◦◦ תתגברו למלחמה ואתם נחשבתם
6] בקואו *vac* משפט צדק תשאלו ועבודת
7] תתנשאו *vacat* ויבחר ב[ם]◦[ ] לזעקה
8] ותשיתׄו֯ [ ]◦מתוק

4Q476 (4QLiturgical Work B) ed. T. Elgvin, *DJD* XXIX

Frg. 1 (formerly frg. 2)

1]◦[
2] [
3]◦◦ ◦◦◦[
4]כ֯ו֯לכם תהיו בשלום [
5 לק]ד֯ש מנוח שבתׄ[ביו]םׄ[השבעי
6]◦ם אהלו֯[

Frg. 2 (formerly frg. 1)

1]]כ֯ו֯[ל
2]]לׄת מלךׄ[
3]]ק֯[ר]ו֯בי אל ל◦[
4 [ו]כול מרוחקי מלך מׄ[
5 הם מאוסי אלוהי[ם
6 כבוד לפני מלך ל◦[

Frg. 3

	Col. i	Col. ii
1	אלו]הׄיׄ	
2	אל]והים ◦◦◦[	
3	]לׄ[ ]ו ה֯וד	בכול תב֯[ל
4	א]ורׄ	וצה◦[
5	]◦ו	הכב֯[וד
6	]יחד	קוד֯[ש
7		ה֯פרׄו֯[כת

4Q**471a** (4QPolemical Text) trans. E. Eshel and M. Kister

1.]when you were commanded not to
2.] *m* And you violated His covenant
3. You] said, 'We shall fight His battles, because He redeemed us'
4.] your [ ] will be brought low, and they did not know that He despised
5.] you become mighty for battle, and you were accounted
6.]*bqwʾw* *vacat* You seek righteous judgement and service of
7.] you are arrogant *vacat* And he chose [them] [ ] to the cry
8.] and You put [ ] sweet

4Q**476** (4QLiturgical Work B) trans. T. Elgvin

Frg. 1

4. [ ]you will all be in peace [
5. [to san]ctify a repose, a Sabbath[on the seventh da]y[
6. [ ] its tent[

Frg. 2

1. [ ]al[l
2. [ ] King[
3. [ ]those n[e]ar to God [
4. [and] all who are rejected by (the) King [
5. they are despised by Go[d
6. glory before (the) King to [

Frg. 3

	Col. i	Col. ii
1.	the Go]d of	
2.	G]od	
3.	] splendour on all the ear[th	
4.	li]ght	and [
5.		the glo[ry
6.	]together	hol[y
7.		the curt[ain

4Q**476a** (4QLiturgical Work C) ed. T. Elgvin, *DJD* XXIX

Frg. 1

1]צדק עם רז֯[
2]עות המרום כ֯ל֯[
3]∘∘∘∘[

Frg. 2

1 משר]ת֯י אל֯[
2] קוד[ש

4Q**478** (4QpapFragment Mentioning Festivals) ed. E. Larson and L. H. Schiffman, *DJD* XXII

top margin

1]לא יעמוד֯[
2] והסמך[
3]∘ ו֯לא ישכח את֯[
4]∘מועדיה ואתה[
5]∘∘[

4Q**479** (4QText Mentioning Descendants of David) ed. E. Larson and L. H. Schiffman, *DJD* XXII

Frg. 1

1 ו֯א֯[
2 ידכ֯[
3 את עבודת֯[
4 זרע דויד֯[
5 דויד יצא[
6 לוא עשה[
7 צפ וש∘[
8 ואת]

Frg. 2

1]∘[
2 ז]ק֯ניו ∘[
3]ש ות֯ ∘[
4]∘∘[

Frg. 3

1 ע֯נ֯ב֯י֯ם֯[
2 וכסוכה[
3 גפנו וכב֯[
4 וחשפו֯[
5 י֯ק֯ום[

4Q476a (4QLiturgical Work C) trans. T. Elgvin

Frg. 1

1.]righteousness with [
2.] the elevated [ ] all[

Frg. 2

1. the serva]nts of God[
2.] holi[ness

4Q478 (4QpapFragment Mentioning Festivals) trans. E. Larson and L. H. Schiffman

1.]he will not stand[
2.] and he/it will be supported[
3.] and he will not forget the[
4.] its festivals/appointed times. And you[

4Q479 (4QText Mentioning Descendants of David) trans. E. Larson and L. H. Schiffman

Frg. 1

2. your hand[
3. the work of[
4. the descendants of David[
5. David, went out[
6. did not do[
7. floating (?) and [
8. and the [

Frg. 2

2.]his [e]lders [

Frg. 3

1. grapes[
2. and like a booth[
3. its (or his) vine [
4. and they uncovered[
5. he will arise

4Q**480** (4QNarrative F) ed. E. Larson and L. H. Schiffman, *DJD* XXII

	Col. i	Col. ii
1	[	בכלֺ נפלֺ[אותיו
2		]יהו֯ה[
3	]ה֯◦[	]לשמי֯[ם
4	]◦וא◦[	]ויכ֯◦◦[
5	]וניסה	אלהים ל◦[
6	]למען	השליכו[

4Q**481** (4QText Mentioning Mixed Kinds) ed. E. Larson and L. H. Schiffman, *DJD* XXII

Frg. 1

1]י֯ זקנים ◦ג֯◦[
2]◦ דייני כלאים א◦[
3]שבאי רשעים[

bottom margin

Frg. 2

1]◦ים[
2]◦ ציון תעלינ֯ה֯[
3]◦ר֯ו]

4Q**481a** (4QapocElisha) ed. J. Trebolle Barrera, *DJD* XXII

Frg. 1

top margin?

1]◦שׂעו לו להנא[
2]◦◦[ ]◦◦◦◦[

Frg. 2

1]י֯א כי
2 אלי]שׂע
3 ו]יעל אלישע ויראו
4 אליש]ע֯ ויבאו לקרת
5]ח֯משים אנשים֯
6 ה]הר]ים

Frg. 3

1]ך֯ והוא
2] לנגדו
3]ך֯ בקינה ויאמר
4]ר֯ב ואדון ולוא
5 נ]שׂא ביהודה
6] *vacat?*

4Q**480** (4QNarrative F) trans. E. Larson and L. H. Schiffman

	Col. i	Col. ii
1.		with all [His] mirac[les
2.		]the Lord (?)[
3.		]to heave[n
5.	]and he tried (?)	God [
6.	]in order that	They cast[

4Q**481** (4QText Mentioning Mixed Kinds) trans. E. Larson and L. H. Schiffman

Frg. 2

2.] Zion, they will ascend[

Frg. 1

1.] elders [
2.] judges (?) of mixed kinds [
3.]captors of evil-doers[

4Q**481a** (4QapocElisha) trans. M. Wise, M. Abegg, and E. Cook

Frg. 1

1.] to him here[

Frg. 2

1.] because
2. Eli]sha
3. and] Elisha arose and they saw
4. Elish]a and they came towards
5.]fifty men,
6. the]mount[ains

Frg. 3

1.] and he
2.] before him
3.] in lamentation, and he said
4.]master and lord, and not
5. li]ft up in Judah
6.] *vacat?*

4Q**481b** (4QNarrative G) ed. E. Larson and L. H. Schiffman, *DJD* XXII

1 י]שׁ֯יב נדחיו לארץ

2 ר]ב֯ ועצום מחניהם

3]ד֯[ ]◦◦[ ]מ֯ה֯ אשר

4]◦ כמדבר ואת

5] מפטיש כ֯ול

6]מיו ו֯[ ]

4Q**481c** (4QPrayer for Mercy) ed. E. Larson and L. H. Schiffman, *DJD* XXII

1]◦[ ]ם ◦[

2]◦נו אוי ד֯י[

3]◦ה אל הר גבה֯[

4]לונו אכלו שנאינו [

5]י֯ר֯ה והללו בכל פיהם[

6]כי רבים רחמיך ומרב אשמ]תם

7]◦א והנה מכה על מכה [

8]ש וקבצנו ◦[

9]ש בכלׄ[

10]ה מים ◦[

4Q**481d** (4QFrags. with Red Ink) ed. E. Larson and L. H. Schiffman, *DJD* XXII

Frg. 1
Underline: words written in red ink

	Col. i	Col. ii
1		נ֯סע]
2	]אחׄי֯	*vacat*
3	]או משחית	עז לנו ב◦לׄ]
4	]ת֯ לחוק	שמנה ה֯]
5	]◦[	דבורת ◦]
6	]◦◦[	

4Q481b (4QNarrative G) trans. E. Larson and L. H. Schiffman

1. He] will return His scattered ones to the land
2. gre]at and mighty, their camps
3.] that
4.] like the desert and the
5.]from a hammer, all
6.] his [ ]

4Q481c (4QPrayer for Mercy) trans. E. Larson and L. H. Schiffman

2.] woe [
3.] to a high hill[
4.]us (?) our enemies consumed [
5.] and they will praise with all their mouths[
6.]for many are your mercies and because of [their] great gui[lt
7.] and behold blow upon blow [
8.] and gather us [
9.] in all[
10.] waters [

4Q481d (4QFrags. with Red Ink) trans. E. Larson and L. H. Schiffman

Frg. 1 Col. i
Underline: words written in red ink

2.]<u>my brother</u>
3.] destroyer
4.] <u>for a law</u>

Frg. 1 Col. ii
1. <u>travelled[</u>
2. *vacat*
3. strength for us [
4. its oil (?) [
5. a bee of [

Frg. 2

1]◦◦[
2]◦ צור לב֯[
3]   vacat חזה בׄה֯[
4]קׄרב כלדבר לאכל[

Frg. 3

1]וׄד[
2 [ ] עונתו ◦[
3]◦ ואהיה עמו ואת[
4]א֯קחה מי֯ד֯ו֯[

Frg. 4

1]◦ נ[
2 [ ] ויקח ל◦[
3]מ֯תחתנו֯[

Frg. 5

1]ת֯ותו ותק֯[
2]ל֯בני יש[ראל
3 [ ] ו◦[

Frg. 6

1]ו֯בם[

Frg. 7

1]שׄ ◦[
2]◦ עמו [
3]ר֯◦[

4Q**481e** (4QNarrative H) ed. E. Larson and L. H. Schiffman, *DJD* XXII

1]בזו לדברי פיכה [לא שמעו
2]ל[עו]לׄם י֯ה֯יה וזרעו לדרות אחריה֯[ם
3]◦ {א֯שר} מחרפו◦[

4Q**482** (4QpapJub[i]?) ed. M. Baillet, *DJD* VII

Frg. 1 Jub 13:29 (cf. Gen 14:22-24)

1]◦עליו[ן
2 אשר ל[כ֯ה ו֯]לוא
3 ומ]מ֯ר֯א ה֯ם֯[
4]י֯ל֯ו֯ד אש[ה
5]ד֯י רצ֯[

Frg. 2 Jub 36:9 (?)

1 [אשר]יחרוש[
2]ש֯מי֯ם֯[
3]ל[

Frg. 2

1.]__[
2.] <u>strength of heart</u>[
3.] *vacat* he saw in[
4.]bring near anything to eat [

Frg. 3

2.] his transgression [
3.] and I will be with him, and I will[
4.]I will take from his hand[

Frg. 5

1.]his[ ]and you[
2.]to the children of Is[rael

Frg. 4

2.] and he took [
3.]from beneath us[

Frg. 7

2.] with him [

Frg. 6

1.]and with them[

4Q**481e** (4QNarrative H) trans. E. Larson and L. H. Schiffman

1.]they despised, to the words of Your mouth [they did not listen
2.]for[ev]er it shall be, and his descendants for the generations after[them
3.] from the reproaches of [

4Q**482** (4QpapJub[i]?) trans. M. Wise, M. Abegg, and E. Cook

Frg. 1

1.] most hig[h
2. which is]yours and[not
3. and Ma]mre they[
4.]born of wom[an

Frg. 2

1. [which]he shall engrave[
2.]heavens[

Frg. 3

1]פניׄ אל ◦[
2]כי לוא [
3]ל הןׄ א[
4]◦א [

Frg. 4

1]בׄרׄי◦[
2]ל חכ◦[
3]◦דפו ד◦[

Frg. 5

1 [בׄ◦◦]
2]כול [
3]ל[

Frg. 6

1 [שמיׄם]
2]גׄבולי יׄ[

Frg. 7

1]◦◦◦◦ ◦[
2]◦ם ב[
3]עליׄ[

Frg. 8

1]◦[
2 א]לׄ עליוׄןׄ[

4Q**483** (4QpapGen° or papJub[j]?) ed. M. Baillet, *DJD* VII

Frg. 1 Gen 1:28 (cf. Jub 2:14)

1]וכׄיבשוׄ[ה
2 ע]לׄ הארץ[
3]◦[ ]◦◦◦[

Frg. 2

1 [דׄ]
2]◦◦◦[

4Q**485** (4QpapProph) ed. M. Baillet, *DJD* VII

Frg. 1

1]וׄ תדורשׄ[
2]אׄיכה כׄ◦[
3]◦ליׄו ושמעת[
4 [וׄשב שבוׄת◦]
5]◦◦◦ם אחר כתוׄבׄ[
6]◦ אשר יביןׄ[

Frg. 2

1]◦ הדׄ?[
2]רׄ אש◦[
3]לרע ל◦[
4]מׄהׄ ל◦[

Frg. 3

top margin?

1 [לאחיׄהׄ]
2]תׄגׄלה [

Frg. 3

1.]before God [
2.]for not [
3.] behold [

Frg. 6

1.] heavens[
2.]boundaries of [

Frg. 5

2.]all [

Frg. 8

2. Go]d Most High[

4Q**483** (4QpapGen° or papJub^j?) trans. M. Wise, M. Abegg, and E. Cook

Frg. 1

1.]and they subdued[her
2. up]on the earth[

4Q**485** (4QpapProph) trans. M. Wise, M. Abegg, and E. Cook

Frg. 1

1.] you shall examine[
2.]how [
3.] his [ ] and [ ] shall hear[
4.] and return the captivity of [
5.] another [ ]it is written[
6.] which he shall understand[

Frg. 3

1.] to her brother[
2.]shall reveal [

Frg. 2

3.]for evil [

Frg. 4

1]◦אף֯ שמע֯[

]◦◦ש֯[

2]◦◦ב֯ו֯ק֯[

Frg. 5

1]◦ר מ◦[

2]ו֯ בתו֯ר֯[ה

4Q**486** (4QpapSap A?) ed. M. Baillet, *DJD* VII

1]◦◦◦◦[

2]ה֯[

3]מ֯◦◦◦[ ]

4]ד֯רׄכיׄהם

5]בסודכם

6]◦ ובחיׄקכם

7]עׄג

8]ם֯

9]◦ם

4Q**487** (4QpapSap B?) ed. M. Baillet, *DJD* VII

Frg. 1 Col. i

1

2]◦◦ו֯ר

3]ה ור֯ו֯מם

4]ב֯כׄול חוקיו

5]עו כימי

6]ל[

Frg. 1 Col. ii

1 מ◦[

2 ברהו לעפר כ֯[

3 יתר בשרירותׄ[לבו

4 בלהבי אש מו֯[

5 בהפכה ושכ[

6 איש אשר [

Frg. 2

1]◦◦[ ]ש֯[ ]◦[

2]ש נדכא בה◦[

3]◦◦מ֯◦ דגלי֯ ב◦◦[

4] גם אל יסתתׄ[ר

5]◦ צרוף בתורת֯[

Frg. 5

2.] in the law[

Frg. 4

1.] listen[

4Q**486** (4QpapSap A?) trans. M. Wise, M. Abegg, and E. Cook

4.]their ways
5.]by your council
6.] and in your embrace

4Q**487** (4QpapSap B?) trans. M. Wise, M. Abegg, and E. Cook with N. Gordon

Frg. 1 Col. i

3.] and praise
4.]in all His statutes
5.] as the days of

Frg. 1 Col. ii

2. He created him for dust [
3. remainder, in the stubbornness[of his heart
4. in flames of fire [
5. in destruction and [
6. a man who [

Frg. 2

2.] crushed by [
3.] banners of [
4.] also let him not hide himse[lf
5.] refined by the law of[

6]ות נפלאות צ[
7]וֹת לב אשמה [
8]אמת וחוכֹ[מה
9]◦ בהשפטֿ[

Frg. 3

1]◦וֹ [
2]ק ש]]ם [
3]ת לוֹ אלוֹ[הים
4] *vacat* [
5] איֹ◦[

Frg. 4

1]◦◦◦ רוח [
2]◦ה חטתוֹ וֹ[
3]בֿיֹת נֹ[

Frg. 5

1]◦רי [
2]תוֹצ◦[
3]הֿ ש◦[
4]ק וע◦[
5]א ייֹרא[
6]ת נפש מעמֿ[
7] ליוֹ◦[

Frg. 6

1]שׁוֹבֿ מֿד◦[
2]חד עריצים[
3]לט לשל[
4]ואל יֹגל[
מת◦◦[
5]בֿ לבו ממח[
6]מוֹיֹם בתעֿ[
7]◦◦[

Frg. 7

1]◦[
2] ולאה[
3]יֹ איש [
4]וֹת חד◦[
5]◦[ ]◦עיל להצ[
6] עולמים ולה[
7]◦ כוֹל[

Frg. 8

top margin

1] יתן לו
2]חמוֹ על
3] *vac* אל
4]◦ו בֿ מכול
5] אל י◦[

Frg. 9

1 שלוֹ[
2 אל [
3 בוֹ [

Frg. 10

1]א◦[
2]ך עונֹ[
3 נ]פֿלאות[
4]לֿבוז א[
5]רֿקים [
6]משמע[

Frg. 11

1]◦ ופהֿ[
2]וֹ תוך ◦◦[
3]ע דבר◦[
4]צים ל◦[
5]לֿ[

Frg. 12

1]◦[
2]◦ יֹמישו ◦[
3]רץ וֹ[
4]ה אותותֿ[

6.] wonders [
7.] guilty heart [
8.]truth and wisd[om
9.] when [ ] enters into judgement[

Frg. 4

1.] spirit [
2.] his sin [
3.]house [

Frg. 3

3.] to him Go[d
4.] *vacat* [

Frg. 6

1.]return [
2.] ruthless ones[
3.] for [
4.]and let him not [
5.] his heart from [

Frg. 5

5.] he shall fear[
6.] person/soul from [

Frg. 8

1.] he shall give to him
2.] upon
3.] *vac* to/God/not
4.] from all
5.] let him not [

Frg. 7

2.] and to [
3.] a man [

5.] to [
6.] everlasting and [
7.] all[

Frg. 10

3. w]onders[
4.]for shame [

6.]hearing[

Frg. 9

2.] to/God/not [
3.] in him [

Frg. 12

2.] they removed [

4.] signs[

Frg. 11

1.] and a mouth[
2.] midst of [
3.] matter [

Frg. 13

]◦[
]◦ה מרפ֯[א
]ה ה֯יות [
]א֯ל ולוא[
]◦חיו ◦[
]ל֯[

Frg. 14

] יסור מש◦[
י]ק֯ו֯ש ללכוד ז֯◦[
]ים רע יחשוב֯[

Frg. 15

]ק֯◦[
]ר אש מעשיו [
]רחוב פי אשמת֯◦[
]◦◦◦◦[

Frg. 16

]◦◦[ ]כ֯י֯ן֯ ל֯א֯[
]מה ואל יפתח א֯[
]ישר ינחלנה ואל י֯◦[
]◦[

Frg. 17

]ע֯ ש֯[
ת]בונן ב[
]◦ו֯ ועש[
]◦ם י֯נ֯◦[

Frg. 18

]א֯יש ◦[
]ו֯ב חיי֯[
]ח עורף [
] ע֯ת֯ה א[

Frg. 19

] מ֯◦[
]ו֯כ֯אחד[
]וא שנ◦[
]◦[

Frg. 20

]ם [
]ם אל ה֯[
]ש֯ע איש[
]◦ו֯ בא◦◦[

Frg. 21

]◦[ ]◦[
] ולמכ◦[
]◦? חוק[

Frg. 22

]◦ב֯◦ [
]לכי [
]א֯ת ◦[

Frg. 13

2.] heali[ng
3.] to be [
4.] and not[
5.] his [

Frg. 14

1.] he shall turn aside from [
2. h]e shall lay a trap to capture [
3.] evil he shall consider[

Frg. 15

2.] fire his deeds [
3.]width of the mouth of [ ] offense[

Frg. 16

2.] and let him not open [
3.]the upright one shall inherit it and let him not [

Frg. 18

1.]man [

3.] neck [
4.] now [

Frg. 20

2.] to/God/not [
3.] man[

Frg. 17

2. you shall] understand [
3.] and [

Frg. 19

2.]and as one[

Frg. 21

2.] and to [
3.] statute[

Frg. 23

1 [ר דבׄ]
2 [נׄוֹ איש ◦]
3 [אל נחלת◦]

Frg. 24

1 [◦]
2 כי[בוד לב ◦]
3 [◦וֹת טוב]

Frg. 25

1 [תו ◦]
2 [וׄ צ◦ד]

Frg. 26

1 [◦] [ש]
2 [מרמׄ]
3 [◦יׄ ד◦]

Frg. 27

1 [◦◦] [רׄ◦◦]
2 [◦אׄ אש]
3 [לוא יׄ]

Frg. 28

1 [שלׄ◦]
2 [ין פלי]
3 [ל ל]

Frg. 29

1 [בׄע◦]
2 [◦רל ◦]
3 [ל]

Frg. 30

1 [הֹ]
2 [וׄש◦]
3 [ם]
4 [ל◦◦]

Frg. 31

1 [◦]
2 [◦ה]
3 [מימ◦]

Frg. 32

1 [◦]
2 [◦ר ◦]
3 [ליׄ]

Frg. 33

1 [◦]
2 [מתו]
3 [◦]

Frg. 34

1 [◦] [◦]
2 [◦תמ]
3 [ל]

Frg. 35

1 [◦◦◦]
2 [◦ כול]

Frg. 36

1 [לשחר]
2 [אוזניוֹ]

Frg. 37

1 [עם כול]
2 [באׄוֹר]

Frg. 38

1 [מֹ◦◦]
2 [?◦ והמקׄ]

Frg. 24

2. har]dness of heart [
3.] good [

Frg. 23

2.] man [
3.] to/God inheritance of [

Frg. 28

2.] wonderful [

Frg. 27

3.]he shall not [

Frg. 36

1.] to seek [
2.] his ears[

Frg. 35

2.] all [

Frg. 38

2.] and the [

Frg. 37

1.]with all[
2.] in the light[

Frg. 39

1]ו֯הב֯[
2 ע]ו֯למים[
3]∘[ ]∘[

Frg. 40

1]ר֯י֯ת[
2] כול[
3]ל֯[

Frg. 41

1]∘[
2]גבו֯ר֯ ∘[
3]∘∘ו֯ א֯∘∘[

Frg. 42

1]∘ מ֯∘[
2]∘י֯ח∘∘[

Frg. 43

1]ו֯דשי֯∘∘[
2]כ֯∘∘[

Frg. 44

1 ∘ב֯[
2 ר∘[

Frg. 45

1]∘[
2]∘∘בב[
3]ש ∘[

Frg. 46

1]א֯ה∘[
2]∘[

Frg. 47

1]יתום֯[

Frg. 48

1]ב֯ש∘[

Frg. 49

1]א֯ה∘∘[

Frg. 50

1] או֯[

Frg. 51

1]ס֯ו֯[

Frg. 52

1]ל֯ מרב[

Frg. 53

1]∘∘[
2]בא∘[

4Q**488** (4QpapApocryphon ar) ed. M. Baillet, *DJD* VII

Frg. 1

1]ד֯ את֯ע֯שק֯ו֯[

Frg. 2

1]ר∘[
2] ∘[

Frg. 3

1] ואנ֯∘[

Frg. 4

1]מ֯∘צר מ֯∘[
2]ב֯ט֯ח∘[

Frg. 40

2.] all[

Frg. 39

2. ev]erlasting[

Frg. 41

2.]warrior [

Frg. 47

1.]orphan[

4Q**488** (4QpapApocryphon ar) trans. E. Cook

Frg. 1

1.] they contended with[

Frg. 5

1]ו֯ר֯ [

2]◦שׁו֯ד֯[

Frg. 6

1]א ו◦[

4Q**498** (4QpapSap/Hymn) ed. M. Baillet, *DJD* VII

Frg. 1 Col. i

top margin

1 חו]ב֯ב כנפשי

2]◦ת֯

Frg. 1 Col. ii

1 ◦[

Frg. 2

1]מבק[

2]ו֯נחלי֯ מ֯]ים

3] י֯ו֯צר כ֯[

4]◦ה כול ◦[

5]◦י֯ו֯ת ל◦◦[

Frg. 3

	Col. ii	Col. i
1	]	]ו֯ה
2	כ֯◦[	]ה כול
3	◦[	]מ֯חש^תב֯

Frg. 4

1]צ֯י֯ל ה֯[

2] הי֯[

Frg. 5

1]◦◦[ה ר◦[

Frg. 6

1] בכול לבבכה [

2]◦[ ]ד֯ב֯ר֯[ ]ל֯[

Frg. 7

1]ה֯ לגי֯ו֯[

2]י֯◦[

Frg. 8

1] במצ֯◦[

bottom margin

Frg. 9

1]◦[

2]כול ו֯בתע[

Frg. 10

1]◦◦לי֯◦◦[

Frg. 11

1]שׁ֯מעו֯ ל◦[

2]◦◦ ב֯ח֯ו֯[

Frg. 12

1]ב֯◦ ש[

Frg. 13

1]עבר[

Frg. 14

1]◦וב [

2]י֯צ◦[

Frg. 15

1] אותו ד [

4Q**498** (4QpapSap/Hymn) trans. M. Wise, M. Abegg, and E. Cook with N. Gordon

Frg. 1 Col. i

1.] my best [fri]end [

Frg. 3 Col. i

2.] all
3.] design

Frg. 2

2.]and brooks of w[ater
3.] creator [
4.] all [

Frg. 4

1. de]liver [

Frg. 7

1.] for a stranger[

Frg. 6

1.] with all your heart [
2.] [ ]matter[ ] [

Frg. 9

2.]all and in [

Frg. 8

1.] with [

Frg. 11

1.]they hear [
2.] with [

Frg. 10

1.] to me [

Frg. 13

1.]passed by[

Frg. 15

1.] him [

4Q**523** (4QJonathan) ed. É. Puech, *DJD* XXV

Frgs. 1–2

1 וי[ק/ש֯]ו[ן֯ ל֯ך֯]
2 [י אוגו/י יהונתׄן֯]
3 [הצבאים גנבו]
4 גנ[בׄו המזלגות ו֯]
5 [גוג וסגוג ◦]
6 [◦] [ב֯י֯ת בטפ֯ם֯]
7 [נתו/ינים֯ ◦]
8 [תסובׄ]בו[ן֯ א֯ת֯]
9 או[צרותיהו סו/ימות֯]
10 [ת/נטון גלו/יקה]
11 [לפקדׄן ט◦]
12 [לׄ]

Frg. 3

1 י[ס֯תׄגון ט/מ]
2 ?א[ל יבטלון פ֯סי/ה]
3 [◦ם ק/ס◦]

Frg. 4

1 הלו֯]
2 ליׄקם֯]
3 [ ]ם֯]

Frg. 5

1 [ה/חם]
2 [◦]

4Q**526** (4QTestament?) ed. É. Puech, *DJD* XXV

top margin

1 [אדני לאבי לוׄ תעשה ל◦]
2 [באשר היתה]

4Q**527** (4QLiturgical Work D?) ed. É. Puech, *DJD* XXV

top margin(?)

1 אשר היו נׄצפנים לחג אׄדׄ[(ו)]ני
2 ◦[ ] לו שלמים כן [
3 [כ֯ן֯ ה֯כ֯ו֯ה֯ן֯ (◦)◦]

4Q523 (4QJonathan) trans. M. Wise, M. Abegg, and E. Cook

Frgs. 1–2

1. [and they]saved you[
2. [ ] they remove (?) Jonathan[
3. [ ]the troops stole[
4. [ ] they [stol]e the flesh-hooks and[
5. [ ]Gog and Magog [
6. [ ] with their children[
7. [ ]stationed [
8. [ ]you go around the[
9. [ ]his [st]orehouses, treasures[
10. [ ] ? [
11. [ ]as a deposit [

Frg. 3

1. [ ] they [shall] multiply themselves [
2. [let]them [n]ot remove [

Frg. 4

2. to [

4Q526 (4QTestament?) trans. M. Wise, M. Abegg, and E. Cook

1.]the Lord to my father, you shall not do [
2.]in that which was[

4Q527 (4QLiturgical Work D?) trans. M. Wise, M. Abegg, and E. Cook

1. that was hidden for the feast of the L[ord
2. [ ] peace offering for him, thus [
3. [ ]thus the priest [

4Q**551** (4QDanSuz? ar) ed. E. Cook

1]◦תתא [ ] ◦רב
2 א]ד̇ין גבר שב̇[ ]מא הוא מן
3] בר יהונתן בר [יהו]שוע בר ישמעאל בר̊[ ] באתר דנה
4] ויתכנשון כל אנש קרתא על ביתא וימרון לה הנפק̊[ ]אלהא ויאמרו
5 אמ]ר להון אחי אל תבאש[ו]ח̊ר תנא
6 ע]ל[ ]◦ש̇לם̊ [ ]שלם להון
7]יא מ̊◦◦
8]ל דנה

4Q**569** (4QProverbs ar) ed. E. Cook

Frg. 1

1]◦◦◦◦◦
2 יקנא אסין[
3 אל [ ] מן[
4 ואל תש̇ת̇פל [
5 והוית כנס̇י̇[
6 הן מרך רחם[
7 למקטלך אנ◦[
8 דכור עני בד[
9 אלף בניכה[

Frg. 2

1]◦[
2]ח̇ט[
3]רך[
4]ד̇ה◦[
5]ת [ר]ש̇ותא [
6]כ̊תה̇ שכב̇[
7]◦א ל̊הוא [
8]ו קדק̇ד̊[

Frg. 3

1]◦◦◦ין לק[
2]ד̊ן שלטנך̇[
3]ט̊ת̇נ̊[
4]ה אנת[ה

4Q**551** (4QDanSuz? ar) trans. E. Cook

1.] you (?) will come [ ] great
2. t]hen an old man[ ] he was from
3.] son of Jonathan son of [Jo]shua son of Ishmael son of[ ] in this place
4.] And all the men of the city gather around the house, and say to him, Bring out[ ]God, and they say
5. sai]d to them, My brothers, do not act wicked[ly] here
6. up]on[ ] peace [ ]peace to them

8. because o]f this

4Q**569** (4QProverbs ar) trans. E. Cook

Frg. 1

2. let him acquire a physician[
3. God/not [ ] (from/who) [
4. and do not be humbled [
5. and I/you have become like a ruler[
6. if your master loves[
7. to kill you [
8. remember the poor in [
9. teach your sons[

Frg. 2

5.] of the [a]uthority [
6.] lie down[
7.] will be [
8.] and crown-of-head[

Frg. 3

2.] your dominion[

4.] (you/woma[n])

5]חׄדה ר[
6]רחך [
7]בקש[טא
8]תיׄ[
9]◦◦[

4Q**578** (4QHistorical Text B) ed. É. Puech, *DJD* XXV

1]◦ת̊[ ]נ̊ה̊[
2a]ןׄ
2]פ̊תלמׄיס[
3 פתל]מׄיס בׄנו̊[
4]◦ה פתל[מיס

4Q**579** (4QHymnic Work?) ed. É. Puech, *DJD* XXV

Frg. 1

1]ב̊כׄלׄ[מ]עשׄ[ה/י־
2]כל מלׄאכים ואׄ[
3]היות לי̊ד̊ו̊ע̊ים מש[
4]ת̊הום ממ{ש}<יט>ה̊ ◦[
5]לׄ[ ]לׄ[

Frg. 2

1]ם̊ ואתם ◦◦[

Frg. 3

1]ם̊ [
2 לימ◦[

4Q**581** (4QTestament? ar) ed. E. Cook

Frg. 1

1]◦◦וי◦[
2] חסיר מנדע[
3]יׄת^ש^רא ברה̊[
4]דׄך על ש[
5]◦◦◦[ ]◦◦[

Frg. 2

1]◦ קדמ[
2]ב̊דיל כדןׄ מללׄ[
3] רברבין [
4]א ואנח̊[נא
5]◦ד◦[

5.]one? [
6.]your [
7.]in tru[th

4Q578 (4QHistorical Text B) trans. M. Wise, M. Abegg, and E. Cook

2.]Ptolemy[
3. Ptole]my his son[
4.] Ptole[my

4Q579 (4QHymnic Work?) trans. M. Wise, M. Abegg, and E. Cook

Frg. 2

1.] and you [

Frg. 1

1.]in all the[d]eed[s of
2.]all the angels and [
3.]becoming known [
4.]the deep making tremble [

4Q581 (4QTestament? ar) trans. E. Cook

Frg. 2

1.] before (?)[
2.]because of this he spoke[
3.] great [
4.] and w[e

Frg. 1

2.] lacking in knowledge[
3.]his son will be released (?)[
4.] upon [

Frg. 3

1]◦◦[
2 א]מר מרי [
3]ח◦◦ מן ב◦[
4]◦◦ו̊ר[ ]מׄנדע מ◦[
5]ל◦◦[

Frg. 4

1 רב]ר̊בין [
2]בשמיא ◦א[
3]◦[

5Q**10** (5QapocrMal) ed. J. T. Milik, *DJD* III

Frg. 1

1] משוחת ל̊א̊[דוני
2]הל̇צ̊ים בבהמת[
3]כיא מלך גדול א[ני] א̇[מר יהוה צבאות
4 א]שר הוא אל חי ו̊הו̊[א
5 ל]מ̇נו̇ת̇ [א]ת̇ הכול [

Frg. 2

1]ה̊◦[
2] השבט̇[

Frg. 3

1] כול̊ [
2]ת [

6Q**10** (6QpapProph) ed. M. Baillet, *DJD* III

Frg. 1

	Col. i	Col. ii
1	]כ̊ל̇י̊	◦[
2	[	ואחרי[
3	]◦ת	הלכתם [
4	[	לשפוך ח̊[מתי עליכם
5	[	בגוי[ם
6	]◦	שמי[
7		ל◦[

Frg. 2

	Col. i	Col. ii
1	]◦תי	◦[
2	[	
3	]◦◦	

Frg. 4

1. g]reat [
2.]in heaven [

Frg. 3

2. h]e said, My lord [
3.] from [
4.] [ ]knowledge [

5Q**10** (5QapocrMal) trans. M. Wise, M. Abegg and E. Cook with N. Gordon

Frg. 1

1.] '*which is blemished to the L*[*ord*' (Mal 1:14)
2.]the ones who scorn with animals[
3.]for [I] am a great King, sa[ys the LORD of Hosts
4. w]ho is a living God and h[e
5. to] distribute all of the [

Frg. 2

2.] the tribe[

Frg. 3

1.] all [

6Q**10** (6QpapProph) trans. M. Wise, M. Abegg, and E. Cook with N. Gordon

Frg. 1

Col. i | Col. ii

2. and after[
3. you walk [
4. pouring out [My] a[nger upon you
5. among the Gentile[s
6. My name[

Frg. 3

1 מׄןׄ]
2 א]

Frg. 4

1]◦◦◦ ◦[
2]הׄןׄ א◦[
3]◦◦יאמ◦[
4]מהוׄןׄ[
5]◦ תׄ◦לׄ◦◦[

Frg. 6

1]◦הי◦[
2]לׄ[

Frg. 7

1] אל ◦[

Frg. 8

1]◦◦◦[
2]אלי◦[

Frg. 9

1]לׄאפׄל ו◦[

Frg. 10

1] אלוׄ[הים

Frg. 11

1]◦לאׄ[

Frg. 12

1 ו◦[
2 [ ]לׄ[

Frg. 13

1]ןׄ לו [
2] כל◦[

Frg. 14

1 ולׄ[
2 א[

Frg. 15

1]ם[
2] ובלות מׄ[
3]סוסיהם[
4]◦◦◦[

Frg. 16

1 ש[מׄואל ◦[
2] הבי◦[
3]◦ ◦[

Frg. 17

1] הצ[
2]◦ וא◦[

Frg. 18

1]◦[
2]◦ ופׄ[
3]ים אׄ[
4]ל ◦[

Frg. 19

1]ושׄ◦[
2]◦ל◦לׄ[

Frg. 20

1]לׄ◦לם [
2]לפנׄ◦[

Frg. 21

1]◦ אשׄ[
2]אשר עׄזׄבׄ[

Frg. 4

4.]of wealth[

Frg. 7

1.] to/God/not [

Frg. 9

1.]to darkness and [

Frg. 13

1.] for him [

Frg. 15

2.] and worn [
3.]their horses[

Frg. 17

2.] and [

Frg. 21

2.]that forsook[

Frg. 3

1. from[

Frg. 10

1. Go[d

Frg. 12

1. and [

Frg. 14

1. and [

Frg. 16

1. Sa]muel [

Frg. 18

2.] and [

Frg. 20

1.] their [
2.]before [

Frg. 22

1]מ֯כל◦[

Frg. 23

2]ר֯י◦[

Frg. 24

1]◦ש[

Frg. 25

1]ח֯ג֯◦[

Frg. 26

1]◦[
2]פׄלא◦[

6Q**11** (6QAllegory of the Vine) ed. M. Baillet, *DJD* III

1]◦נׄיות [
2]ה֯ ע֯ם֯[
3]ובקציר באׄתׄ[י
4 מן הב]קר עד הערב ◦[
5 חב]לה ילדה חבל ילד ית[
6]ואמרתה הגפן הנטעת אשמ֯[ר

bottom margin

6Q**12** (6QApocryphal Prophecy) ed. M. Baillet, *DJD* III

1 ביום ההו]א֯ה יהיה ישראל ע◦◦[
2] *vacat* [
3 מאין]יושב ואחר היובלים[
4 להאבי]ד֯ם בגויים ולזרותׄ[ם בארצות
5]◦◦◦◦◦◦◦◦◦[

6Q**13** (6QPriestly Prophecy) ed. M. Baillet, *DJD* III

1]]◦[ ]ע֯ל[[
2] א]רץ[ ]◦ ◦[[
3]]בל ◦[[
4 מבני פינחס וש[ישוע]
5 בן יוצדק אשר[ ]
6 [ביר]וׄ[ש]ל[י]ם֯ ביום[ ]

6Q11 (6QAllegory of the Vine) trans. M. Wise, M. Abegg, and E. Cook

2.] with/people[
3.]and with the harvest [I] came[
4. from the mor]ning until the evening [
5.] a girl [des]troyed, a boy destroyed [
6.]and you shall say, 'I shall gua[rd] the planted vine[

6Q12 (6QApocryphal Prophecy) trans. M. Wise, M. Abegg, and E. Cook with N. Gordon

1. on tha]t [day] Israel shall [
2.] *vacat* [
3. without]inhabitants. And after the jubilees[
4. to destro]y them among the Gentiles and to scatt[er them among the nations

6Q13 (6QPriestly Prophecy) trans. M. Wise, M. Abegg, and E. Cook with N. Gordon

1.]upon[
2. l]and[

4. from the sons of Phinehas and [Jeshua]
5. the son of Jehozadak who[ ]
6. in Jer]u[sa]l[e]m on the day[

7 [ש]נ֯יבצ֯ר לי◦[… [
8 ו֯היה בימ֯[ים ההם … [
9 בימים [ההם … [

6Q**14** (6QApocal. ar) ed. M. Baillet, *DJD* III

Frg. 1

1]בל֯ל֯◦[
2]מן די ◦[
3]פ֯ה לגב[ה] כפיל֯[
4]יא יפוק מן א◦[
5]ה יבדה ע֯[
6] כול חות ב֯[רא
7]עמי֯ן מן ◦[
8]יא[

Frg. 2

1]ע֯ק יקום [
2]עד די כ֯[
3 א]ב֯ל ובכי [
4]◦◦ב֯ל֯א֯ כ֯[

6Q**19** (6QText Related to Genesis ar) ed. M. Baillet, *DJD* III

1] … ארעא]
2 די בני חם[… [
3] ע]ממיא[… [
4]]א ח֯◦[… [

6Q**20** (6QDeut?) ed. M. Baillet, *DJD* III

1]
2 כי הא֯[רץ
3 ארץ נחל[י מים
4 בית האו֯[
5 התהמות [
6 חדשה ו֯[
7 וה֯תנחל֯[תם
8 ח֯[
9 ◦[
10 ו֯◦[
11 חק֯[

7. [She]nibazzar [ ]
8. and it shall come to pass in [those] da[ys]
9. in [those] days [ ]

6Q**14** (6QApocal. ar) trans. M. Wise, M. Abegg, and E. Cook

Frg. 1

2.]from which [
3.] to the height doubled (?) [
4.] he will go out of [
5.] he will destroy him [
6.] every beast of th[e field
7.]peoples from [

Frg. 2

1.] he will rise [
2.]until [
3. m]ourning and weeping [

6Q**19** (6QText Related to Genesis ar) trans. M. Abegg

1. [the land]
2. of the sons of Ham[ ]
3. [ ]the [p]eoples[ ]

6Q**20** (6QDeut?) trans. M. Wise, M. Abegg, and E. Cook

1. *vacat* [
2. for the l[and
3. a land of brook[s of water
4. house of the [
5. the deeps [
6. new [
7. and [you] may possess[

6Q**21** (6QProphetic Text?) ed. M. Baillet, *DJD* III

top margin

נפשו֯תי[
את עמי֯ [
לקצו֯ר ל[

11Q**29** (11QFragment Related to *Serekh ha-Yaḥad*) ed. F. García Martínez, E. J. C. Tigchelaar, and A. S. van der Woude, *DJD* XXIII

]◦ ◦◦◦[
]רׄוחו לבגׄו֯ד֯ ב֯[
]ם֯ בראי֯[שונה

XQ**6** (XQOffering ar) ed. A. Lemaire, *DJD* XXXVI

] לש֯[ ]◦ [
]ו֯ כשלו ו֯כש[
]ח֯י֯ לקורבא קו֯[
]לארמא[
]ע֯י֯ן [

6Q**21** (6QProphetic Text?) trans. M. Wise, M. Abegg, and E. Cook

1.]selves [
2. My people [
3. to reap/cut short [

11Q**29** (11QFragment Related to *Serekh ha-Yaḥad*) trans. F. García Martínez, E. J. C. Tigchelaar, and A. S. van der Woude

2.]his spirit to betray [
3.] in the fir[st (year)

XQ**6** (XQOffering ar) trans. E. Cook

2.] they stumbled and [
3.] to sacrifice (?) [
4.]to lift up[

Contents of Complete Edition

Part 1: Texts Concerned with Religious Law

4QWar Scroll-like Text B (4Q**471**) (*DJD* XXXVI, 2000)
4QM[a–e] (4Q**491–495**) (4Q**491–495,** *DJD* VII, 1982; WAC with Gordon)
4QpapM[f] (4Q**496**) (*DJD* VII, 1982; WAC with Gordon)
4QpapWar Scroll-like Text A (4Q**497**) (*DJD* VII, 1982; WAC with Gordon)
11QSefer ha-Milḥamah (11Q**14**) (*DJD* XXIII, 1998)

C. Purity Rule

4QTohorot A (4Q**274**) (*DJD* XXXV, 1999)

D. Other Rules

4QOrdinances[a–c] (4Q**159**, **513–514**) (4Q**159**, *DJD* V, 1968; Allegro with Gordon); (4Q**513–514**, *DJD* VII, 1982; WAC with Gordon)
4QHalakha A (4Q**251**) (*DJD* XXXV, 1999)
4QMiscellaneous Rules (4Q**265**) (*DJD* XXXV, 1999)

E. Epistolary Treatise Concerned with Religious Law
Miqṣat Maᶜaśe Ha-Torah = MMT

4QMMT[a–d,f], 4QpapMMT[e] (4Q**394** 3–10, **395–399**) (*DJD* X, 1994)
4QcryptA MMT[g]? (4Q**313**) (*DJD* XXXVI, 2000)

F. Unclassified Texts Concerned with Religious Law

4QTohorot B[a–b] (4Q**276–277**) (*DJD* XXXV, 1999)
4QTohorot C (4Q**278**) (*DJD* XXXV, 1999)
4QFour Lots (4Q**279**) (*DJD* XXVI, 1998)

Part 2: Exegetical Texts

A. Pesharim: Thematic Pesharim

4Q**174** (4QFlor = 4QMidrEschat[a]?), **177** (4QCatena A = MidrEschat[b]?), **178** (4QUnclass. frags. = 4QMidrEschat[c]?), **182** (4QCatena B = 4QMidrEschat[d]?) (4Q**174**, **177**, *DJD* V, 1968; WAC with Gordon); (4Q**178**, *DJD* V, 1968; Gordon); (4Q**182**, *DJD* V, 1968; Allegro with Gordon)
4QAgesCreat A (4Q**180**) (*DJD* V, 1968; Allegro with Gordon)
4QAgesCreat B (4Q**181**) (*DJD* V, 1968; Allegro with Gordon)
11QMelch (11Q**13**) (*DJD* XXIII, 1998)

B. Pesharim: Continuous Pesharim

Isaiah (1): 4Qpap pIsa[c], 4QpIsa[e] (4Q**163**, **165**, **515** [4QpapUnclassified frags.]) (4Q**163**, **165**, *DJD* V, 1968; WAC with Gordon); (4Q**515**, *DJD* VII; Gordon)
Isaiah (2): 4QpIsa[a–b,d] (4Q**161–162**, **164**) (*DJD* V, 1968; Allegro with Gordon)

2QJub^{b} (2Q**20**) (*DJD* III, 1962; WAC with Gordon)
3QJub (3Q**5**) (*DJD* III, 1962; WAC with Gordon)
4QJub$^{a–h}$ (4Q**216–224**) (*DJD* XIII, 1994)
11QJub + XQText A (11Q**12** + XQ**5a**) (11Q**12**, *DJD* XXIII, 1998); (XQ**5a**, *DJD* XXXVI, 2000)

Apocryphon of Moses
1QDM (1QapocrMoses^{a}?) (1Q**22**) (*DJD* I, 1955; WAC with Gordon)
1QLiturgy of 3 Tongues of Fire (1QapocrMoses^{b}?) (1Q**29**) (*DJD* I, 1955; WAC with Gordon)
4QapocrMoses$^{a,b?,c?}$ (4Q**375–376**, **408**) (4Q**375–376**, *DJD* XIX, 1995); (4Q**408**, *DJD* XXXVI, 2000)

4QpsJub$^{a–c?}$
4QpsJub$^{a–c?}$ (4Q**225–227**) (*DJD* XIII, 1994; 4Q**226** 6a?: Eshel–Eshel, *DSD* 11 [2004], forthcoming)

4QapocrPent. A
4QapocrPent. A (4Q**368**) (*DJD* XXVIII, 2001)

Temple
4QT^{a}? (4Q**365a**) (*DJD* XIII, 1994)
4QT^{b} (4Q**524**) (*DJD* XXV, 1998; WAC with Gordon)
11QT$^{a–b}$, 11QT^{c}? (11Q**19–21**) (11Q**19**, Yadin); (11Q**20–21**, *DJD* XXIII, 1998)

Reworked Pentateuch
4QRP$^{a–e}$ (4Q**158,** 4Q**364–367**) (*DJD* V, 1968; WAC; *DJD* XIII, 1994; WAC)

Apocryphon of Joshua
4QapocrJosh$^{a–b}$ (4Q**378–379**) (*DJD* XXII, 1996)
4QProphecy of Joshua (4QapocrJosh^{c}?) (4Q**522**) (*DJD* XXV, 1998; WAC with Gordon)
5QWork with Place Names (5QapocrJosh?) (5Q**9**) (*DJD* III, 1962; WAC)

Samuel
4QVisSam (4Q**160**) (*DJD* V, 1968; Allegro with WAC and Gordon)

Pseudo-Ezekiel
4QpsEzek$^{a–e}$ (4Q**385**, **386**, **385b**, **388**, *DJD* XXX, 2001); (4Q**391**, *DJD* XIX, 1995)
4QpsEzek: Unid. Frags. (4Q**385c**) (*DJD* XXX, 2001)

Prayer of Enosh
4QPrayer of Enosh (4Q**369** [4QPrayer Concerning God and Israel?]) (*DJD* XIII, 1994)

B. Narratives Based on Biblical Themes

Birth of Noah
1QapGen ar (1Q**20**) I–V 27: see section A
4QBirth of Noah$^{a–c}$ ar (4Q**534–536**) (*DJD* XXXI, 2001; Cook)

Aramaic Levi Document
1QTLevi ar (1Q**21**) (*DJD* I, 1955; Cook)
4QLevi$^{a–f}$ ar (4Q**213**, **213a**, **213b**, **214**, **214a**, **214b**) (*DJD* XXII, 1996)

C. Testaments

Testament of Jacob

4QTJacob? ar (4Q**537**) (*DJD* XXXI, 2001; Wise)

Testament of Judah

3QTJud? (3Q**7**) (*DJD* III, 1962; WAC)

4QpapTJud? (4Q**484**) (*DJD* VII, 1982; WAC)

(Testament of Benjamin)

4QTJud ar (4Q**538**) (*DJD* XXXI, 2001; Wise)

Visions of ʿAmram

4QVisions of ʿAmram$^{a–f, g?}$ ar (4Q**543–549**) (*DJD* XXXI, 2001; Cook)

(Unidentified Testament)

4QapocrLevi$^{a–b}$? ar (4Q**540–541**) (*DJD* XXXI, 2001; Cook)

D. Texts of Mixed Genre

Book of Watchers (*1 Enoch* 1–36)

4QEn^{a} ar (4Q**201**) (Milik, *BE*; Milik, rev. Cook [frg.1]; *DJD* XXXVI, 2000 [frgs. 2–8])

4QEn^{b} ar (4Q**202**) (Milik, *BE*; Milik, rev. Cook)

4QEn^{c} ar (4Q**204**) 1 (Milik, *BE*; Milik, rev. Cook): see Letter of Enoch

4QEn^{d} ar (4Q**205**) 1 xi–xii (Milik, *BE*; Milik, rev. Cook) *Complete text of 4Q**205** provided

4QEn^{e} ar (4Q**206**) 1 xx–xxii, xxvi–xxviii (Milik, *BE*; Milik, rev. Cook): see Book of Giants

XQpapEn (XQ**8**) (Eshel–Eshel, *DSD* 11 [2004], forthcoming)

Book of Giants (*1 Enoch* 37–71)

1QEnGiants$^{a–b?}$ ar (1Q**23–24**) ([re-edition] *DJD* XXXVI, 2000)

2QEnGiants ar (2Q**26**) ([re-edition] *DJD* XXXVI, 2000)

4QEnGiants$^{a–f}$ ar (4Q**203**, **530–533**, **206** 2–3) (4Q**203**, frg. 1 [re-edition] *DJD* XXXI, 2001; frgs. 2–13 *DJD* XXXVI, 2000) (4Q**530–533**, *DJD* XXXI, 2001; Cook) (4Q**206** 2–3, *DJD* XXXVI, 2000) *Complete text of 4Q**206** provided

6QpapGiants ar (6Q**8**) ([re-edition] *DJD* XXXVI, 2000)

Enastr (*1 Enoch* 72–82)

4QEnastr$^{a–b}$ ar (4Q**208–209**) (*DJD* XXXVI, 2000)

4QEnastr$^{c–d}$ ar (4Q**210–211**) (Milik, *BE*; Milik, rev. Cook)

Book of Dreams (*1 Enoch* 83–91)

4QEn^{c} ar (4Q**204**) 4 (Milik, *BE*; Milik, rev. Cook): see Letter of Enoch

4QEn^{d} ar (4Q**205**) 2 (Milik, *BE*; Milik, rev. Cook): see Book of Watchers

4QEn^{e} ar (4Q**206**) 4 (Milik, *BE*; Milik, rev. Cook): see Book of Giants

4QEn^{f} ar (4Q**207**) 4 (Milik, *BE*; Milik, rev. Cook)

4QEn^{g} ar (4Q**212**) 1 i 1–ii 21 (Milik; Milik, *BE*; rev. Cook): see Letter of Enoch

Letter of Enoch (*1 Enoch* 92–108)

4QEn^{c} ar (4Q**204**) 5 (Cook; cf. Milik, *BE*) *Complete text of 4Q**204** provided

4QEn^g ar (4Q**212**) 1 ii 21–v 26 (Cook; cf Milik, *BE*) *Complete text of 4Q**212** provided
7QpapBiblical Text? gr (7QpapEn gr?) (7Q**4**); 7QpapUnclass. frags. gr (7QpapEn gr?) (7Q**8**, **11–14**) (*DJD* III, 1962)

Naphtali

4QNaph (4Q**215**) (*DJD* XXII, 1996)

Testament of Joseph

4QTJoseph ar (4Q**539**) (*DJD* XXXI, 2001; Wise)

Testament of Qohath

4QTQohath ar (4Q**542**) (*DJD* XXXI, 2001; Cook)

E. Unclassified and Fragmentary Texts

4QParaphrase of Gen and Exod (4Q**422**) (*DJD* XIII, 1994)
4QAdmonFlood (4Q**370**) (*DJD* XIX, 1995)
4QText Mentioning the Flood (4Q**577**) (*DJD* XXV, 1998; WAC)
1QNoah (1Q**19**, **19bis**) (*DJD* I, 1955; WAC with Gordon)
4QExposition on the Patriarchs (4Q**464**) (*DJD* XIX, 1995)
4QText Concerning Rachel and Joseph (4Q**474**) (*DJD* XXXVI, 2000)
2QapocrMoses? (2Q**21**) (*DJD* III, 1962; WAC with Gordon)
4Qpap paraExod gr (4Q**127**) (*DJD* IX, 1992)
4QapocrPent. B (4Q**377**) (*DJD* XXVIII, 2001)
6Qpap apocrSam–Kgs (6Q**9**) (*DJD* III, 1962; WAC with Gordon)
4Qpap paraKings et al. (4Q**382**) (*DJD* XIII, 1994)
2QapocrDavid? (2QNarrative and Poetic Composition?) (2Q**22**) (*DJD* III, 1962; WAC with Gordon)
4QText Mentioning Zedekiah (4Q**470**) (*DJD* XIX, 1995)
4QNarrative and Poetic Composition$^{a–d}$ (4Q**371–373**) (*DJD* XXVIII, 2001) (4Q**373a**: Tigchelaar, *RevQ* 21 [2004] 477–85)
4QNarrative Work and Prayer (4Q**460**) (*DJD* XXXVI, 2000)
4QNarrative D (4Q**463**) (*DJD* XIX, 1995)

Part 4: Calendrical Texts and Sapiential Texts

I. Calendrical Texts

A. Calendrical Texts Concerned with Mishmarot (Temple Watches)

1. Lists of Mishmarot

4QOtot (4Q**319**) (*DJD* XXI, 2001)
4QcryptA Mishmarot J (4Q**324i**) (Abegg; WAC)

2. Times of Service

Days

4QMishmarot A (4Q**322**) (*DJD* XXI, 2001)

Days and Festivals

4QMishmarot C (4Q**324**) (*DJD* XXI, 2001)

Days, Sabbaths, and Festivals

4QCal. Doc./Mishmarot D (4Q**325**) (*DJD* XXI, 2001)

Festivals

4QCal. Doc./Mishmarot A (4Q**320**) 4 ii–vi (*DJD* XXI, 2001)

4QMishmarot H (4Q**329a**) (*DJD* XXI, 2001)

3. Beginnings of Calendrical Units

Years

4QMishmarot I (4Q**330**) (*DJD* XXI, 2001)

Quarter-Years

4QMishmarot F (4Q**328**) (*DJD* XXI, 2001)

Months

4QMishmarot B (4Q**323**) (*DJD* XXI, 2001)

4QMishmarot D (4Q**324a**) (*DJD* XXI, 2001)

4. List of Months and Days Connected with Mishmarot

4QCal. Doc./Mishmarot A (4Q**320**) 3 ii–4 i (*DJD* XXI, 2001)

5. Equation Tables

4QCal. Doc./Mishmarot A (4Q**320**) 1 + 2 (*DJD* XXI, 2001)

4QCal. Doc./Mishmarot C (4Q**321a**) (*DJD* XXI, 2001)

4QMishmarot E (4Q**324c**) (*DJD* XXI, 2001)

6. List of Mishmarot Combining Different Categories

4QCal. Doc./Mishmarot B (4Q**321**) (*DJD* XXI, 2001)

4QMishmarot G (4Q**329**) (*DJD* XXI, 2001)

4QcryptA Lit. Cal.^{c}? (4Q**324f**) (Abegg; cf. *DJD* XXVIII, 2001, pl. LXI)

4QcryptA Cal. Doc. F? (4Q**324g**) (Abegg; cf. *DJD* XXVIII, 2001, pl. LXII)

4QcryptA Cal. Doc. G? (4Q**324h**) (Abegg; cf. *DJD* XXVIII, 2001, pl. LXII)

B. Calendrical Texts Not Concerned with Mishmarot

1. Tables of Festivals and Sabbaths

4QcryptA Lit. Cal.$^{a–b}$ (4Q**324d–e**) (Abegg; cf. *DJD* XXVIII, 2001, pls. LIX–LXI)

4QCal. Doc. C (4Q**326**) (*DJD* XXI, 2001)

4QCal. Doc. D (4Q**394** 1–2) (*DJD* XXI, 2001)

2. Various Calendrical Texts

4QcryptA Lunisolar Calendar (4Q**317**) (Abegg; WAC; cf. *DJD* XXVIII, 2001, pls. LII–LVIII)

4QOrdo (4Q**334**) (*DJD* XXI, 2001)

C. Calendrical Texts Too Fragmentary for Further Characterization

4QCal. Doc./Mishmarot A (4Q**320**) 3 i + 6–9 (*DJD* XXI, 2001)

4QpapCal. Doc. A? (4Q**324b**) (*DJD* XXI, 2001)

4QCal. Doc. E? (4Q**337**) (*DJD* XXI, 2001)

6QpapCalendrical Document (6Q**17**) (*DJD* III, 1962; WAC with Gordon)

II. SAPIENTIAL TEXTS

A. SAPIENTIAL INSTRUCTIONS

Instruction (*Mûsār lᵉMēvîn*)

1QInstruction (1Q**26**) ([re-edition] *DJD* XXXIV, 1999)
4QInstruction[a–e] (4Q**415–418**, **418a**) (*DJD* XXXIV, 1999)
4QInstruction[f]? (4Q**418c**) (*DJD* XXXIV, 1999)
4QInstruction[g] (4Q**423**) (*DJD* XXXIV, 1999)

Book of Mysteries

1QMyst (1Q**27**) (*DJD* I, 1955; WAC with Gordon)
4QMyst[a–b] (4Q**299–300**) (*DJD* XX, 1997)
4QMyst[c]? (4Q**301**) (*DJD* XX, 1997)

Ben Sira

2QSir (2Q**18**) (*DJD* III, 1962; Gordon)

Other Sapiential Instructions

4QSapiential-Didactic Work A (4Q**412**) (*DJD* XX, 1997)
4QSapiential-Hymnic Work A (4Q**426**) (*DJD* XX, 1997)
4QBeatitudes (4Q**525**) (*DJD* XXV, 1998; WAC with Gordon)

B. COLLECTION OF PROVERBS

4QInstruction-like Composition B (4Q**424**) (*DJD* XXXVI, 2000)

C. DIDACTIC SPEECHES

Treatise of the Two Spirits

1QS(erekh) III 13–IV 26 (Abegg; WAC with Gordon)
4QpapS[a] (4Q**255**) (*DJD* XXVI, 1998)
4QS[b] (4Q**256**) (*DJD* XXVI, 1998)
4QpapS[c] (4Q**257**) (*DJD*, 1994; WAC)

Other Didactic Speeches

4QSapiential Work (4Q**185**) (*DJD* V, 1968; Allegro with Gordon)
4QcryptA Words of the Maskil to All Sons of Dawn (4Q**298**) (*DJD* XX, 1997)

D. SAPIENTIAL POETIC TEXT

4QSapiential Hymn (4Q**411**) (*DJD* XX, 1997)

E. SAPIENTIAL TEXTS TOO FRAGMENTARY FOR FURTHER CLASSIFICATION

4QWiles of the Wicked Woman (4Q**184**) (*DJD* V, 1968; Allegro with Gordon)
4QpapAdmonitory Parable (4Q**302**) (*DJD* XX, 1997)
4QMeditation on Creation A (4Q**303**) (*DJD* XX, 1997)
4QMeditation on Creation C (4Q**305**) (*DJD* XX, 1997)
4QComposition Concerning Divine Providence (4Q**413**) (*DJD* XX, 1997)
4QSapiential-Didactic Work B (4Q**425**) (*DJD* XX, 1997)
4QThe Two Ways (4Q**473**) (*DJD* XXII, 1996)

Part 5: Poetic and Liturgical Texts

A. Poetic Texts

1. Hodayot, Hodayot-like, and Similar Texts

Hodayot

1QH^{a} (Abegg; WAC with Gordon)
1QH^{b} (1Q**35**) (*DJD* I, 1955; WAC with Gordon)
4QH$^{a–f}$ (4Q**427–432**) (*DJD* XXIX, 1999)
4QHodayot-like Text A (4Q**433**) (*DJD* XXIX, 1999)
4QpapHodayot-like Text B (4Q**433a**) (*DJD* XXIX, 1999)
4QHodayot-like Text C (4Q**440**) (*DJD* XXIX, 1999)
4QHodayot-like Text D (4Q**440a**) (*DJD* XXXVI, 2000)

4QBarkhi Nafshi$^{a–e}$ (4Q**434–438**) (*DJD* XXIX, 1999)
4QLament by a Leader (4Q**439**) (*DJD* XXIX, 1999)
4QNarrative I (4Q**469**) (*DJD* XXXVI, 2000)

2. Laments

4QapocrLam A (4Q**179**) (Bernstein, 2004)
4QLament A (4Q**445**) (*DJD* XXIX, 1999)

3. Collections of Psalms

4QNon-Canonical Psalms A–B (4Q**380–381**) (*DJD* XI, 1998)
4QWorks of God (4Q**392**) (*DJD* XXIX, 1999)
4QCommunal Confession (4Q**393**) (*DJD* XXIX, 1999)

4. Various Poetic Texts

4QApocryphal Psalm and Prayer (4Q**448**) (*DJD* XI, 1998)
4QTime of Righteousness (4Q**215a**) (*DJD* XXXVI, 2000)
11QPs^{a} (11Q**5**) (non-canonical segments) (Abegg; WAC)
11QPs^{b} (11Q**6**) (non-canonical segments) (*DJD* XXIII, 1998; WAC)
4QPs^{f} (4Q**88**) (non-canonical segments) (*DJD* XVI, 2000)

B. Liturgical Texts

1. Collections of Daily Prayers

4QpapPrQuot (4Q**503**) (*DJD* VII, 1982; WAC with Gordon)
4QDibHam^{a}, 4QpapDibHam^{c} (4Q**504**, **506**) (4Q**504**, *DJD* VII, 1982; and Chazon, 2004; WAC) (4Q**506**, *DJD* VII, 1982; WAC with Gordon)

2. Collections Concerned with Various Festivals and Festivities

PrFêtes

1QLiturgical Prayers$^{a–b}$ (1Q**34** + **34bis**) (1Q**34**, *DJD* I, 1955; Gordon) (1Q**34bis**, *DJD* I, 1955; WAC)
4QPrFêtes$^{a–b}$ (4Q**507–508**) (4Q**507**, *DJD* VII, 1982; WAC) (4Q**508**, *DJD* VII, 1982; WAC with Gordon)
4QpapPrFêtes^{c} (4Q**509**) (*DJD* VII, 1982; WAC with Gordon)
4QpapDibHam^{b} (4Q**505**) (*DJD* VII, 1982; WAC with Gordon)

4QLiturgical Work A (4QLiturgy) (4Q**409**) (García Martínez–Tigchelaar, 1998)

4QpapRitual of Marriage (4Q**502**) (*DJD* VII, 1982; WAC with Gordon)

3. COLLECTIONS CONCERNED WITH THE SABBATH SACRIFICE

ShirShabb

4QShirShabb$^{a–h}$ (4Q**400–407**) (*DJD* XI, 1998)

11QShirShabb (11Q**17**) (*DJD* XXIII, 1981)

4. COLLECTIONS AND TEXTS CONCERNED WITH COVENANTAL CEREMONIES

1QSb (1Q**28b**) (*DJD* I, 1955; WAC)

4QBer$^{a–e}$ (4Q**286–290**) (*DJD* XI, 1998)

5. RITUALS OF PURIFICATION

4QPurification Liturgy (4Q**284**) (*DJD* XXXV, 199)

4QRitual of Purification A (4Q**414**) (*DJD* XXXV, 1999)

4QpapRitPur B (4Q**512**) (*DJD* VII, 1982; WAC with Gordon)

C. FRAGMENTARY POETIC OR LITURGICAL TEXTS

1QHymns (1Q**36**) (*DJD* I, 1955; Gordon)

1QHymnic Composition? (1Q**39**) (*DJD* I, 1955; WAC with Gordon)

3QHymn (3Q**6**) (*DJD* III, 1962; Gordon)

4QWork Containing Prayers A (4Q**291**) (*DJD* XXIX, 1999)

4QWork Containing Prayers B (4Q**292**) (*DJD* XXIX, 1999)

4QWork Containing Prayers C (4Q**293**) (*DJD* XXIX, 1999)

4QIndividual Thanksgiving A (4Q**441**) (*DJD* XXIX, 1999)

4QIndividual Thanksgiving B (4Q**442**) (*DJD* XXIX, 1999)

4QPersonal Prayer (4Q**443**) (*DJD* XXIX, 1999)

4QPoetic Text A (4Q**446**) (*DJD* XXIX, 1999)

4QPrayer A (4Q**449**) (*DJD* XXIX, 1999)

4QPrayer B? (4Q**450**) (*DJD* XXIX, 1999)

4QPrayer C (4Q**451**) (*DJD* XXIX, 1999)

4QHalleluyah (4Q**456**) (*DJD* XXIX, 1999)

4QPrayer Concerning God and Israel (4Q**471c**) (*DJD* XXIX, 1999)

4QpapHymns/Prayers (4Q**499**) (*DJD* VII, 1982; WAC with Gordon)

4QpapBenediction (4Q**500**) (*DJD* VII, 1982; WAC with Gordon)

4Qapocryphal Lamentations B (4Q**501**) (*DJD* VII, 1982; WAC)

4QHymnic or Sapiential Work B (4Q**528**) (*DJD* XXV, 1998; Gordon)

6QpapBenediction (6Q**16**) (*DJD* III, 1962; Gordon)

11QHymns A (11Q**15**) (*DJD* XXIII, 1998)

11QHymns B (11Q**16**) + XQText B (XQ**5b**) (*DJD* XXIII, 1998; *DJD* XXXVI, 2000)

Part 6: See pp. iv-ix

INDEX OF THE QUMRAN TEXTS INCLUDED IN *DSSR*

Item No.	**Name**	**Part**
1Q**14**	pMic	2
1Q**15**	pZeph	2
1Q**16**	pPs	2
1Q**17**	Jub^{a}	3
1Q**18**	Jub^{b}	3
1Q**19**	Noah	3
1Q**19bis**	Noah	3
1Q**20** I–V 27	apGen ar	3
1Q**21**	TLevi ar	3
1Q**22**	DM (apocrMoses^{a}?)	3
1Q**23**	EnGiants^{a} ar	3
1Q**24**	EnGiants^{b}? ar	3
1Q**25**	Apocr. Prophecy	6
1Q**26**	Instruction	4
1Q**27**	Myst	4
1Q**28a**	Sa	1
1Q**28b**	Sb	5
1Q**29**	Lit. of 3 Tongues of Fire (apocrMoses^{b}?)	3
1Q**30**	Liturgical Text A?	6
1Q**31**	Liturgical Text B?	6
1Q**32**	NJ? ar	6
1Q**33**	M	1
1Q**34** + **34bis**	LitPr^{a-b}	5
1Q**35**	H^{b}	5
1Q**36**	Hymns	5
1Q**37**	Hymnic Composition?	6
1Q**38**	Hymnic Composition?	6
1Q**39**	Hymnic Composition?	5
1Q**40**	Hymnic Composition?	6
1QH^{a}	H^{a}	5
1QpHab	pHab	2
1QS I 1–III 12,	S I 1–III 12	1
1QS III 13–IV 26	S III 13–IV 26	4
1QS V 1–XI 22	S V 1–XI 22	1
2Q**18**	Sir	4
2Q**19**	Jub^{a}	3
2Q**20**	Jub^{b}	3
2Q**21**	apocrMoses?	3
2Q**22**	apocrDavid? (Narrative and Poetic Composition?)	3
2Q**23**	Apocr. Prophecy	6
2Q**24**	NJ ar	6
2Q**25**	Juridical Text	6

4Q325	Cal. Doc./Mishmarot D	4
4Q326	Cal. Doc. C	4
4Q328	Mishmarot F	4
4Q329	Mishmarot G	4
4Q329a	Mishmarot H	4
4Q330	Mishmarot I	4
4Q331	papHistorical Text C	6
4Q332	Historical Text D	6
4Q333	Historical Text E	6
4Q334	Ordo	4
4Q337	Cal. Doc. E?	4
4Q338	Genealogical List?	6
4Q339	List of False Prophets ar	2
4Q340	List of Netinim	6
4Q341	Exercitium Calami C	6
4Q342	Letter? ar	6
4Q343	Letter nab	6
4Q344	Debt Acknowledgement ar	6
4Q345	Deed A ar or heb	6
4Q346	Deed of Sale ar	6
4Q347	papDeed F ar (= part of XHev/Se 32)	6
4Q348	Deed B heb?	6
4Q350	Account gr	6
4Q351	Account of Cereal A ar	6
4Q352	papAccount of Cereal B ar or heb	6
4Q352a	papAccount A ar or heb	6
4Q353	papAccount of Cereal or Liquid ar or heb	6
4Q354	Account B ar or heb	6
4Q355	Account C ar or heb	6
4Q356	Account D ar or heb	6
4Q357	Account E ar or heb	6
4Q358	papAccount F? ar or heb	6
4Q359	papDeed C? ar or heb	6
4Q360	Exercitium Calami B	6
4Q364	RP[b]	3
4Q365	RP[c]	3
4Q365a	T[a]?	3
4Q366	RP[d]	3
4Q367	RP[e]	3
4Q368	apocrPent. A	3
4Q369	Prayer of Enosh (Prayer Concerning God and Israel?)	3
4Q370	AdmonFlood	3
4Q371	Narrative and Poetic Composition[a]	3
4Q372	Narrative and Poetic Composition[b]	3
4Q373	Narrative and Poetic Composition[c]	3
4Q373a	Narrative and Poetic Composition[d]	3

4Q**484**	papTJud? (papJub[k]?)	3
4Q**485**	papProph	6
4Q**486**	papSap A?	6
4Q**487**	papSap B?	6
4Q**488**	papApocryphon ar	6
4Q**489**	papApocalypse ar	6
4Q**491**	M[a]	1
4Q**492**	M[b]	1
4Q**493**	M[c]	1
4Q**494**	M[d]	1
4Q**495**	M[e]	1
4Q**496**	papM[f]	1
4Q**497**	papWar Scroll-like Text A	1
4Q**498**	papSap/Hymn	6
4Q**499**	papHymns/Prayers	5
4Q**500**	papBened	5
4Q**501**	apocrLam B	5
4Q**502**	papRitMar	5
4Q**503**	papPrQuot	5
4Q**504**	DibHam[a]	5
4Q**505**	papDibHam[b]	5
4Q**506**	papDibHam[c]	5
4Q**507**	PrFêtes[a]	5
4Q**508**	PrFêtes[b]	5
4Q**509**	papPrFêtes[c]	5
4Q**510**	Shir[a]	6
4Q**511**	Shir[b]	6
4Q**512**	papRitPur B	5
4Q**513**	Ordinances[b]	1
4Q**514**	Ordinances[c]	1
4Q**515**	papUnclassified frags.	2
4Q**521**	Messianic Apocalypse	6
4Q**522**	Prophecy of Joshua (apocrJosh[c]?)	3
4Q**523**	Jonathan	6
4Q**524**	T[b]	3
4Q**525**	Beatitudes	4
4Q**526**	Testament?	6
4Q**527**	Liturgical Work D?	6
4Q**528**	Hymnic or Sapiential Work B	5
4Q**529**	Words of Michael ar	6
4Q**530**	EnGiants[b] ar	3
4Q**531**	EnGiants[c] ar	3
4Q**532**	EnGiants[d] ar	3
4Q**533**	EnGiants[e] ar	3
4Q**534**	Birth of Noah[a] ar	3
4Q**535**	Birth of Noah[b] ar	3